Feminism and Its Fictions

Feminism and Its Fictions

The Consciousness-Raising Novel and the Women's Liberation Movement

Lisa Maria Hogeland

PENN

University of Pennsylvania Press

Philadelphia

10 9 8 7 6 5 4 3 2 1

Published by
University of Pennsylvania Press
Philadelphia, Pennsylvania 19104-4011

Library of Congress Cataloging-in-Publication Data
Hogeland, Lisa Maria.
    Feminism and its fictions : the consciousness-raising novel and the women's liberation
movement / Lisa Maria Hogeland.
        p.   cm.
    Includes bibliographical references and index.
    ISBN 0-8122-3429-4 (cloth : alk. paper). — ISBN 0-8122-1640-7 (pbk. : alk. paper)
    1. American fiction—Women authors—History and criticism.   2. Feminism and
literature—United States—History—20th century.   3. Women and literature—United
States—History—20th century.   4. American fiction—20th century—History and
criticism.   5. Interpersonal relations in literature.   6. Group identity in literature.
I. Title.
PS374.F45H64   1998
813′.54099287—dc21

97-39291
CIP

In memory of my mother
Sharon Maria Meade Hogeland
with love

Contents

Preface

This book argues that the women's and feminist fiction of the 1970s was dominated by what I call the consciousness-raising (CR) novel; it traces the movement of ideas back and forth between the Women's Liberation Movement and these novels. The CR novel in some cases depicted the protagonist's process of consciousness raising explicitly. In others, it shaped its narrative according to the structure of consciousness raising, the process by which participants come to see the personal as political. In still others, it was designed to transact CR with its readers. The CR novel was important and influential in introducing feminist ideas to a broader reading public, and particularly in circulating feminist ideas beyond the small-group networks that made up radical feminism in the early part of the decade.[1] The novels played an important role in feminism in the decade, but they did not do so in isolation, for, as I argue in Chapter One, the widespread media coverage of the Movement, especially in the early part of the decade, provided a basic awareness of feminist issues. Like the media coverage, many of the CR novels enabled a wider circulation of ideas from the Women's Liberation Movement by moderating those ideas, by softening their political edges, by personalizing and novelizing feminist social criticism. Identifying but not overestimating the work these novels performed has been a difficult task; it remains a central task for feminists engaged in tracing histories of the second wave.

Unlike most of the scholarly works that examine feminist fiction from the 1970s, this study attends far more to popular and bestselling novels than to the more canonical feminist metafiction. Dorothy Bryant's *Ella Price's Journal*, Marilyn French's *The Women's Room*, Erica Jong's *Fear of Flying*, Marge Piercy's *Woman on the Edge of Time*, Joanna Russ's *The Female Man*, and Alix Kates Shulman's *Burning Questions* appear far more frequently than novels by Doris Lessing or Margaret Drabble. Other novels I discuss include Kathy Acker's *Blood and Guts in High School*, Lisa Alther's *Kinflicks*, Margaret Atwood's *Lady Oracle*, E. M. Broner's

Her Mothers, Rita Mae Brown's *Rubyfruit Jungle,* Bryant's *The Kin of Ata Are Waiting for You,* Suzy McKee Charnas's *Walk to the End of the World* and *Motherlines,* Joan Didion's *Play It As It Lays,* Zoe Fairbairns's *Benefits,* Sally Gearhart's *The Wanderground,* Mary Gordon's *Final Payments,* Lois Gould's *Such Good Friends* and *Final Analysis,* Margaret Laurence's *The Diviners,* Ursula K. Le Guin's *The Left Hand of Darkness,* Alison Lurie's *Real People* and *The Truth About Lorin Jones,* Piercy's *Braided Lives,* and Fay Weldon's *Down Among the Women* and *Praxis.* Alice Walker's *The Color Purple* is an important counterpoint to the overwhelming number of novels by white women. Most of the novels are American, with a small number from Britain and Canada, and all were written in English.

As this list suggests, the CR novel as a fictional form crossed established genres, and crossed as well divisions between "literary" and "popular" fiction. This study does not attend to questions of literary quality; whether novels like *Fear of Flying* or *The Women's Room* are "good" novels is far less interesting to me than the ways these novels shaped and were shaped by feminist ideas and discourses. I am thus less interested in the aesthetics of the CR novel than in its politics—the political and rhetorical meanings of its narrative strategies, or what we might call, paraphrasing Jane Tompkins in *Sensational Designs,* the (counter) cultural work these novels performed.

Though the CR novel was a specific and historically short-lived fictional form, it and the theories of CR that were foundational to it continue to shape feminist critical understandings of the relationship between reading and social change. Joanne S. Frye, in *Living Stories, Telling Lives: Women and the Novel in Contemporary Experience* (1986), lays out this relationship in these terms:

> The fullest participation of the novel in feminist change derives from the reader, especially the woman reader, who might find through the reading of novels the growing edge of her own humanity, extending beyond available roles and categories and into a renewed future. As she learns from female characters new ways to interpret her own and other women's experiences, she helps to reshape the culture's understanding of women and participates in the feminist alteration of human experience. (191)

Frye's articulation of this process of change (reading, reflecting, reshaping culture) echoes quite closely Cheri Register's 1975 discussion of the relationship between feminist fiction and consciousness raising. Register argued that feminist fiction should "serve as a forum for women," thus enabling readers better to "understand what female experience is." "Once literature begins to serve as a forum," she continues, "it can assist in humanizing and equilibrating the culture's value system, which has historically served predominantly male interests" (19). A significant difference between the two arguments is that Register specifically noted that feminist fiction must be supplemented by "factual information about the status of women from other sources" in order to perform its consciousness-raising function (23). By the mid-1980s, Frye's woman reader need only read fiction, and the explicit reference to CR has dropped away. Reading had by then *become* consciousness raising.

I examine the increasing metaphorization of CR in Chapter Two, tracing its slippage from the "hard," theory-building CR in the early part of the decade to the "soft," self-esteem-building CR later on. What interests me about Frye's formulation—which is by no means unique in feminist literary criticism—is the way it enlists the assumptions of CR, the assumptions of a direct relationship between individual consciousnesses and social change that were created in feminist theorizations of the process. Frye need not even invoke CR directly to enlist its resonances, so commonplace have these assumptions become—and so foundational to our notions of feminist reading.

We can also see the importance of the consciousness-raising novel of the 1970s in Ellen Cronan Rose's 1993 Review Essay in *Signs*, where she reads a dozen works of "American Feminist Criticism of Contemporary Women's Fiction." She concludes by identifying "the task confronting feminist scholars of contemporary women's fiction at this time: to theorize and historicize today's novels rather than to memorialize a feminist high renaissance of the 1970s" (375). Rose misses a middle step in this process of dethroning the 1970s renaissance as the centerpiece of the "contemporary," however, and that is the central task of this book: the high renaissance of the 1970s must be theorized and historicized.

Rose notes that Doris Lessing's *The Golden Notebook* seems to have lost its power for her students—who "read it as a historical document that may have been relevant to their mothers . . . , but not to them" (370). How has Lessing's novel lost its power, its effectivity as "one of the most profound explorations of a woman's complex consciousness that exists in fiction" (370), as Rose quotes Roberta Rubenstein's description of the novel's importance? More precisely, we might ask, what were the conditions—of reading, of feminist politics, and of the relations between the two—that made *The Golden Notebook* so powerful in its day, and that make it less powerful for readers today? Perhaps the most obvious difficulty that Lessing's novel poses for contemporary students is its concern with the fundamental contradiction that Anna Wulf experiences between *woman* and *writer*. The very courses in which students are most likely to read *The Golden Notebook*—courses called "Women's Literature" or "Women Writers," for instance—make that contradiction difficult to engage, and mark very clearly a significant difference in the conditions for reading during the 1970s from those conditions today. The very successes of feminism in the academy, especially in literary studies, can work to make the novels that were so important to feminism in the 1960s and 1970s strange to our students, who read them as history rather than as the stories of their own lives.

A panel at the 1994 Modern Language Association convention addressed the continuing relevance of women's fiction from the feminist high renaissance of the 1970s using the case of *Fear of Flying*. (Evidence for the novel's embattled status in the academy was provided by the MLA's refusal to accept a panel the previous year celebrating the novel's twentieth anniversary.) *Fear of Flying*, ran the essence of the panelists' arguments, could now be reclaimed in the aftermath of the sex-wars of the 1980s and the increasing engagement of feminism with issues of censorship as, essentially, "prematurely pro-sex."[2] My analogy here is, of course, to the McCarthyite term, "prematurely anti-fascist." *Fear of Flying*, in this logic, was targeted for the political purposes of the anti-pornography movement, and may now be returned to its honorable place in literary-political history. Reading *Fear of Flying* as "pro-sex" is, as I argue in Chapter Three, partially true and partially appropriate to what Alice Echols names the "stereographic" view of sexuality in the radical feminism of the 1970s—but only partially so. In large part, though, such attempts to claim or reclaim the novel's argument about sexuality as if it had predicted (and won) the sex-wars exemplify Rose's argument about the hegemony of the feminist renaissance of the 1970s.

The canon of contemporary women's fiction is relatively stable, as Rose reads it out of the twelve critical works she discusses, and it is substantially made up of novels from the 1970s. Insofar as the contemporary can have a canon, critics have constructed it as much by the standards of 1970s feminism as they have constructed it from 1970s novels. Rose identifies an "exhilaration" which "many of us felt in the early 1970s, when novels like *The Golden Notebook*, Atwood's *Surfacing*, Marge Piercy's *Small Changes* . . . , and Drabble's *The Waterfall* corroborated what we were learning in consciousness-raising sessions and movement activism—that change was possible" (373). That has become for many critics of contemporary women's fiction not a specific, historically located way of feminist reading, but rather feminist reading itself. Thus Gayle Greene dismisses novels that do not perform consciousness-raising as "postfeminist" in *Changing the Story: Feminist Fiction and the Tradition* (1991), an argument greatly facilitated by reading only white women novelists of the 1980s.[3] Thus Rose herself structures her essay around the reading strategies of Lessing's Martha Quest, who asks of novels, "What has this got to do with me?" (Lessing quoted in Rose 347), despite Rose's evidence that her students read differently. Thus Rose's intention to shift the focus of the contemporary away from the 1970s is thwarted by her use of reading strategies forged in 1970s CR. And thus the canon of contemporary women's fiction remains particularly resistant to engaging works by women writers of color, which frequently require different reading strategies from white women readers than do works from the white feminist 1970s renaissance.

My feminist students today read in ways different from the ways I read as an undergraduate feminist in the late 1970s. Reductively (and polemically) put, I see our reading strategies as shaped by this disjunction: my students read for difference where I read for identity. Or, perhaps more accurately, my students read for specificity where I read for universality. In part, this difference is shaped by a different dominant narrative about both race and gender: my teachers understood difference as a problem of equality-as-assimilation, whereas my students' teachers understand it as a problem of equality-as-diversity. This is not surprising; as Rose herself points out in noting a generational difference among the critics she surveys, the "younger generation of scholars" were not trained in the New Critical formalism and were not constructed as feminist political readers whose lives were saved by women's novels (368).[4] My students' reading strategies are both formed by different literary training and shaped by different political concerns of feminism from those prevalent in the 1970s.[5] This is not to say that consciousness raising is not still central to the practice of feminist reading—quite the contrary, in fact— but rather that it works very differently in contemporary feminism compared with the CR of the 1970s. CR in contemporary feminism has been reconstructed by anti-racist work in the Movement, and by "unlearning racism" workshops.[6] Contemporary CR has become a dialectic of difference and identification, forged in understanding the range of gendered experience differently constructed by race and class, among other social forces at work.[7]

Implicit in my sense of these differences is a strong sense that the early 1980s marked a watershed in feminism. The outpouring of works by women of color, Jewish women, working class women, lesbian women, disabled women—who insisted that *women* could not be unmodified without enacting an exclusionary hegemony that feminism was committed to overturning—radically changed our notions of feminism. I discuss the impact of these works in Chapter Six, focusing on African-American women's work in particular, as part of my exploration of the sex/race analogy. Even when those changes are not (always) successfully enacted in feminist practices and organizations, they are (at least unevenly) enacted in our reading strategies and reading lists, our theorizing, our discourse, our ideas. The overmapping of feminism and anti-racism, moreover, on which feminist women of color have been insisting for more than fifteen years, has gained sufficient power as a vision of feminism that it erupts into even the most mainstream varieties of feminism. An example of this growing importance of anti-racist politics can be seen in the censuring of Los Angeles NOW president Tammy Bruce in December 1995, over comments she made after the O. J. Simpson verdict that were perceived to claim sexism to be more important than racism.[8] In *Prime-Time Feminism* (1996), Bonnie J. Dow similarly finds anti-racist politics making their way into contemporary women's television;[9] it is thus small wonder that reading strategies would be influenced.

One of the central problems with critics who base their notions of the "contemporary" on the 1970s renaissance is that, as many feminists did in that decade, they come to conflate *women* with *feminism*. Frye's "woman reader" is clearly a *feminist* reader—a reader at least amenable to imagining a life beyond available roles for women. Much of the women's fiction of the 1970s is strongly influenced by the Women's Liberation Movement, but not all of it is feminist in the sense of advocating specific feminist political agendas. Many novels by women in the decade demonstrate the dangers and difficulties of illegal abortions, for instance, but, as I argue in Chapter Three, few novels connect abortion rights with other issues of reproductive freedom. Similarly, many novels by women illuminate and demonstrate specific aspects of women's oppression, especially in heterosexual relationships, but few novels explicitly forward ideas about these forms of oppression in relation to systemic analyses. Register explained in 1975 that "No feminist critic insists that a fictional work include political analysis" (24), citing Kate Millett's notion that art should "*express* female experience [rather] than analyze it" (Register, 28 n. 81). Thus, Register argues, "The remaining tasks involved in consciousness-raising are left to the reader: to compare the problems encountered by female literary characters with her own, to explain similarities in terms of causes, and to decide on appropriate political action" (24). What makes a novel feminist in this analysis is what a reader can do with it.[10]

There were, however, any number of other criteria for defining feminist fiction in the period. Many novels were, to name one standard, written by women with clear and well-known ties to the women's movement. Rita Mae Brown's membership in The Furies and Alix Kates Shulman's in Redstockings exemplify one such tie. Feminist essays by Marge Piercy ("The Grand Coolie Damn" in *Sisterhood Is Powerful* [1970]) and Joanna Russ ("What Can a Heroine Do? or Why Women Can't Write" and "Images of Women in Science Fiction," in *Images of Women in Fiction: Feminist Perspectives* [1972]) exemplify another, as readers could seek out these writers' fiction on the basis of their political affiliations. Relationships to feminist publications, such as E. M. Broner's ties to *Chrysalis* and *New Women's Times' Feminist Review*, exemplify yet another, as readers could follow the circulation of signature in the feminist press and commercial fiction publishing. Other writers, like Erica Jong, Lois Gould, and Doris Lessing, published work in *Ms.* magazine, demonstrating (at least) a sense of feminist audience; the magazine may also have served to provide an explicitly feminist imprimatur for the authors' work. Marilyn French's *The Women's Room* (1977), Alix Kates Shulman's *Burning Questions* (1978), and Fay Weldon's *Praxis* (1978) set their characters in the Women's Movement, explicitly depicting feminism as their subjects. It is not difficult to claim such writers and/or their novels as "feminist."

There are, however, more complex examples. Gayle Greene identifies the complicated relationships to feminism of several of the writers whose work she studies: of Doris Lessing, Margaret Drabble, Margaret Laurence, and Margaret Atwood, only Laurence "unequivocally identifies with feminism" (2).[11] Greene nonetheless proposes that these writers' metafictions do fall under the rubric of feminist fiction, whatever the equivocations of the writers themselves: "we may term a novel 'feminist' for its analysis of gender as socially constructed and its sense that what has been constructed may be reconstructed—for its understanding that change is possible and that narrative can play a part in it" (2). Greene's is, of course, a definition of feminist fiction that need not rely on authorship or signature, and indeed, that may have little to do with women at all, since the gender that can be shown to be "reconstructable" with the participation of narrative could be masculine.[12]

Greene's definition is, however, a problematic one for the period of second-wave feminism which this study addresses. Only in the 1980s did feminist critics begin taking seriously the possibility of reading works written by men as feminist fiction. Only in the 1980s, for instance, does Samuel Delany "count" as a feminist writer in Donna Haraway's "Manifesto for Cyborgs." Similarly, Kate Millett's reading of Genet's work as a radical critique of patriarchy had little importance in U. S. feminism until a version of it resurfaced "around 1981" (in Jane Gallop's reckoning) with the appearance of Hélène Cixous's work in *New French Feminisms: An Anthology,* and the wide circulation that volume had in academic feminism. The "images of women" feminist literary criticism of works by men writers emphasized "resisting readings" of stereotyped, sexist, damaging depictions of women, even when they became (as in Judith Fetterley's reading of Norman Mailer in *The Resisting Reader*) so parodic that they could be seen to unmask as much as to further patriarchal ideas.[13]

The feminist criticism of the 1970s nearly always insisted that feminist fiction be written by and about women, in part because, as Register explained, "female writers are seldom reviewed in major literary publications, included in literary histories, or read in college English classes"

(11), so that the simple presence of women writers and the women characters they depicted was seen to be serving the movement.[14] Over the course of the decade, the argument for fiction by and about women as potentially serving the cause of feminism became transformed in some circles into an argument that fiction by and about women was feminist by definition. Joan Didion, for example, was widely regarded in the popular press as a feminist novelist, despite her attack on Women's Liberation in the *New York Times Book Review* in 1972, and despite Catharine R. Stimpson's analysis of the anti-feminism of her work in *Ms.* in 1973; by 1977, Didion was reclaimed as a feminist writer in *Ms.* That reclamation, as I argue in Chapter Four, was based on a vision of feminism that the magazine (and much of the Movement) developed over the course of the decade: the belief that all women are feminists, and a corollary belief that all women-authored or women-centered fiction has a necessary relationship to feminism.[15]

What I hope is clear from this range of definitions of feminist fiction is their very lack of clarity, for what constituted feminist fiction, like what constituted feminism itself, was hotly contested over the course of the decade. Rather than providing a stipulative definition of feminist fiction, as Greene does, for example, or ignoring the definitional question entirely, I want to point out that the task of a historicist study such as *Feminism and Its Fictions* is to address the range of fictions that counted as feminist in the decade, together with the range of feminisms by which they were shaped and which they forwarded.

At the same time, inescapably, my attention to the conflation of *women* and feminism has been shaped by the intense questioning that the term *women* has undergone as part of rethinking racism and racist exclusionary practices.[16] Such a conflation naturalizes *feminism* as political, intellectual, and discursive practices (among the other things that feminism is) by collapsing it into *women* as a social, historical, or biological category. Such a conflation naturalizes and makes inevitable the relation between *feminism* and *women* as if all women were feminists, as if there were not powerful political interests at work, as well as choices that women make in identifying and not identifying as feminists.[17] I see a direct and troubling relationship between this conflation and the slippage to "soft" CR, the slippage of feminism itself into a movement more concerned with women's self-esteem than with social justice.[18] As Dow points out in the conclusion to *Prime-Time Feminism*, "It would be nice if the majority of women in this country felt comfortable saying, 'Yes, I am a feminist'; but if the way to make that happen is to empty the term of all political implications so that all it really means is 'I like myself,' then feminism has not gained much" (213).

An exchange in the Letters section of *Chrysalis* 4 in 1977 locates this

problem in the decade of the 1970s, where it takes shape in conflicting uses of *female* (a word well worth resisting, in my view). The discussion focuses on Alice Bloch's review of Erika Duncan's (admittedly
pre-feminist) novel, *A Wreath of Pale White Roses*, which Bloch criticized
for its lack of a "female vision." The defenders of the novel, Duncan
herself and Gloria Feman Orenstein, both suggest in different ways that
the novel indeed has a *female* (though not a *feminist*) vision in its archetypal explorations of women's pain. Bloch in reply essentially refuses
the usefulness of the archetypal altogether, suggesting that the "stereotypical nature of these images of women was [not] being confronted
and transcended" (9). Since the archetypal is stereotypical (and thus
inauthentically "female"), Bloch defines her notion of (presumably authentic) "female vision" as "look[ing] at women's experience from the
inside rather than from the outside." This "female vision," she suggests,
is not the same as a more explicitly feminist demand for the "overtly
political" in fiction (9). At the same time, of course, such an implied criterion of authenticity must necessarily be feminist to the extent that it
requires a resistance to hegemonic notions of femininity. By the end of
this rather dizzying three-page exchange, all three writers acknowledge
the issue—"how to criticize nonfeminist writing from a feminist point
of view," as Bloch puts it—but the conflicting uses of *female* in their different relations to *feminist* is the problem none will acknowledge.[19]

In order to historicize the feminist renaissance of the 1970s, I attend to ways that ideas, discourses, problems, and issues circulated
between the writings of the Women's Liberation Movement and the
consciousness-raising novel. I use the popular feminist anthologies of
the decade, most notably *Sisterhood Is Powerful* and *Radical Feminism*,
along with other works of feminist criticism and theory, feminist jour-
nalism, and book reviews. Historicist scholars working on the Women's
Liberation Movement have the advantage of working on a movement
that developed an extensive independent press; I have relied in particular on *off our backs*, the longest-running feminist newspaper, founded in
1970 and still publishing today, as well as on other publications available
in microfilm in the Women's Herstory Archives. Two important literary-
critical studies to the shaping of my arguments are Rita Felski's *Beyond
Feminist Aesthetics: Feminist Literature and Social Change* (1989), with its brilliant analysis of the feminist public sphere, and Rachel Blau DuPlessis's
*Writing Beyond the Ending: Narrative Strategies of Twentieth-Century Women
Writers* (1985), with its crucial formulation of unfinished endings as a
kind of textual feminism. I have also relied on recent historical accounts
of feminism's second wave, including Flora Davis's *Moving the Mountain:
The Women's Movement in America Since 1960* (1991), and Barbara Ryan's
Feminism and the Women's Movement: Dynamics of Change in Social Move-

ment Ideology and Activism (1992), as well as such accounts dating from the 1970s as Jo Freeman's *The Politics of Women's Liberation* (1975), and Leah Fritz's *Dreamers and Dealers: An Intimate Portrait of the Women's Movement* (1979).

Perhaps the most important history of second-wave feminism has been Alice Echols's controversial book, *Daring to be BAD: Radical Feminism in America, 1967–1975* (1989). The distinction Echols draws between radical feminism as "a political movement dedicated to eliminating the sex-class system" and cultural feminism as "a counter-cultural movement aimed at reversing the cultural valuation of the male and the devaluation of the female" (6) is an enormously useful heuristic device, but it is also an extremely difficult distinction to work with outside her precise Movement history. For cultural feminism tended to come later than 1975 on the West Coast (the belatedness of West Coast feminism is something historians often note without examining[20]), and to take somewhat different forms in Midwestern communities like Columbus and Cincinnati, perhaps because the project of community-building may have been more important than it was in New York, especially for lesbian women in the Midwest.[21]

Too, the versions of radical and cultural feminisms Echols identifies need not be mutually exclusive. As is the case with any such typology—like the conventional set of divisions between liberal, radical, and socialist feminisms—the tidiness of the typology belies the messiness of experience, the shiftiness of circumstance, and the specificity of individual and institutional locations. Katie King's critique of Echols's book—that it "gives edges and borders to threads of connection: tendency becomes sect" (10)—makes this point more elegantly.

And yet, it is simply impossible to write a book about the Women's Liberation Movement without some recourse to typologies, and the term *radical feminism* is the most indispensable. The term is highly contested in contemporary accounts of second-wave feminism, whether its opposite term is *liberal, socialist,* or *cultural* feminism. My use in the book is somewhat less related to ideological typologies than to institutional locations, though the former is not entirely irrelevant; by *radical feminism* I mean both the small groups of Women's Liberation (as distinct from NOW or WEAL) and the analysis of sexual politics (as *sometimes* distinct from analyses of discrimination). My use, then, is more descriptive than prescriptive, and is meant to cover a variety of radical feminisms rather than to produce a particular radical feminism as the best or only kind.[22]

I began my work with a sense that the novels could usefully be recontextualized by setting them back into their dialogues with the writings of the Women's Liberation Movement. This book has taken shape in relation to the emergence of a substantial and growing body of work on the Women's Liberation Movement in the 1970s, in a wide range of disciplines. Academic and non-academic feminists alike are turning increasingly to histories and accounts of the Movement's crucial decade for clues about some of the tensions and contradictions in contemporary feminism, much as feminism's second wave produced a large body of work devoted to the first wave. If feminism has begun something like a third wave—a postulation subject to no small debate [23]—it is the more logical that we turn to mining our recent past. For if it is true, as Gerda Lerner has famously argued, that a knowledge of women's history is foundational to feminist consciousness, this recent move to re-examine and reprint important works from feminism's recent past is a crucial task for the survival of the Movement.

It is my hope that studies like mine will enable feminist scholars better to historicize the present—to see generational differences as more than divisive, to trace out more nuanced and complete visions of what constituted feminist fiction, and by which and whose criteria. As I suggested earlier, I also hope that by historicizing the feminist high renaissance of the 1970s, we can make more space for contemporary women writers of color in our discussions of feminist fiction. The feminist renaissance was overwhelmingly white: most of the bestselling novels and works of feminist theory were by (and about) white women, even when attentive to race and ethnicity. I address some of the reasons for the prominence of works by white women, and for the back-grounding of issues of ethnicity and class, in Chapter One. Feminism has changed since the 1970s, and changed in ways we cannot recognize nor attend to unless we theorize and historicize the movement's crucial decade—not, as Adrienne Rich wrote of re-reading canonical literary works, "to pass on a tradition but to break its hold over us" ("When We Dead Awaken" 35).

Notes

1. See Jo Freeman's chapter, "The Small Groups," in *The Politics of Women's Liberation*, for an account of these networks.

2. The phrase "sex-wars" here stands in for a complicated history and debate within feminism in the 1980s over the relationship of sexuality to women's freedom and self-determination, as "sex-radical" and "anti-porn" feminists faced off over pornography and a variety of other issues. See, e.g., B. Ruby Rich, "Review Essay: Feminism and Sexuality in the 1980s," for an overview.

3. Greene argues that her focus on metafiction necessarily results in a focus on white, middle-class women writers. "Not that they [African American women] do not write metafiction," she adds, pointing to works by Toni Morrison, Alice Walker, and Paule Marshall, but she omits these works from her study because of their different order of concern ("less urgent") with "white male tradition" (23–24). Greene's book ends with the hope that "the fiction of minority women

may take over from where white women's fiction left off" (220)—which it is, to say the least, unlikely to do.

4. Rose's implication that such critics are essentially insincere about political change because of their training in literary theory marks the depth of that generational divide; her implication also marks the difficulty of making mutually intelligible different theories about the relationship between fiction and social change, as those theories have emerged from different moments in feminism.

5. Again, this is reductive and polemical: my students include a very large number of students who were trained in New Critical reading strategies in high schools, and some who would identify with the Martha Quest reading strategies that Rose names. The tendency to read for difference is uneven, but sufficiently true, I think, for the purposes of my argument.

6. See, e.g., Tia Cross, Freada Klein, Barbara Smith, and Beverly Smith, "Face-to-Face, Day-to-Day—Racism CR." Most such workshops use CR techniques, particularly the sharing and interrogating of personal narratives.

7. When my Feminist Theory class "did CR" in 1996, for example, my students identified the single most important piece of knowledge produced by the exercise to be the impact of race, class, and nation on sexuality.

8. For a "pro-Bruce" view, see Toni Cabrillo, "N.O.W.'s Rush to Judgment: The *American Psycho* Connection"; for Bruce's self-defense, see "Can We Talk? An *OTI* Dialogue with Tammy Bruce and Julianne Malveaux"; for an "anti-Bruce" view, see Helen Zia, "How Now?"

9. See her discussion of *Dr. Quinn, Medicine Woman* in *Prime-Time Feminism*, especially 176–78.

10. It is, of course, extremely difficult to ascertain what readers actually do with fiction. I have longed for the imagined comfort of empirical evidence as I have worked on this project, fantasizing being able to do something with CR novels along the lines of Janice Radway's exploration of romance novels in *Reading the Romance*. The students who read various of the novels in my classes did provide me with "real" readers and "real" readings in their journals, though ones located differently historically. Discussions of the novels with second-wave feminists proved to be always already reconstructed; what we remember doing with fiction can be very different from what we did with it upon first reading.

11. This would be a surprise, I suspect, to many of Atwood's readers; Greene overreads Atwood's critiques of some kinds of feminism as disaffiliation (3).

12. For an example of precisely this kind of reading, see Myra Jehlen's reading of *The Adventures of Huckleberry Finn* in her entry "Gender," in *Critical Terms for Literary Study*. Though Jehlen's is a delightful and compelling reading of portions of Twain's novel, I remain unconvinced of the value of claiming *Huck Finn* as a feminist text; because a clever reader can make any novel do and undo gender, this seems to me an insufficient definition of feminist fiction.

13. Haraway discusses Delany briefly (220); Millett reads Genet in *Sexual Politics*, and Cixous notes his version of *écriture féminine* in "The Laugh of the Medusa" (255–56); Fetterley reads Mailer in *The Resisting Reader*.

14. An important exception is "Theories of Feminist Criticism: A Dialogue," in which Carolyn Heilbrun and Catharine Stimpson imagine two types of feminist criticism, and critics X and Y both debate the usefulness to feminism of both men writers and men characters.

15. See Rosalind Coward's "Are Women's Novels Feminist Novels?" (1980) for a critique of this position.

16. There is considerable debate among contemporary scholars about whether

this rethinking of "women" has its origins in the emergence of feminism's ties with post-structuralism or in the writings of women of color from the early 1980s. I want to claim both these origins, but to prioritize the political. For an account of feminism and post-structuralism, see Alcoff.

17. See my essay, "Fear of Feminism," where I draw a distinction between gender consciousness and feminist consciousness, for a further discussion of this question.

18. The obvious rejoinder—that self-esteem for women *is* an issue of social justice—takes us back to the important distinction between individual and collective struggles and solutions. As Dow and I have argued elsewhere, "individual solutions" are "hardly the political answer to a political struggle for justice" (13).

19. Of course, the different valuations of the archetypal are also at stake here. Duncan and Orenstein want to find a continuum from the archetypally female to the politically feminist (a sort of add-politics-and-stir position); Bloch sees them in opposition, implicitly taking a position more like Lillian Robinson's in "Dwelling in Decencies: Radical Criticism and the Feminist Perspective" (1971), where she argues: "There are, indeed, parallel characteristics in the lives of fictional women. We should not make a mythic fetish of these, but consider why they exist" (Brown and Olson 28). A later and (typically) more belligerent formulation of this position can be found in Angela Carter's *The Sadeian Woman* (1978), where she calls attempts to make myths and archetypes workable for feminism "consolatory nonsense" (5), further suggesting that "these archetypes serve only to confuse the main issue, that relationships between the sexes are determined by history and by the historical fact of the economic dependence of women upon men" (6–7).

20. As does Echols, for example (20–21); see also Katie King's critique of "the priority these cities [New York, Washington, D.C., and Chicago, where Echols did her interviewing] already had in movement histories, as *publication* as well as political centers" (23).

21. On Columbus, see Verta Taylor and Leila J. Rupp, "Women's Culture and Lesbian Feminist Activist: A Reconsideration of Cultural Feminism"; and Nancy Whittier, *Feminist Generations: The Persistance of the Radical Women's Movement*; on Cincinnati, see Susan Kathleen Freeman, "From the Lesbian Nation to the Cincinnati Lesbian Community: Lesbian Feminists' Construction of a Local Discourse in the 1970s."

22. I have in mind here a question King asks in relation to her critique of Echols' book: "How does one contend that a single term can refer to more than one political object?" (11).

23. A great deal of the "Feminist Generations" Conference in February 1996 at Bowling Green State University was devoted to the relationships between second- and third-wave feminism; particular examples include the fabulous multi-media presentation, "We Learn America Like a Script: Activism in the Third Wave, or, Enough Phantoms of Nothing," by Leslie Heywood and Jennifer Drake; and the panel, "Perspectives on the Second Wave," which included papers by Sylvia Bryant, Jennifer Wiley, 'Becca Cragin, and myself. For a sampling of "third wave" feminism, see Rebecca Walker's essay, "Becoming the Third Wave," and her edited collection, *To Be Real: Telling the Truth and Changing the Face of Feminism*, as well as Barbara Findlen's anthology, *Listen Up: Voices from the Next Feminist Generation*.

Chapter One
Feminism and/as Literacy

Feminism exploded in the first half of the 1970s. One way of accounting for this spectacular, exponential growth is to see it as a kind of literacy: a way of reading both texts and everyday life from a particular stance. The development over the second half of the decade of what would come to be called the "feminist public sphere" marks the institutionalization of that literacy, with, I will argue, the attendant problems of containment; moreover, this process of institutionalization was hotly contested within radical feminism. One of the peculiar features of the emergence of the feminist public sphere was the privileging of literature—of reading, writing, and critiquing literature as feminist activities. The importance that many feminists accorded to literary endeavors derived from an overinvestment in literacy, from the belief that literacy was feminism, rather than its precondition.

The 1970s was a crucial period for feminism in the United States, a period in which feminist issues and ideas from the small groups of radical feminists and the founding members of the National Organization for Women moved quickly into the mainstream. Fueled by extraordinary media coverage, membership in Women's Liberation groups grew spectacularly through the first half of the decade, and feminism in various forms filtered into virtually every area of U.S. life. Feminism moved into sports, for instance, in the 1973 tennis match between Billie Jean King and Bobby Riggs, played before thirty thousand spectators in the Houston Astrodome, plus a television audience of millions; into fiction television, in series such as *Maude* and a huge array of made-for-tv movies; into Hollywood film, in films such as *Alice Doesn't Live Here Anymore* and *An Unmarried Woman*; into the academy, in Women's Studies courses and programs, as well as in lawsuits to enforce Title IX; into the fine arts; and into the professions, as women entered professional schools in increasing numbers over the decade. Mainstream politics also were affected, both in Shirley Chisholm's bid to become the Democratic Party's first African-American woman nominee for the Presidency in 1972, and in the Democratic Party's fight over the inclusion of abortion rights in its party platform that same year.[1]

During this time, mainstream reforms proliferated and feminist institutions began to be founded. Among the reforms were Congressional passage of the Equal Rights Amendment (1972), Title IX and the Equal Credit Opportunity Act (1972 and 1974), the relegalization of abortion in the *Roe v. Wade* and *Doe v. Bolton* decisions (1973), and childcare bills passed by Congress (though vetoed by Presidents Nixon and Ford in 1971 and 1975). Feminist organizations sprang up, ranging from the National Women's Political Caucus (founded in 1971), to feminist women's health centers (about 50 by 1976), to rape crisis centers (about 400 centers, and an estimated 1500 antirape projects nationwide by 1976), to feminist periodicals like *off our backs* (1970) and *Ms.* magazine (1972), among the more than a hundred feminist publications founded in the early 1970s. Membership in NOW increased from three thousand in 1970 to over fifty thousand in 1974. In the academy, the Women's Equity Action League (WEAL, formed out of a split with NOW over abortion rights in 1968) filed a class-action complaint with the U. S. Department of Labor against all American universities and colleges, charging them with sex discrimination against academic women (1970); courses on women in U. S. universities increased from a handful in 1969 to over two thousand by 1973.[2]

Such a listing is, of course, only partial, but it does suggest the range of activities in which feminists engaged, and that located feminisms of various kinds in the public arena. The Movement's early period of growth was fueled by media coverage, as every major newsmagazine, from *Life* to *Time* to *Newsweek* to *Playboy*, ran a cover story on feminism in 1969–1970; Jo Freeman suggests that the Movement policy of speaking only to women reporters resulted in nearly all the initial magazine stories' being "personal conversion stories" (*Politics* 114).[3] In some cases, these conversion stories had ramifications for other women who worked for the magazines; Freeman notes that the women at *Newsweek* chose to file their EEOC complaint of discrimination on the same day the magazine's special issue on the women's movement came out (*Politics* 114–15). *Ladies' Home Journal* ran an eight-page feminist insert in response to a sit-in by a coalition of diverse feminist groups in 1970.[4] Three major works of radical feminism—*Sexual Politics*, *The Dialectic of Sex*, and *Sisterhood Is Powerful*—were published in 1970, widely reviewed in the mainstream media, and became best-sellers. Novels by self-identified feminist writers Alix Kates Shulman (*Memoirs of an Ex-Prom Queen* [1972]), Marge Piercy (*Small Changes* [1972]), and Erica Jong (*Fear of Flying* [1973]), and novels by women who were widely regarded as feminist writers, such as Joan Didion (*Play It As It Lays* [1971]), were similarly widely reviewed and read. Such media attention had both positive and negative effects on Women's Liberation. On the one hand, it meant that feminism was everywhere, was reaching, even if in watered-down or ridiculed versions, an enormous audience, and bringing far more women into the Movement than the recruiting strategies of the radical small groups, based in friendship- and activist-networks, could ever have reached.[5] Certainly, the coverage of Women's Liberation by the mainstream media helped contribute to the formation of a feminist public sphere, what Rita Felski has described as "an oppositional discursive space within contemporary society grounded in gender politics" (155).

On the other hand, this media attention created tremendous problems for radical feminists in particular, many of whom were caught in the cross-fire between radical groups' "structurelessness" and increasing phobia of leadership and the fact that, as Alice Echols puts it, "the one thing feminists could peddle were their ideas" (206).[6] Movement historians agree that this divisiveness, because it worked to silence radical feminists in the media, was responsible in part for the emergence by default of media figures like Gloria Steinem—women who were named feminist "leaders" without a Movement or even an organization behind them (Echols 210, F. Davis 118–19). In turn, the silencing of radical feminists led to the "deradicalization" of the Movement—whether in favor of liberal feminism, as Flora Davis argues, or of cultural feminism, as Echols argues.[7] This deradicalization process was also a product of the large numbers of women coming into Women's Liberation with no background in or experience with other political movements—women who had participated in neither the anti-racist work of the civil rights movement nor the critiques of capitalism and class of the New Left.[8]

It is useful to ask, though, what "coming into the movement" could actually mean during a time when, as Jo Freeman pointed out in 1975, "Membership in the movement is purely subjective—the participants are those who consider themselves participants" (*Politics* 104), regardless whether they belonged to any organized group. Similarly, Robin Morgan argued in the Introduction to *Sisterhood Is Powerful,*

This is not a movement one "joins." There are no rigid structures or membership cards. The Women's Liberation Movement exists where three or four friends or neighbors decide to meet regularly over coffee and talk about their personal lives. It also exists in the cells of women's jails, on the welfare lines, in the supermarket, the factory, the convent, the farm, the maternity ward, the streetcorner, the old ladies' home, the kitchen, the steno pool, the bed. It exists in your mind, and in the political and personal insights that you can contribute to change and shape and help its growth. It is frightening. It is very exhilarating. It is creating history, or rather, *herstory.*
And anyway, you cannot escape it. (xli; emphasis original)

Such a notion of *subjective membership*—of membership not only without formal organizational or institutional affiliations but also without necessarily any active participation in political work—illuminates a central problem in the history of feminism in the period: the problem of the definitional question itself. For what is feminism if feminism is everywhere? If feminism existed in any gathering of women, regardless of their politics, then feminism really was nothing more than gender consciousness.[9] If feminism were defined by individual acts of belief ("in your mind"), then it could be whatever anyone who called herself a feminist said it was.[10] If feminism were an inescapable force of history, then the definitional question was largely irrelevant; if feminism were inevitable, then only history (or herstory) could teach us what it meant in retrospect. These visions of subjective membership enabled feminists to side-step the definitional question, and thus to overlook or to downplay real debates in the Movement about politics.

Such a notion of subjective membership may have facilitated the Movement's explosive growth in the first half of the decade; the central message of the statement, *anyone can be a feminist*, is, of course, that *you* can be one too.[11] But this question of subjective membership with its attendant definitional problems might more usefully be recast as a question of *literacy*. That is, rather than seeing allegiance to the Women's Liberation Movement in terms of activity, we should see it in terms of a set of reading and interpretive strategies that people who identified themselves as feminists applied both to texts and to the world around them. In that sense, Women's Liberation really did exist "in your mind." Mass media coverage of the Movement helped make these strategies widely available, as did best-selling works of feminist theory, feminist anthologies, and the consciousness-raising novel; by mid-decade, the contours and conventions of feminist literacy were pervasive.

Part of the case for understanding feminism as literacy can be seen in Linda Alcoff's account of "becoming feminist" from an article on feminist theory in the late 1980s:

When women become feminists the crucial thing that has occurred is not that they have learned any new facts about the world but that they come to view those facts from a different position, from their own position as subjects. . . . This difference in positional perspective does not necessitate a change in what are taken to be facts, although new facts may come into view from the new position, but it does necessitate a political change in perspective since the point of departure, the point from which all things are measured, has changed. (434–35)[12]

Alcoff's sense of the shift in world view tallies nicely with a central convention of *Ms.* magazine's letters pages—the "click!" experience, which records "a moment of feminist insight" from everyday life, as it does with consciousness-raising, which I'll discuss in the next chapter.[13] More important is her sense that it is not information but positionality that creates feminist awareness—and what positionality means in this sense is a shift in interpretive frames, a shift in the site of interpretation.

The pervasive feminist literacy of the 1970s was based on gender consciousness, on women's sense of themselves *as women*—as members of a group socially, politically, and economically positioned differently from the group *men*. Alix Kates Shulman's *Burning Questions* (1978) illuminates the positional shift that feminist literacy entailed, when Zane describes becoming a feminist this way: "The truth was, I'd never thought women treated unfairly given their difference; I'd only thought me treated unfairly to have been born one" (236). Zane's shift here—from gender as an individual misfortune to gender as a political category—is precisely the baseline feminist literacy of the decade. Feminist writers built on that feminist literacy in a variety of ways, in part by the ways they named the political situation of the group *women*. As "an oppressed majority," women needed only to band together to create a powerful block for reform; as a "caste," as Simone de Beauvoir had named women in *The Second Sex*, women needed to refuse the "otherness" that kept them trapped in immanence (as well as a socialist revolution); as victims of the "sex/gender system," in Gayle Rubin's felicitous phrase, women needed nothing less than a total social transformation to achieve equality.[14] These are, of course, only a few of the wide range of political positions that feminist literacy could lead to—though it did not necessarily have to lead to any particular political stance. The very ubiquity of the Women's Liberation Movement in Robin Morgan's description reflects the open-endedness of feminist literacy.[15]

In the first half of the 1970s, both new facts and new ways of reading the world were made widely available in media coverage of the Movement, and the two combined in the "personal conversion stories" that Jo Freeman argued were central to that media coverage. As a set of interpretive strategies, as a kind of literacy, feminism could be far more widely available to women than membership in specific groups or participation in specific activities. What Gloria Steinem would later call "everyday rebellions" in the title of a collection of her essays—small, individual acts of resistance—could be for many who identified themselves as feminists the sum total of their feminist practice, as could reading feminist books. Robin Morgan's Introduction to *Sisterhood Is Powerful* exemplifies the range of such rebellions in this catalogue of everyday oppressions:

Everything, from the verbal assault on the street, to a "well-meant" sexist joke your husband tells, to the lower pay you get at work (for doing the same job a man would be paid more for), to television commercials, to rock-song lyrics, to the pink or blue blanket they put on your infant in the hospital nursery, to speeches by male "revolutionaries" that reek of male supremacy—everything seems to barrage your aching brain, which has fewer and fewer protective defenses to screen such things out. (xviii)

Joanna Russ's *The Female Man* (1975) demonstrates this notion of "everyday rebellions" when her character Joanna asserts: "I committed my first revolutionary act yesterday. I shut the door on a man's thumb" (203). The pervasiveness of women's oppression thus could be matched by the pervasiveness of opportunities for resistance and rebellion.

It is in the context of a widespread and growing feminist literacy that we can best understand the institutionalization of feminist practice over the second half of the decade. As some radical feminist ideas and issues were taken up or taken over by liberal feminists, specialized groups and institutions were increasingly formed to address them, as exemplified by the battered women's and women's health movements. This move to institutionalization and specialization tended to emphasize reform feminism on the one hand, in lobbying and other kinds of negotiations with the state, and (more or less) separatist cultural work, on the other, in the founding of women's businesses, bookstores, publishing houses, and record companies.[16] Both of these feminist strategies differed from the theory-building intellectual work and zap-action demonstrations of the earlier radical groups. Reform feminism, because of its practical need for numbers in order to make a case to powerful anti-feminist interests, tended to shy away from some radical ideas and issues for fear of alienating "mainstream" women and men, as NOW's "purge mentality" toward lesbians in the early 1970s exemplifies (Echols 219). Separatist cultural feminism, in which feminist groups, as Echols points out, came to exist more like communities than movements, tended to be "small, self-contained subcultures that proved hard to penetrate, especially to newcomers unaccustomed to their norms and conventions" (281), and moved in precisely the opposite direction toward exclusivity.

The moves to institutionalization and specialization in the second half of the 1970s created what Rita Felski and others have called a feminist public sphere: a loose network of feminist-oriented institutions—reform and separatist, capitalist and non-profit, political and cultural. Rather than a unified and autonomous counter-public sphere, Felski argues, this loose network of institutions can better be understood as "a series of cultural strategies which can be effective across a range of levels both outside and inside existing institutional structures" (171). Felski specifies three parts of this feminist public sphere: "an infrastructure of decentralized collectively organized projects, such as women's groups, feminist publications, day-care and health centers, and bookstores"; institutions such as battered women's shelters and rape crisis centers that "function with a degree of autonomy but within the framework of existing social welfare bureaucracies"; and the "feminist activity . . . within existing state institutions, including bureaucracies and universities," such as women's studies and affirmative action programs (170).

Feminist service provision—in examples like rape crisis centers and battered women's shelters—began with a complicated justification. Such centers and shelters were understood to be a logical outgrowth of feminist work on these issues, and a home for feminist analyses of the political implications of rape and violence against women. These institutions had the dual function of meeting women's needs and performing educational work. Additionally, as Carol Anne Douglas pointed out in 1976, providing services to women in crisis sent "a political message":

Women who are in difficulties should be able to turn to the feminist movement for support—providing support for them is a political message. I don't want those women who feel they have no place to go or no one to listen to them to have to turn to the Catholic Church or Rev. Moon. . . . I don't want women to have to turn to the patriarchy for care; we know what kind of "care" they will provide. ("how feminist is therapy?" 23)

Implicit in the recruitment-oriented "political message" of feminist service provision was a sense that women should be able to get their needs met within Women's Liberation, enabling them to turn away from patriarchy. This required that feminist institutions be autonomous. As Felski points out, however, the autonomy of such institutions—arguably, of all feminist institutions in the feminist public sphere—was (and continues to be) constantly under negotiation, especially in relation to questions of funding and of the professionalism and professional training of staff and administrators.

Indeed, the problem of the feminist autonomy of such institutions was a central issue in the debates within radical feminism over the process of institution building. Echols addresses specifically the debates over the Feminist Economic Network (FEN) in the context of debates over feminist businesses generally (269–81); she argues that the increasing emphasis on institution building fed the ascendence of cultural feminism and led ultimately to the deradicalization of the women's movement.[17] One of the central issues at stake in the radical feminist debates about institutionalization was the question of containment: the fear that *a place* for feminist work created in the process of institutionalization would become *the only place* for a kind of feminist work that was thoroughly compromised and coopted by its location within a larger institution. As feminist work inside feminist institutions became in many instances increasingly mainstreamed—as crisis work, for instance, became increasingly funded by state and local government, or as Women's Studies became increasingly imbricated in traditional disciplines—much feminist work has become professionalized in ways that were anathema to radical feminists at mid-decade.[18]

At the heart of this feminist public sphere, Felski argues, is a fundamental duality: "*internally*, it generates a gender-specific identity grounded in a consciousness of community and solidarity among women; *externally*, it seeks to convince society as a whole of the validity of feminist claims, challenging existing structures of authority through political activity and theoretical critique" (168). Both the internal and external practices contribute to feminist literacy, both consolidating literacy and publicizing it. Felski's argument about this duality is crucial to understanding how the feminist public sphere actually did (and does) function. Whatever the orientation of its specific institutions—from NOW to the Michigan Womyn's Music Festival—many feminist women moved among and between them, buying books and attending readings in women's bookstores, sending money (whether dues or donations) to NOW for its ERA campaign, volunteering at rape crisis centers, subscribing to both *Ms.* and *off our backs*.[19] This duality is at the heart not only of the diversity and contradictions of the movement as a whole, but also of individual women's experiences as feminists within it. Felski points out that one's membership in the feminist public sphere "is conditional not on the acceptance of a clearly delineated theoretical framework, but on a more general sense of commonality in the experience of oppression" (167).

The feminist public sphere was frequently imagined as a (or the) feminist *community* in the 1970s, even before the institution building at mid-decade, a community constructed precisely by the feminist literacy that Felski names "a commonality in the experience of oppression." Shulamith Firestone in *The Dialectic of Sex* (1970), for instance, described feminist community as a defense against the painful realization of women's oppression: "The first women are fleeing the massacre, and, shaking and tottering, are beginning to find each other. Their first move is a careful joint observation, to resensitize a fractured consciousness" (2). Sherry Sonnett Trumbo's essay, "A Woman's Place is in the Oven," brought the anthology *Radical Feminism* (1973) to rest with its vision of a feminist community of struggle:

We must remember that we are only one of a larger group and that our strength as individuals is directly proportional to our strength as a group. We must learn to speak to each other, to make each other aware of our possibilities, capabilities, and alternatives. Our freedom will not be handed to us by society, but it will be taken when we as a group have the strength and force to demand it. . . .

No matter which road we follow, we all have two things to do: to liberate ourselves and to liberate each other. We can't do one without the other and we can't
do either unless we do both. (Koedt, Levine, and Rapone 424)

Trumbo unites the personal and the political, the individual and the
collective, in this vision of the possibility for change; her image of feminist community is created discursively—in speaking to each other—and
moves outward from there into the act of "taking our freedom." Susan
Koppelman Cornillon's introduction to *Images of Women in Fiction: Feminist Perspectives* (1972) provides a similar vision of feminist community,
and locates it specifically in the anthology itself:

The people who have written this book range in age from twenty one to the late
sixties. Some of us haven't gone in formal education beyond high school and
some of us have Ph.D.'s. Some have been published before and some of us have
never written before. Some are married, some single, some divorced. All of us
are trying to belong to ourselves. About half of us are parents with children
ranging from infancy to adulthood. Many of us are teachers, some are students,
some are writers, some librarians, some waitresses, some full-time mothers at
home. We are from all over the country and are all excited and happy to have
found one another. (xi–xii)

Publishing feminist essays enables women to "find one another" despite
their differences; what unites them besides appearing in the same anthology is their common struggle "to belong to ourselves" and their
pleasure in this vision of community itself.

Such visions of community and of "sisterhood" are central to feminist
literacy, even when they depend less on memberships in organizations
that perform feminist work than on a more abstract sense of "commonality" in Felski's term. If, as Josephine Donovan argues in *Feminist
Theory*, "Feminism is a political interpretation of the condition of being a
woman, and it urges recognition of that condition as the basis for political identity," then what subtends both "interpretation" and "identity"
as feminist practices is collectivity, is a community of (feminist) women
(2nd ed., 199).[20] The assertion of feminist identity turns on the interplay of the individual and the collective, as that interplay was concisely
caught in the emergence of Helen Reddy's 1972 Grammy-winning song,
"I Am Woman," as a feminist anthem.[21] The initial assertion of gender
identity was a crucial first step in attaining feminist literacy, as well as in
developing a vision of feminist community.

Moreover, for (relatively) privileged white women, the assertion of
gender identity *was* the assertion of political identity. Identifying with
the category *women* could require, in radical feminism at least, the un-
doing of certain kinds of bourgeois individualist assumptions. For Red-

stockings and New York Radical Women, for example, a political vision of membership in the group *women* meant identifying with women more oppressed than oneself: "We define our best interest as that of the poorest, most brutally exploited women," Redstockings argued in "Redstockings Manifesto" (R. Morgan 600); "We define the best interests of women as the best interests of the poorest, most insulted, most despised, most abused woman on earth," New York Radical Women argued in "Principles" (R. Morgan 583–84). The logic of this analysis led Redstockings to call on women to "repudiate all economic, racial, educational or status privileges that divide us from other women" (R. Morgan 600) in order to participate in a sisterhood based on this refiguration of women's interests.

Feminist community, sisterhood, was a fantasy—a fantasy that feminists of all kinds tried in various ways to concretize over the course of the second wave. Its importance can be demonstrated by the effectivity of appeals to sisterhood, as my discussions of the sex/race analogy in Chapter Six reveal.[22] The institution-building strategies at mid-decade that gave rise to the feminist public sphere worked to concretize the fantasy of sisterhood within the larger arena of widespread feminist literacy. Literature and literary criticism were central to these endeavors. Felski specifically points to "the importance that literature has assumed in the development of an oppositional women's culture"; she argues that

the feminist novel focuses upon areas of personal experience which women are perceived to share in common beyond their cultural, political, and class differences. The feminist public sphere exemplifies a repoliticization of culture which seeks to relate literature and art to the specific experiences and interests of an explicitly gendered community. (167)

Producing, critiquing, interpreting, and teaching literature were often perceived as front-line activities in the 1970s, especially among theorists and the growing number of feminist academics. Many feminist theorists directly linked women's oppression in the world to women's depiction in literary works written by men, and nearly all early works of feminist theory found some way that literature oppressed women.[23]

The most significant example is Kate Millett's *Sexual Politics*, which derived a theory of patriarchy from Millett's readings of literature. D. H. Lawrence, Henry Miller, and Norman Mailer, for Millett, were writers who helped to build the "vast gray stockades of the sexual reaction"; as "counterrevolutionary sexual politicians," they "both reflected and actually shaped attitudes" toward women and toward sexuality (329). Such reading strategies for literary texts required major changes in the practice of literary criticism, as Millett argued:

It has been my conviction that the adventure of literary criticism is not re-
stricted to a dutiful round of adulation, but is capable of seizing upon the larger
insights which literature affords into the life it describes, or interprets, or even
distorts. . . . I have operated on the premise that there is room for a criticism
which takes into account the larger cultural context in which literature is con-
ceived and produced. (xiv)

Millett's reading strategies in *Sexual Politics* were foundational to feminist literary criticism. Her readings of Lawrence, Mailer, and Miller set
the stage for Adrienne Rich's notion of "re-vision" from her influential
essay, "When We Dead Awaken: Writing as Re-Vision" (1971), and for
Judith Fetterley's practice in *The Resisting Reader* (1978); Millett's reading
of Genet, moreover, strongly parallels Hélène Cixous's argument that
his work represents *écriture féminine* in "Laugh of the Medusa."[24]

Millett's attack on New Critical "adulation" of the text was designed
to open up new ways of reading for academic critics; in 1975, Cheri
Register suggested that feminist criticism was only just beginning to be
an academic endeavor. Register provides a non-academic context for
emergent feminist literary criticism in the opening paragraph of her
"American Feminist Literary Criticism: A Bibliographic Introduction":

A young woman is sitting on the bus reading Doris Lessing's *The Golden Notebook*. Her young male seat companion comments, "You must be into women's
lib." At a workshop on sexism in education, an English teacher asks what she can
give her seventh graders—in addition to *Little Women*—to counter the influence
of *Double Date* and *Double Feature*. The members of a feminist collective circu-
late among themselves a well-worn volume of Sylvia Plath's poetry. The women's
magazine *Redbook* [in 1972] prints an excerpt from Kate Chopin's *The Awakening*, which has been ignored since the controversy following its publication in
1899. (1)

These "incidents," Register argues, "signal the emergence of *feminist
criticism*, a new literary analysis based on the tenets of the American
women's movement." Register notes the importance of "the informal
feminist grapevine" as it provides "the impetus to read Doris Lessing,"
even without supplying an "analytical method" for feminist reading. Implicit in Register's opening paragraphs is an argument that the feminist
grapevine also provides a model for "instructors of female studies" to
exchange syllabi, reading lists, and pedagogical advice, a grapevine that
had only begun to be "organized" since the founding of the Modern
Language Association's Commission on the Status of Women in 1970
(1–2). The emergence of feminist criticism in academic institutions was
thus both preceded by and dependent upon feminist literacy.

"Whenever I talk about feminist criticism, I am amazed at how high a moral tone I take," Carolyn Heilbrun and Catharine Stimpson wrote in 1975 (72). The link feminists found between women's oppression and women's depiction helps account for this tone, the dominant tone of feminist literary criticism in the 1970s. This passage from Marcia Holly's "Consciousness and Authenticity: Toward a Feminist Aesthetic" (1975) was typical, with its rhetoric of repudiation, radicalism, and authenticity:

Feminist criticism represents the repudiation of previous formulations about women. It has emerged from a radical perspective about literature and sex roles, and is a tentative beginning in the development of a feminist literary aesthetic — one that is fundamentally at odds with masculinist value standards, measuring literature against an understanding of authentic female life. (46)

The link feminist critics made between women's oppression and women's depiction also reflected a particular notion of the way literature works in the world. In *The Feminine Mystique*, Betty Friedan asked, "What is missing from the image that mirrors and creates the identity of women in America today?" (29). In her survey of feminist work on literature through about 1973, Register identified "the factors most frequently cited in discussing literature's social implications" as the "use of female stereotypes as tools in sex-role socialization, the need for positive role-models, [and] male authors' failure to provide realistic solutions to common female problems" (7). "Mirroring" and "creating" female identity was clearly at issue in feminist criticism, as this focus on role models and stereotypes makes clear.

But the feminist critical project was also profoundly utopian, as Holly's essay points out:

I found myself wondering about all those professors who had pronounced literature psychologically real, presenting themselves as humanists unmoved by conventional wisdom and ideology. I wondered what it would *take* to make literature realistic, literary critics humanist; what would it really *mean* for writers to present us with the 'truth' we seek in literature. (38–39; emphasis original)

Were literature to reflect women's "truths," according to Register, it would bring about nothing less than the radical transformation of culture itself: "Once literature begins to serve as a forum, illuminating female experience, it can assist in humanizing and equilibrating the culture's value system, which has historically served predominantly male interests" (19).

Feminist criticism's utopian project of total social transformation rested on an enormous faith in the power of texts to make change. That faith in turn rested on a belief in feminist literacy *as* social change: providing new ways of mirroring and creating women's identity could tranform culture only insofar as "your mind" was the real battleground of feminism. The belief that feminist literacy *was* feminism—that women's interpretive strategies were equivalent to social change—privileged literature and literary criticism not only as means but in some sense as ends in themselves. Bonnie Zimmerman's argument in *The Safe Sea of Women: Lesbian Fiction, 1969–1989* (1990) about reading as identity clarifies this logic; Zimmerman writes, "Lesbian novels are read by lesbians in order to affirm lesbian existence. Conversely, the books a woman reads are what makes her a lesbian feminist, or a member of 'the lesbian community'" (15). My intention here is not to collapse the distinction between lesbian and feminist (though Zimmerman's use of "lesbian feminist" hints at such a collapse), but rather to argue that the political import of reading as a practice of identity affirmation is underpinned by a belief in feminism as literacy.

The sense of feminist criticism as a revolutionary activity continued throughout the decade. In her essay, "Personally Speaking: Feminist Critics and the Community of Readers" (1981), Jean Kennard quotes one of her students identifying feminist criticism as a kind of "Underground":

This spring, I found a group of women who are just like me. We read, we write, and once a week we slink upstairs to a seminar room where we discuss contemporary women's fiction. No matter that this seminar is approved by the graduate school of English, that all its participants function respectably outside the course, that the professor is chair of the English department. We behave as if we are part of The Underground. We're suspicious of auditors. We meet in twos and threes outside class in a seedy diner and whisper rude things about Saul Bellow. (140)

No matter how respectable or authorized feminist criticism might be by the early 1980s, as the student points out, women still could experience it as a metaphoric underground—as subversive, as secretive, as a sort of academic equivalent to armed struggle against an occupying power. "Underground" in this instance was an empowering metaphor for feminist criticism's marginality within the English department, as it enlisted resonances of important political struggle to describe even the practice of "whisper[ing] rude things about Saul Bellow."

Despite the centrality of literature to feminism in the 1970s, successful women writers in the radical groups in the Movement, including theorists as well as novelists, found themselves in a difficult position. Because of the Movement's radical egalitarianism, or what Joreen [Jo Freeman] called its "tyranny of structurelessness," success was often viewed as selling out, or cashing in on the Movement. As Women's Liberation struggled over leadership, the media's creation of Movement "stars," and its fears of being co-opted, women writers came to be "especially mistrusted" (Echols 206). According to Echols, this "distrust of writers was so great that Alix Kates Shulman recalls being 'terrified' that she might have to choose between being a writer and being an activist in the movement" (206). In "The Grand Coolie Damn," Marge Piercy identified her writing—"[I] make a living off my writing and care about it"—as one of several factors that initially prevented her from joining Women's Liberation (R. Morgan 482). Brooke [Williams] and Hannah Darby, writing in *off our backs* in 1976, articulate what they see as the "dichotomy" between art and politics, suggesting that the emergence of local Movement leaders who "are all self-defined poets rather than politicos" created a situation where "Instead of having competent political workers in positions of power, we have people who, in an attempt to overcome the divide between politics and art, bring the values of their art to bear on the movement, and, as a result, are killing off politics" ("business" 28). Despite this distrust, literature, literary criticism, and writers remained central to the Movement.

We can see women writers' centrality to the Movement enacted in the number of protagonists in the feminist novels of the 1970s who are writers. The important example from the 1960s is, of course, Doris Lessing's Anna Wulf, in *The Golden Notebook* (1962); Lessing's novel and its centrality to emergent feminist literary criticism helped set the stage for the feminist writer-protagonists of the next decade.[25] These include Dorothy Bryant's diarist in *Ella Price's Journal* (1972), Erica Jong's poet Isadora in *Fear of Flying* (1973), Fay Weldon's feminist journalist Praxis Duveen in *Praxis* (1978), Alix Kates Shulman's memoirist Zane in *Burning Questions* (1979), and even Christa Wolf's report-writing scientist "Anders" in "Selbstversuch: Traktatt zu einam Protokoll" (1972). Alice Walker later adapted this tradition for African-American women in Celie's letters to God and to her sister in *The Color Purple* (1982). The protagonist of E. M. Broner's *Her Mothers* (1975) is working on *Unafraid Women*, an historical study of heroic women of the past; just as Jong's Isadora reads the lives and works of women writers before her, so Broner's protagonist interrogates the lives of the women she studies, looking for role models and for strategies for living. Margaret Atwood's *Lady Oracle* (1976) gives us another woman writer, Joan Foster, whose depiction suggests several important ways that women writers are central to feminism in the 1970s. Joan writes romances under a pseudonym, and publishes a collection of automatic writings as well. When Joan fakes her own death, the press quickly calls it a suicide, and transforms her into a Plathian suicide-goddess:

I'd been shoved into the ranks of those other unhappy ladies, scores of them apparently, who'd been killed by a surfeit of words. . . . The curse, the doom. I began to feel that even though I hadn't committed suicide, perhaps I should have. They made it sound so plausible. (346)

Atwood's parody of the woman-poet-suicide association here serves several purposes. It underlines feminism's project of interrogating cultural assumptions about women writers (that writing—like any other achievement—is fatal to women in this example), and reminds us as well that Sylvia Plath was a crucial figure in the literary feminism of the 1970s.

Plath was invoked repeatedly as the archetypal victim of patriarchy, whose work and life were seen to "delineate the psychological and emotional horror of a woman living in a society that keeps women down," as Anita Rapone argued in an essay on her work in the anthology *Radical Feminism* (407). Two of the major early feminist anthologies—*Radical Feminism*, in Rapone's essay, and *Sisterhood Is Powerful*, which reprinted "The Jailor"—located Plath in relation to the Women's Liberation Movement. Moreover, discussions of *The Bell Jar*, as well as of Plath's poetry, were a staple of emergent feminist literary criticism.[26] The narrative inevitability that woman + genius = suicide, which Atwood so brilliantly parodies in *Lady Oracle*, emblemizes a particular conception of pre-Movement feminist struggle: one of the goals of Women's Liberation was precisely to break that equation, to make more space in the world for gifted women.[27]

More recent discussions of the writer-protagonist in feminist fiction help to clarify my argument here. Peter J. Rabinowitz notes in *Before Reading: Narrative Conventions and the Politics of Interpretation* that Erica Jong's *Fear of Flying*, like so many modern novels with women artists as protagonists, makes it difficult "to tell to what extent Isadora Wing's problems result from her being a woman and to what extent they stem from her being an artist" (215). Rabinowitz argues that because artists are supposed to suffer (a modern truism), novels that focus on the woman artist's sufferings confuse their feminist message that women suffer because they are women. But Rabinowitz misses the logic of feminist novels about women artists: it is precisely the presumably greater "freedom" of women writers that makes them the perfect protagonists for the feminist fiction of this period. For the same modern conventions about artists' suffering also establish the artist as socially (at least) unconventional, as potentially "freer" from strict gender codes and traditional femininity. "You might expect," wrote Elaine Showalter in 1971, "that women writers would be the most emancipated women in the world" (Koedt, Levine, and Rapone 391). Rachel Blau DuPlessis argues in *Writing Beyond the Ending* that "Making a female character be a 'woman of genius' sets in motion not only conventional notions of womanhood but also conventional romantic notions of the genius, the person apart, who because unique and gifted, could be released from social ties and expectations" (84–85).[28]

The "woman of genius" or the writer protagonist was thus precisely positioned to enact the "resistances to consciousness" Irene Peslikis laid out in her essay of the same title in *Sisterhood Is Powerful.* The artist's (relative) release from social conventions functioned politically as a temptation to false consciousness—as a temptation to believe, falsely, *"that individual solutions are possible,* that we don't need solidarity and a revolution for our liberation," in Peslikis's terms (R. Morgan 379; emphasis original). For such a writer-protagonist to be or to become a feminist thus demonstrated the overcoming of false consciousness, and proved that even "free women" (in the title of Anna Wulf's novel) could not be free without the Movement. Moreover, as the repeated invocations of the Plath mythos made clear, the personal solutions available to "women of genius" were lethal. Nothing less than "how to save your own life," in the title of Jong's second novel (1977), was at stake.

Two of the other resistances Peslikis identified are relevant here: the belief that "education privilege" could leverage women out of their oppression, and the intellectual snobbery that divides women politically (379). While the struggles of privileged women—women privileged by race, class, ethnicity, ability, sexual identity—dominate the feminist fiction of the period, even the exceptions—Rita Mae Brown's lesbian Molly Bolt or Marge Piercy's working-class and Jewish protagonists, for example—have or attain "education privilege," and the struggle to get it is often central to the novels. Education privilege in these novels is clearly not liberation, but rather only another aspect of the protagonists' struggles.

Focusing on such privileged women characters was related to a particular rhetorical strategy of (some kinds of) feminism in the period. By the same logic that writer-protagonists served to demonstrate the distinction between privilege and liberation, demonstrating the oppression of privileged women "proved" the existence of a purely gender-based oppression, an oppression uncomplicated by race or class factors. The refiguration of women's "best interests" that Redstockings and New York Radical Women advocated in their manifestos—which required privileged women to identify with others more oppressed than they—is reversed in this logic: less privileged women could be taught their oppression by identifying the struggles of the privileged as evidence of sexism. If such *purely female*—because "unraced" and "unclassed"—protagonists were oppressed, then surely women's oppression must be real—and the more real for women less "purely female" because less privileged.[29]

The critique of intellectual snobbery—which parallels the critique of professionalism in radical feminist debates about institution building— may help account for the number of women writer-protagonists who are not "women of genius" in DuPlessis's sense, but rather more "amateur" writers. The diarists, memoirists, and letter-writers in particular exemplify and enact in strikingly clear ways the primacy of the personal narrative in feminist discourses. Moreover, the protagonists who write diaries, memoirs, and letters parallel the interest in emergent feminist criticism in reclaiming these forms as specifically "women's" or "female" literary forms—as forms that were historically available to women (and available to greater numbers and a greater diversity of women than poetry or the novel), and as forms that were particularly amenable to recording and representing the realities of women's lives.[30] The "amateur" writer-protagonists could enable feminist fiction to have it both ways: both to enlist the logic of oppression-despite-privilege of the woman artist novel and at the same time to maintain that this logic applied as well to ordinary women.

The novels with writer-protagonists, amateur or not, provide striking evidence of the centrality of literary endeavor to feminism in the 1970s. The broader social forces at work in "mirroring" and "creating" women's identities, to return to Friedan's terms, were brought home in the novels depicting individual women's struggles to tell their stories. The struggle for narrative *was* the struggle for identity; the struggle for consciousness *was* the struggle for total social transformation. Both linkages between these sets of struggles depended on an overinvestment in feminist literacy: an understanding that feminist literacy, as a set of interpretive strategies for reading both texts and everyday life, was feminism.

The institutionalization of feminist literacy at mid-decade contributed to this overvaluation. For if feminist thinking could create feminist institutions—could create real and material alternatives to patriarchy—then, by a logic of "critical mass," it could create enough such alternatives to overthrow patriarchy. Importantly, many of the material alternatives to patriarchy created in the feminist public sphere were institutions of cultural production: not only shelters for battered women providing an alternative to abusive familial situations, but also publishers and record companies, bookstores and music festivals, made up the feminist public sphere. Thus the institutionalization of literacy ensured its continued circulation, while also demonstrating its materiality.

These arguments about literacy and institutionalization are a necessary background for the next chapter's discussion of consciousness-raising (CR). For CR has too often been understood metaphorically, as if the term named any way of producing knowledge about feminism or about women, rather than the precise and specific practice that it was;

the next chapter traces the increasing metaphorization of CR over the course of the decade. The media, which played such an important role in creating feminist literacy in the early 1970s, did not raise consciousness as such, nor, as Dow and I have argued, does it today ("When Feminism Meets the Press"). Rather, CR is best understood in its distinctiveness against the background of other kinds of knowledge production and knowledge circulation.

Notes

1. For media coverage of the movement in the 1970s, see Susan J. Douglas, *Where the Girls Are: Growing Up Female with the Mass Media*, especially 166–85 for a summary of major media coverage during 1970 alone; see also Flora Davis, *Moving the Mountain: The Women's Movement in America Since 1960*, 106–20. The term "Women's Liberation" was originally used by radical feminists to distinguish themselves from reform-oriented groups like the National Organization for Women, but was later both applied to and used by a wide range of feminist groups, including NOW. For a discussion of the King-Riggs match-up in relation to other feminist inroads in sports, see F. Davis, 215–16. On made-for-television movies, see Elayne Rapping, *The Movie of the Week: Private Stories, Public Events.* On women protagonists in Hollywood film, see Charlotte Brunsdon, "A Subject for the Seventies." For an account of feminist impact on education, see F. Davis, 205–6. On feminism and the fine arts in the United States, see Lucy R. Lippard, "Sweeping Exchanges: The Contribution of Feminism to the Art of the 1970s." On women in professional schools, see F. Davis, 218. On Chisholm, see F. Davis, 188–90. On abortion rights, see Chapter Three.

2. These figures are a compilation of statistics and information from Jo Freeman, *The Politics of Women's Liberation*, Chapter Six, "The Policy Impact of the Women's Liberation Movement," and F. Davis, *Moving the Mountain.* On NOW membership, see F. Davis, 108; on feminist publications, see J. Freeman, 109–11, and F. Davis, 117; on *off our backs* in particular, see Jennie Ruby, "*Off Our Backs*"; on the ERA, see J. Freeman, 238–39, and F. Davis, 121–36; on Title IX, see F. Davis, 212–13; on the ECOA, see F. Davis, 147–52; on abortion, see F. Davis, 157–83; on childcare bills and vetoes, see F. Davis, 280–85; on the NWPC, see J. Freeman, 160–62; on feminist women's health centers, see J. Freeman, 158, and F. Davis, 234; on rape crisis centers, see F. Davis, 314–15; on WEAL, see J. Freeman, 152–54; on Women's Studies, see F. Davis, 220.

3. For a much less positive view of the effectivity of this and other media strategies of radical feminists (and a wonderful analysis of NOW's media strategies), see Bernadette Barker-Plummer, "News as a Political Resource: Media Strategies and Political Identity in the U.S. Women's Movement, 1966–1975."

4. See Echols, 195–97 and F. Davis, 111–14 for contrasting discussions of the sit-in; Davis also notes that the insert itself became a resource for the Women's Bureau to refer letter-writers to Women's Liberation groups.

5. Jo Freeman discusses the "radical community" out of which independent feminism emerged as "like-minded women" who "had participated in one or more of the many protest activities of the 1960s"; this community "had established its own ethos and its own institutions" by the late 1960s, and was co-optable by feminists (58). As large numbers of women came into Women's

Liberation from outside the radical community, they brought with them very different assumptions about politics and social change; Jo Freeman suggests that the CR group served as an "artificial institution" that "provides some degree of structured interaction" as the Movement expanded beyond the radical community (117). See Chapter Two for a discussion of CR.

6. The term "structurelessness" comes from Joreen's [Jo Freeman's] essay, "The Tyranny of Structurelessness," where she specifically critiques the Movement's radical egalitarianism as disabling; see Echols 204–10, for a discussion of crises in radical groups over leadership and media-star issues.

7. Liberal and cultural feminism are not so easily separable, as I argue in discussing *Ms.* in Chapter Four; Echols herself sees their relation when she argues that the ascendence of cultural feminism led to liberal feminism's prominence.

8. Rather than simply blaming radical feminists for their tendency to focus on gender to the exclusion of race and class—an analysis that usually assumed if it only rarely attended to these issues—it seems to me that the large numbers of women who had never paid any attention to race or class issues or analyses and who came into Women's Liberation in the period 1970–1975 must be accounted a factor.

9. For an incisive critique of this notion in contemporary popular feminism, see bell hooks's essay on Naomi Wolf's *Fire with Fire*, "Dissident Heat," in *Outlaw Culture: Resisting Representations*, especially 98–101; for a discussion of the distinction between gender consciousness and feminist consciousness, see my "Fear of Feminism."

10. This position, according to Echols, was a central problem in the struggles among radical feminists over feminist businesses (see below).

11. This notion of subjective membership has continued to be problematic—to say the least—in mid-1990s debates about feminism, in which seemingly anyone who claims to be a feminist can purport to speak for the Movement, even when her views are funded by right-wing institutions like the Olin Foundation. See, e.g., Christina Hoff Sommers, *Who Stole Feminism?* (1994); for an account of the Olin Foundation's politics, see Ellen Messer-Davidow, "Manufacturing the Attack on Liberalized Higher Education," especially 59–63.

12. Alcoff attempts in this article to steer a course between cultural feminism and post-structuralism/postmodernism; she compares this change in consciousness to "colonial subjects" who "begin to identify with the colonized rather than the colonizer" (434)—an analogy between "women" and "the colonized" that is similar to the sex/race analogy I discuss in Chapter Six.

13. In the Introduction to *Letters to Ms. 1972–1987*, editor Mary Thom explains that the use of "click!" to describe "a moment of feminist insight" was coined by Jane O'Reilly in "The Housewife's Moment of Truth" from the *Ms.* Preview Issue in 1972. Thom notes that such letters continued to make up a staple of the letters pages into the late 1980s (xvii).

14. Evelyn Reed's "Women: Caste, Class, or Oppressed Sex?" (1970) presents this range of terms; Rubin's "sex/gender system" is from "The Traffic in Women: Notes on the 'Political Economy' of Sex" (1975). A section of *Sisterhood Is Powerful* is called "The Oppressed Majority."

15. My thinking on feminist literacy has greatly benefited from working with Bonnie J. Dow; see our essay, "When Feminism Meets the Press, Our Real Politics Get Lost," for a discussion of contemporary feminist literacy and its political limitations. For another view of feminist literacy, one shaped both by a cultural feminist understanding of women's history and culture and by the development

of Women's Studies as an institutional site for educating women, see Josephine Donovan's suggestion in the Preface to *Feminist Theory* (1986, 1993) that "literacy" for women requires a knowledge of the history of feminist theory (xi). While my use of the term differs substantially from Donovan's, her brief discussion of this notion in the Preface was tremendously helpful to me.

16. Echols notes that radical feminists—former Furies members—"founded Diana Press, Olivia Records, Women in Distribution, and *Quest/a feminist quarterly* which encouraged the growth of feminist businesses" (273). Her discussion of the controversies over feminist businesses, especially the Feminist Economic Network (FEN), makes an important distinction between businesses and institutions—between the for-profit work of feminist capitalists and the not-for-profit work of rape crisis centers (a distinction that may account for the absence of women's bookstores from this discussion, as bookstores most thoroughly blur that distinction).

17. One way to recast and recontextualize Echols's argument about the ascendence of cultural feminism at mid-decade, however, and the move from radical feminist movement to cultural feminist community, is to see these developments as institutionalizing the fantasies of community and sisterhood that underlay feminist literacy into the material community of a specific group of women. Such a reading of Echols's specific history of radical feminism places it firmly within the larger history of feminism in the decade that I'm drawing here, where literacy became institutionalized in the feminist public sphere, and institutions themselves became increasingly professionalized.

18. Felski's analysis of the feminist public sphere takes this professionalization for granted, and the radical critique of professionalism nowhere enters her analysis. From the vantage point of the 1990s, informed by Estelle B. Freedman's analysis in "Separatism as Strategy: Female Institution Building and American Feminism, 1870–1930" (1979), it seems clear to us today that these institution-building strategies enabled feminism to survive the backlash of the 1980s so thoroughly documented by Susan Faludi in her best-selling book, *Backlash: The War Against American Women* (1991). Then again, it may be difficult for any professional (or professorial) feminist to take seriously the radical feminist dismissal of professionalism *tout court*.

19. Not all feminist women, of course, performed any or all of these activities; nonetheless, my listing here is meant to suggest the ways feminists inhabited and moved through (as many continue to do) a variety and multiplicity of these institutions, something for which no simple political typology of feminist institutions (or, for that matter, of feminist theoretical positions) can account. Such a multiplicity of institutional affiliations need not be uncritical; many feminists were quite cynical about the ERA as a vehicle for change, for example, but supported the drive to pass the Amendment nonetheless. See J. Freeman, 239–40 for a critique of the ERA drive in 1975; F. Davis, in a chapter called "Why the ERA Lost" (385–411), puts a positive spin on the campaign.

20. Note the slippage here: my phrase "(feminist) women" attempts to mask the conflation of feminist and women even while it performs it. This conflation is not so simply the province of cultural feminism—*all* varieties of feminism in the 1970s (and arguably, today) depend upon it. Even recent theoretical attempts to interrogate the term "women" as the grounding for feminist theory and politics (Alcoff's article, for example) mask the conflation in performing it, rather than addressing the possibility that feminism is a politics not solely (even perhaps primarily) built on a reading out of "women"—the possibility, in other

words, that feminist politics are not "about" women but are "about" politics. See Diana Fuss, "Reading like a Feminist," for a version of this argument.

21. For a discussion of Reddy's song as "anthem," see S. Douglas, 165. Susan Freeman's research on lesbians in Cincinnati, Ohio, during the 1970s uncovered a suggestive difference. For the lesbian women writing in to Cincinnati's lesbian magazine, *Dinah*, it was "We Are Family" that became the community's anthem in the late 1970s (23), a factoid that suggests, first, the increased importance of community in the latter part of the decade, and second, perhaps the greater importance of community to lesbians (especially in beleaguered communities like Cincinnati).

22. For a good example of the power of the appeal to sisterhood, see Margaret A. Simons, "Racism and Feminism: A Schism in the Sisterhood."

23. Betty Friedan's *The Feminine Mystique* (1963) is one example; her chapter on women's magazine fiction ("The Happy Housewife Heroine" 28–61) explores the depiction of housewifery in these stories as a tool for teaching women traditional femininity. For a critique of Friedan's readings and research in that chapter, see Joanne Meyerowitz, "Beyond the Feminine Mystique: A Reassessment of Post-War Mass Culture, 1946–1958."

24. Cixous alludes to a reading of Genet similar to Millett's in "Sorties," 98, and "The Laugh of the Medusa," 255–56; see Millett's chapter on Genet in *Sexual Politics*, 470–505.

25. Among discussions of *The Golden Notebook* in the early 1970s are these, all reprinted in Brown and Olson: Annis Pratt, "The New Feminist Criticism" (1971); Ellen Morgan, "Alienation of the Woman Writer in *The Golden Notebook*" (1973); and Agate Nesaule Krouse, "Toward a Definition of Literary Feminism" (1974).

26. Paging through the early anthologies of feminist criticism turns up these discussions of Plath (a list that is by no means exhaustive): Nancy Burr Evans, "The Value and Peril for Women of Reading Women Writers" (in Koppelman Cornillon); Heilbrun and Stimpson 70–71; Suzanne Juhasz, *Naked and Fiery Forms: Modern American Poetry by Women, a New Tradition* (1976, excerpt rpt. in Brown and Olson); Annette Kolodny, "Some Notes on Defining a 'Feminist Literary Criticism'" (1975, rpt. in Brown and Olson). In "Reconsidering Sylvia Plath" (1972), Harriet Rosenstein summed up one view of Plath as heroine: "To those feminists who unfurl Plath's name like a battle banner, who read her writings and her biography as a single manifesto, who interpret her suicide as a function of her sexual oppression, Sylvia Plath has become an icon" (214–15).

27. The enduring popularity of Virginia Woolf's *A Room of One's Own* in Women's Studies classes—including ones that are not primarily focused on literature—may suggest the continuing influence of this vision of pre-Movement feminist struggle; Alice Walker has also adapted this tradition for African-American women in her important (and enduring) essay, "In Search of Our Mothers' Gardens" (1974).

28. DuPlessis examines an earlier tradition in her chapter on *Kunstlerromane* by women writers; I want to address ways that the more general problematic she so nicely lays out takes on particular political meanings in the feminist *Kunstlerromane* of the 1970s. For another view of women's artist novels, see Linda Huff, *A Portrait of the Artist as a Young Woman: The Writer as Heroine in American Literature*. To be fair to Rabinowitz's *Before Reading* (a work I find quite splendid and useful), I should point out that his argument about the woman writer-protagonist is in the service of recovering an obscure feminist novel.

29. The "pure" femaleness of white privileged women writers is the logic that underpins Ellen Moers's much criticized formulation that "Historians of the future will undoubtedly be satisfied with the title of Lorrain Hansberry's posthumous volume, *To Be Young, Gifted, and Black* . . . but of Sylvia Plath they will have to say 'young, gifted, and a woman'" (xviii). See Alice Walker's critique in "*One* Child of One's Own: A Meaningful Digression Within the Work(s)."

30. See, for example, Ann Snitow, "Women's Private Writings: Anais Nin," which the editors of *Radical Feminism* note was part of a series of radio talks on women's diaries and letters; and the debate over "grandmother's letters" in Heilbrun and Stimpson's "Theories of Feminist Criticism: A Dialogue" (66–67).

Chapter Two
Consciousness Raising and the CR Novel

Women talking together doesn't beget radical feminism. But it did back in 1970.

—Vickie Leonard[1]

The most important novel form for feminist writers in the 1970s—and for many non-feminist women writers as well—was what I call the consciousness-raising (CR) novel. The CR novels depict a woman's process of consciousness raising, more or less explicitly engaging the Women's Liberation Movement's concern in the 1970s with CR as a wholly new way of understanding and of making political change. The process of consciousness raising, according to the CR outline published in *Radical Feminism* in 1973, was "one in which personal experiences, when shared, are recognized as a result not of an individual's idiosyncratic history and behavior, but of the system of sex-role stereotyping. That is, they are political, not personal, questions" (Koedt, Levine, and Rapone 280–81). The women in the group shared and analyzed personal narratives in order to shift the terrain of their interpretation from the personal to the political. The "overplot" of the CR novel traces a similar trajectory, as the protagonist moves from feeling somehow at odds with others' expectations of her, into confrontations with others and with institutions, and into a new and newly politicized understanding of herself and her society.[2]

Feminist literary criticism in the early 1970s was often concerned with defining and typologizing feminist and/or women's fiction, and several critics drew relationships between fiction and consciousness raising.[3] One of these important essays is Cheri Register's "American Feminist Literary Criticism: A Bibliographic Introduction" (1975), which has been most noted for its discussion of "prescriptive criticism."[4] Register argued that one of literature's specific uses for feminism was that it could "augment consciousness-raising" by providing "realistic insights into female personality development, self-perception, interpersonal relationships, and other 'private' or 'internal' consequences of sexism" that readers could then balance with "factual information about the status of women from other sources" (19, 22–23). Register insisted that such novels not be simply "didactic"; they should instead be similar to the "personalized polemic" of black writers like Baldwin and Ellison.[5] What novels could provide was more personal narratives, more and more extended versions of the testimony that women provided in the face-to-face group meetings which were the basis of CR. Like the personal essays that were a staple of feminist periodicals in the 1970s— the "click!" letters to *Ms.,* for example, in which women described some small experience that crystalized their understandings of women's oppression[6]—the novels were to function as testimony of the absent member. Whether the novels depicted explicitly their protagonists' process of CR or not, then, novels that would augment CR would enact it as a transaction between character, author, and reader.

Before I turn to an analysis of the conventions of the CR novel, I want first to explore the history and theory of CR itself in the Movement. For despite feminist theory's enshrining of CR as feminism's central method by the end of the decade, CR's usefulness as a practice was the subject of considerable debate. Moreover, as CR itself became highly conventionalized over the course of the decade (a process, I will argue, aided by the ubiquity of the CR novel), its usefulness as a technique for theory-building became further problematized.

Historians of feminism's second wave agree that CR was central to Women's Liberation, though they disagree about its origins. According to Alice Echols,

> The proponents of consciousness-raising took their inspiration from the civil rights movement where the slogan was "tell it like it is," the Chinese revolution when peasants were urged "to speak pains to recall pains," and from the revolutionary struggle in Guatemala where guerrillas used similar techniques. (84)

In *Personal Politics: The Roots of Women's Liberation in the Civil Rights Movement and the New Left* (1979), Sara Evans traced consciousness raising's origins to Students for a Democratic Society (SDS), as it developed an "essentially intellectual notion of the process of radicalization" by which "People first had to understand that their problems were social and not personal in nature and that only collective action could solve them" (133–34). In *Woman's Estate* (1971), Juliet Mitchell argued that CR was "the reinterpretation of a Chinese revolutionary practice of 'speaking bitterness'" (62). Studying gender differences in conversational style led Dale Spender to argue in *Invisible Women: The Schooling Scandal* (1982) that CR emerged from women's conversational style, rather than from other political movements. Consciousness raising, for Spender, was "merely an extension of the co-operative turn-taking talk that women normally engage in." "Women did not think out an egalitarian and considerate arrangement and then try and implement it," Spender argued, "rather they found themselves engaged in this form of talk and attempted to describe and analyze it" (136–37).

These different accounts of CR's origins demonstrate the particular politics of the writers or their interview subjects; as Katie King has pointed out in *Theory in Its Feminist Travels*, "origin stories" about the Women's Movement are always "interested stories" (124). Echols bases her account on interviews with radical feminists in the Women's Liberation Movement in the late sixties, who were likely to be closer to the Civil Rights Movement than women who came to feminism later. Evans's book is an account of Women's Liberation's roots in these other political movements; her account is unusual in specifying SDS rather than the Civil Rights Movement (specifically the Student Non-Violent Coordinating Committee [SNCC]). Mitchell's account, though it specifies CR's origins in the United States, is also influenced by British feminism's much stronger alliance with Marxism. Spender's account is the most influenced by cultural, perhaps even separatist, feminism in its insistence that CR is specifically and uniquely—even perhaps "naturally"—female.[7]

Most radical feminists in the late 1960s and early 1970s theorized the relationship between CR and social change in highly practical terms: CR was a starting point for feminism, a place from which to begin doing more public, activist organizing, rather than an end in itself or an investigative model. The consciousness raising outline in *Radical Feminism*, for example, suggested that CR groups spend their first three to six months "talking about personal experiences and then analyzing those experiences in feminist terms" (Koedt, Levine, and Rapone 280). After that period, the CR group was to shift its focus away from CR itself, to

working on specific projects and activities including such activities as reading, analyzing and writing literature; abortion law repeal projects; setting up child care projects; organizing speak-outs (rape, motherhood, abortion, etc.); challenging sex discrimination in employment, education, etc. (Koedt, Levine, and Rapone 280)[8]

Consciousness raising, then, would open out to specific activist projects, a transition that proved more difficult in practice than in theory.

The Boston Women's Health Book Collective may be the most well-known example of a CR group making the transition, publishing *Our Bodies, Ourselves* in 1973. Other groups were not so successful. As early as 1968, some feminists were becoming convinced that CR, at least in some groups, was leading only to more CR (Echols 113–14). Carol Williams Payne, in an essay called "Consciousness-Raising: A Dead End?" (1971) identified the central problem of her CR group as

a conflict between those who favored the personal, psychological approach and those who felt that a women's group should be building a bridge between the personal insight gained by being in a small group and political action with a larger body of women. (Koedt, Levine, and Rapone 283)

Joreen [Jo Freeman] argued that the difficulty in making the transition from CR to activism was inherent in the "structurelessness" of the groups: at the point of transition, she argued, "they usually floundered because most groups were unwilling to change their structure when they changed their task" ("Tyranny" 285).[9] The editorial from *Notes from the Third Year* (1971) called for the movement as a whole to make the transition from CR to organizing:

women are beginning to see that consciousness-raising is meant as a stage of growth. It is limited as a tool. If we don't move on from consciousness-raising, both as individuals and as groups, we face the danger of stagnation. (Koedt, Levine, and Rapone 300)

Jo Freeman argued that CR "as a major movement function started to become obsolete" by about 1971, its "educational work" becoming less necessary as "women's liberation became a household word" in the explosion of press attention at that time (128). CR was thus, in her view, superseded by feminist literacy, and the Movement needed to focus on other work. As a means of "introducing basic women's liberation issues to women who might be intimidated by militant groups," though, CR was still frequently cited in the radical feminist press as important, even if as limited.[10]

Despite these and other feminist critiques of CR, its perceived limitations in building a movement or in making social change, CR spread throughout the movement in the first half of the decade, filtering into reformist organizations like NOW (Echols 199).[11] The enormous popularity of the practice had its price, however, as CR became increasingly therapeutized, whether subtly so in a shift in its emphasis, or more blatantly so in the enlistment of therapist-facilitators to "lead" CR groups in the latter part of the decade.[12] Here, Claudia Dreifus's distinction between "soft" and "hard" CR in *Woman's Fate: Raps from a Feminist Consciousness-Raising Group* (1975) is particularly important. "Soft" CR was so intensely focused on personal experience that the rules for its practice disallowed theorizing, generalizing, and challenging. "Hard" CR, by contrast, called for group members "always [to] test generalizations on women's personal experience," as Brooke Williams describes Redstockings' practice in reviewing Dreifus's book for *off our backs*. "Soft" CR resolved the debates over the purpose of CR by seeing the practice as an end in itself, rather than as a political strategy, a recruitment device, or a resource for feminist theory-building, as "hard" CR was theorized.[13] The conflict Payne identified in her CR group was thus a conflict between "soft" and "hard" CR—between the "personal, psychological" version of it, and the version of it as a "bridge" between personal insight and collective political action. Importantly, "soft" CR was subject, as Williams pointed out, to the "rule of Niceness," in which support for one's sisters outweighed political analysis (18).

Part of the reconstituted Redstockings attack on *Ms.* magazine in 1975 (overshadowed by the allegations of Gloria Steinem's CIA connections), involved this de-politicization of CR. *off our backs* published a long portion of the attack in 1975; it included portions of a previously unpublished *Village Voice* interview with Kathie Sarachild, "who originated the program of consciousness-raising in the movement" (Redstockings ,*Ms.*" 32).[14] Sarachild charged that *Ms.* had recast the politics of CR into "a change yourself line," which she distinguished from the Redstockings "pro-woman line" this way:

The *Ms.* line is the prevailing line in the movement. Women are psychologically damaged and therefore unqualified right now for jobs and relationships. *Ms.* is telling women to try to get over their hang-ups due to male supremacy. These aren't hang-ups. They are reactions to a reality. The thing to do is analyse the reality. And fight. *Ms.* tells women to fight *individually*. We have a *movement* to fight these forces. (32)[15]

The therapeutizing of CR deserves some attention here, for it marks a number of major changes in how CR was conceptualized, and the kind of work it was perceived to accomplish.

CR had long been recognized to have, at least incidentally, a particular kind of therapeutic effect —specifically, it was understood to replace therapy, in the sense that the assurance women received from CR that they were not crazy would enable them to forgo patriarchal therapy's enforced reconciliation with gender-based systems of domination. Attacks on conventional, patriarchal psychiatry and psychology abounded in the feminist theory of the early 1970s, and feminist writing—literary, political, personal, and theoretical—was pervaded by the haunting suspicion that the disjunctures between women's feelings and the ideologies of gender meant that women were really "crazy." In "Woman and Her

Mind" (1973), Meredith Tax applied R. D. Laing's analysis of schizophrenia as a social process to feminist analyses of women's roles, arguing that the "contradictory instructions and conflicting descriptions" women receive produce a kind of schizophrenia in women: "Our society could be described as one which drives women crazy" (Koedt, Levine, and Rapone 34; 32).[16] Similarly, Sally Kempton, in "Cutting Loose" (1970), identified feminism as the only alternative to masochism.

Feminism's concern with women's feeling crazy may help account for Women's Liberation's initial hostility toward psychiatry and psychoanalysis. In *The Dialectic of Sex* (1970), Shulamith Firestone read the history of "first wave" feminism as a battle with what she calls "Freudianism"; feminism, she argued, lost that battle. Most feminist writers in the early second wave devoted significant attention to Freud, as did Friedan, and Millett, for example, and as had de Beauvoir before them. *The Dialectic of Sex* was typical in arguing that psychoanalytic theory, especially in the United States, served to enforce and reinforce sex roles, and that psychoanalysis as therapeutic practice worked against feminism by "adjusting" women to their roles in a system of unjust power relations. Firestone used the explanatory power of psychoanalysis against psychoanalysis itself throughout *The Dialectic of Sex*, using ideas about family romance to explain race relations and to argue for abolishing the nuclear family, childhood, and pregnancy, even while she rejected its application to individuals as therapeutic practice. Because psychoanalytic theory and practice stop "short of revolution," Firestone argued, they work to "stem the flow of feminism" (76). Both "Freudianism" and feminism, according to Firestone, were "explosive," but "Freudianism . . . had a safety catch that feminism didn't—it never questioned the given reality," and thus "flourished at the expense of Feminism, to the extent that it acted as a container of its shattering force" (79).[17] The difference between first and second wave feminism, for Firestone, was that the second wave would turn away from therapy to "the only thing that can do any good: political organization" (80).

An important feminist critique of psychology was Naomi Weisstein's " 'Kinde, Kuche, Kirche' as Scientific Law: Psychology Constructs the Female," widely circulated in the Movement and then anthologized in *Sisterhood Is Powerful*. Weisstein argued that theories of gender differences were neither empirically true nor based in examinations of the social context of gender roles; instead, theories of gender difference merely reflected the researchers' prejudices about women. Because "psychologists' ideas of women's nature fit so remarkably the common prejudice and serve industry and commerce so well," Weisstein pointed out, psychology itself was "less than worthless in contributing to a vision which could truly liberate—men as well as women" (230–31). Where

Firestone (among others) critiqued psychoanalytic practice, Weisstein critiqued psychological research; both were found to reinforce sex roles and gender inequality, and both worked to make women feel crazy when they didn't fit gender stereotypes.

Given the strength of the feminist critiques of psychoanalysis and psychological research, it is not surprising that feminists were quick to defend CR against the charge that it was nothing more than therapy. Irene Peslikis suggested in "Resistances to Consciousness" (1969) that *"Thinking that women's liberation is therapy"* marked both women's resistance to feminism, in believing in individual solutions to political problems, and men's resistance, in belittling CR techniques when women used them but not when Chinese peasants did (R. Morgan 379, emphasis original). Feminists defended the radicality of CR by comparing it to techniques used in China or Guatamala, part of their defense of Women's Liberation itself against charges from the left that it was bourgeois. "We aren't sick, we are oppressed," argued Beverly Jones in "The Dynamics of Marriage and Motherhood" (1970), making a distinction between women's small group work in the Movement and "group therapy," just as Robin Morgan did in the Introduction to *Sisterhood Is Powerful* (66; xxvi). In 1980, Vickie Leonard invoked the political context of the early 1970s to defend her CR group's practice:

In this militant and activist era, the women's liberation movement was surrounded by radical ideas—sharing the ownership of children, humane jobs for all, individuals changing the course of history. All the while, American soldiers were slaughtering the Viet Namese. In such a milieu to sit down and speak of personal matters smacked of self indulgence. That's why CR groups never became therapy sessions. Speaking of oneself as one person with *choices* and not seeing oneself in a broader perspective was frowned upon and considered "individualistic." ("cr" 17)

Leonard here invokes an implicit sense of the difference between "hard" and "soft" CR; "hard" CR was for her an extension of the political thinking of radical movements in the early 1970s.

By the end of the 1970s, CR was firmly enshrined in feminist theory as feminist method, as Catharine A. MacKinnon's important article, "Feminism, Marxism, Method, and the State" (1981), exemplifies:

Consciousness-raising is the major technique of analysis, structure of organization, method of practice, and theory of social change of the women's movement. In consciousness raising, often in groups, the impact of male dominance is concretely uncovered and analyzed through the collective speaking of women's experience, from the perspective of that experience. . . . Women's powerlessness had been found through consciousness raising to be both internalized and externally imposed, so that, for example, femininity is identity to women as well as desirability to men. The feminist concept of consciousness and its place in social order and change emerge from this practical analytic. What marxism conceives as change in consciousness is not a form of social change in itself. For feminism, it can be, but because women's oppression is not just in the head, feminist *consciousness* is not just in the head either. (5–6; emphasis original)

MacKinnon's argument about CR as feminism's *method* is a typical move in turn-of-the-decade feminist theory, in which a specific Movement practice comes to take on enormous theoretical weight. At a conference on Women and Science in 1979, Susan Leigh Star made a similar case for CR as a rigorous investigative process, suggesting that feminists replace the "male paradigm or model" of scientific method with the "feminism/science" of CR (in Segerberg 12).

Marsha Segerberg, the reporter from *off our backs* at this conference on Women and Science, however, expressed some concern about CR, noting its limited ability to account for difference when CR groups were "comprised mostly of cultural and racial peers," and suggesting that CR had stopped short, and nearly vanished from the Movement: "Now there are no more CR groups" (Segerberg 29). Similarly, Rosalind Coward argued in 1980 that "consciousness-raising no longer forms the heart of feminism; small groups which do still have a central place in feminist politics are now often either campaigning groups or study groups" (237).[18] At the same time that organized, non-therapeutic CR was disappearing, feminist theorists like MacKinnon came to enshrine it as feminism's central method. How did this disjunction between perceptions of CR and its practice come about?[19]

One phrase from the passage of MacKinnon's essay I quoted provides a starting point for addressing this question: "often in groups." While MacKinnon does emphasize the importance of feminist collectivity—"the collective speaking of women's experience"—raising one's consciousness had become, by the early eighties, something one could undertake alone, not necessarily in a group of other women. If not in a group, then presumably one experienced the collective speaking of women's experiences in the activities of reading and writing—so that feminist literacy came to replace, or at least to supplement, the CR group. Such solitary consciousness raising was not, however, an invention solely of early-eighties cultural feminism. As early as 1970, Morgan's introduction to *Sisterhood Is Powerful* located Women's Liberation "in your mind"—in individual consciousnesses—and the notion of subjective membership that I discussed in the previous chapter also suggests that CR could be undertaken alone. Kempton's "Cutting Loose" concludes with a vision of individual change: "Women's liberation is finally only personal. It is hard to fight an enemy who has outposts in your head" (57). The CR that could be undertaken in solitude was more likely to be "soft" than "hard," especially when it engaged novels—with their focus on the "private" and "internal" aspects of women's oppression—as testimony of the absent member. Karlyn Kohrs Campbell's 1973 analysis of the rhetoric of Women's Liberation, which focuses on essays and speeches from the Movement, links the practice of CR with the style of Movement texts, creating a vision of CR that may be based in reading.[20]

Moreover, CR's "softening" was an instance in which radical feminists lost a contest for meaning in the Movement, even while their accounts of CR's political function remain dominant in feminist theory. That is, the "hard" CR practiced by some radical feminist groups came to be enshrined as CR in feminist theory, even while "soft" CR dominated Movement practice. The "soft" CR of Movement practice could then be understood politically as if it were the "hard" CR of feminist theory, and thus overestimated in its political value and importance. Women talking about their lives—and women reading about women's lives—thus came to take on revolutionary import in the slippage from "hard" to "soft" CR.

The exact role of feminist consciousness in making social change continues to be debated widely by feminist theorists; feminists agree that it is necessary, but not whether it is sufficient. Even Coward, whose criticism of CR is one of the strongest, argues that "the question of how to articulate the discoveries of consciousness-raising with struggles over financial, legal, and other forms of social and sexual oppression is still crucial" (237). Theorists also agree on the nature of the feminist consciousness achieved through CR. The most frequent images used to describe feminist consciousness were images of duality and splitness. Influential literary depictions of this duality include Doris Lessing's *The Four-Gated City* (1969), when Martha Quest describes the part of herself that always "watches," and the moment Virginia Woolf describes as the "splitting off of consciousness" in *A Room of One's Own*. In 1975, Annette Kolodny notes the pervasiveness of "reflexive perceptions" in women's fiction, in which "character after character is depicted discovering herself or finding some part of herself in activities she has not planned or in situations she cannot fully comprehend" ("Some Notes" 41). Discussing the dual consciousness of the feminist literary critic in 1979, Elaine Showalter writes:

We are both the daughters of the male tradition, of our teachers, our professors, our dissertation advisors, and our publishers—a tradition that asks us to be rational, marginal, and grateful; and sisters in a new women's movement which engenders another kind of awareness and commitment, which demands that we renounce the pseudo-success of token womanhood and the ironic masks of academic debate. ("Toward" 141)

She goes on to suggest that "this divided consciousness is sometimes experienced by men," but also suggests that few academic men experience the division as precisely as she did, during the year she was a Visiting Minority Professor.[21] Sheila Rowbotham describes feeling "sliced in two," a sensation clarified for her by her double-identification process in watching a woman in a movie: "I could see through their [men's] eyes but I could feel with her body. I was a man-woman" (*Woman's Consciousness* 40–41). In 1971, Caroline Bird uses a similar image of dividedness in describing her feelings when her article on women was rejected by a publisher: "I accepted—half of me, at least—the verdict of incompetence. But the other half of me was furious" (ix). These feelings of dividedness also make the women who experience them doubt their own perceptions, as Bird explains: "All along I had to fight the consensus. Maybe I *was* incompetent. Maybe I *was* some kind of nut" (ix; emphasis original). Perhaps the most vivid image of feminist consciousness as divided comes from the cover of *Radical Feminism*, designed by Anne Koedt, which shows a woman's face and head divided in half: one side of her wears make-up, an elaborate hairstyle, and a magazine-model expression, while the other side has no make-up, messy hair, and a grin that shows lines in her face. This image highlights the disjunction between conventional femininity and women's reality, figured here as a disjunction between how women "should" look and how women "do" look.

Early critiques of the role of psychoanalysis and psychology in maintaining women's oppression gave way to later explorations of feminism as kind of (valued and celebrated) madness. In "Toward a Phenomenology of Feminist Consciousness" (1977), Sandra Lee Bartky argued that "Feminist consciousness is something like paranoia" (28). In *Gyn/Ecology: The Metaethics of Radical Feminism* (1978), Mary Daly argued that what she calls "woman-identification" was a kind of "positive paranoia" (125), another example of the recuperation of paranoia to describe feminist consciousness. According to Bartky, feminists who understood "the full extent of sex discrimination and the subtle and various ways in which it is enforced" would necessarily become "vigilant and suspicious" of the world around them, and "fall prey to self-doubt or to a temptation to compliance" in examining their own motives. Because sexism "is everywhere, even inside her own mind," feminists experience every interaction, the most ordinary situations, as fraught with "the possibility of attack, of affront or insult, of disparagement, ridicule, or the hurting blindness of others" as well as with opportunities "for struggle against the system" (30).

When feminists began to analyze their own participation in their oppression, according to Bartky, they were subject to a "double ontological shock" resulting from "an inability to know how to classify things."

Bartky gives these examples of this double-thinking, self-doubting process:

The timidity that I display at departmental meetings, for instance—is it nothing more than a personal shortcoming, or is it a typically female trait, a shared inability to display aggression, even verbal aggression? And why is the suggestion I make ignored? Is is intrinsically unintelligent or is it because I am a woman and therefore not to be taken seriously? The persistent need I have to make myself 'attractive,' to fix my hair and put on lipstick—is it the false need of a chauvinized woman, encouraged since infancy to identify her value as a person with her attractiveness in the eyes of men? Or does it express a wholesome need to express love for one's own body by adorning it, a behavior common in primitive societies, allowed us but denied to men in our own still-puritan culture? (29)

Bartky's example of "attractiveness" exemplifies the variety of possible and contradictory readings of any individual woman's behavior, and even the variety of readings that can be aligned with feminist values. It is thus not surprising that Women's Liberation was subject to splits and schisms, that the movement could produce an extraordinary range of often contradictory beliefs and programs; the potential for such contradictions was built into the structure of feminist consciousness itself.

A consciousness raising group could often accommodate these contradictory readings. Folklorist Susan Kalčik analyzed the style of women's "rap" or CR groups in an essay called ". . . like Ann's gynecologist or the time I was almost raped" (1975), and her analysis demonstrates ways that CR groups both generated and accommodated multiple readings of individual stories. Kalčik suggested that "the underlying aesthetic or organizing principle" in all the rules, outlines, and suggestions for conducting women's rap groups was "harmony," and she explained several ways that groups maintain their harmony. These included verbal strategies like "filling in, tying together, and serializing" the narratives (6), and using humor "supportively to keep the group close and to underline the feeling of 'we're all in this together'" (5). Kalčik quotes specific examples of this humor, including these: "'Well, you know how we women are; our hormones get up into our brain and fuck up our thinking'" and "'My doctor thinks my vaginal infection is all in my head; he has a strange picture of my anatomy'" (5). Both these examples use impersonations of stereotypical masculinist discourses to underline what the women in the group share: the oppression by and opposition to the power relations these discourses represent. It is also important that these examples play off ideas about "anatomy as destiny": the crucial discourses for harmonizing feminist opposition tended to be medical and therapeutic, as the pervasiveness of critiques of psychiatry suggests.

These examples suggest that consciousness raising is a fundamentally heteroglossic process. In the ways these groups use humor, in impersonating masculinist discourses, they make the power relations of these discourses "sound" within the group to unify it in opposition.[22] CR was designed, even in its "soft" version, to bring individual personal narratives into dialogue not only with other such narratives, but also with the public and political discourses in relation to which they would yield new feminist meanings. In the dividedness of feminist consciousness itself we can find competing discourses: "maybe I really was crazy" and "is [my suggestion] intrinsically unintelligent" compete with "is it because I'm a woman and therefore not to be taken seriously?" The process of shifting the terrain of investigation from the personal to the political sets discourses in dialogue.

Some of these dialogues were more agonistic than others. Because consciousness raising, in both its style and its content, focussed on eliciting women's shared experiences of oppression, differences between women—of race, class, ethnicity, sexual identity, age, for example— were more likely to be minimized than differences between women and men. These differences between women could be minimized within the CR group because of the group's interest in maintaining its harmony— a harmony that could over-ride the differences between women, even as those differences erupted in other settings.[23] One letter-writer to *off our backs* describes the sense of sisterhood in CR groups as "that smiling loving high of being with other women," even as she critiqued its limitations in addressing women's differences and building feminist theory (J. Stein). Consciousness raising thus both created and contained, or set limits on, heteroglossia, and the feminism that was based in CR tended to emphasize gender more than other differences.

Another way that CR worked to contain heteroglossia was that it became increasingly conventionalized over the course of the decade, and became, in effect, highly manipulable. A striking example is the use of CR in the anti-pornography movement of the late 1970s. Brooke Williams's *off our backs* coverage of a Women Against Pornography [WAP] conference in 1979 evidences the importance of CR to the anti-pornography movement by the end of the decade; Williams notes that WAP's "slide-show parties"—"their initial organizing tool"—were followed up by "anti-porn CR."[24] WAP reproduced this organizing strategy at the conference's opening session; after two opening speeches, the slide show followed, and then the organizers performed a "speakout" about women's experiences with pornography. Williams notes, "This was *not* a speakout from the audience"; instead, a series of "excerpts from letters from women around the country were read, describing harrowing incidents with porn" ("porn again" 24). Implicit here is a point Williams makes explicit in analyzing the CR sessions and workshops that followed: CR at this conference was very carefully managed. "I felt," Williams writes,

and I think this was true throughout the conference, a subtle pressure that the only admissible experiences with porn were real horror stories, as in previous examples from the speakout, and that women like myself who had few bad experiences directly linked to porn were out of it. ("porn again" 25)

The WAP conference demonstrates two crucial facts about CR by decade's end. First, the conference's performed speakout—*not* from the audience, as Williams notes—demonstrates that CR techniques had become so conventional that the *representation* of a speakout (reading letters aloud) could stand in for enacting one (in which women from the stage and from the audience would speak). Even when the technique was being used "in groups" (to return to the discussion of individualized CR), then, it could be done *for* rather than *by* those groups. Second, the representation of the speakout not only modelled the actual CR sessions that followed, but more importantly served to control and limit the kinds of narratives and interpretive practices that were "admissible" in those sessions. CR as a practice could thus be manipulated, could be managed to produce (only) certain kinds of narratives.[25]

The popularity and ubiquity of the consciousness-raising novel helped to make CR so highly conventionalized over the course of the decade. Best-selling and less well-known novels by feminist and non-feminist writers alike used the process of CR as a structural device for their narratives, depicted or described CR groups, or used Women's Liberation as a backdrop for their protagonists. CR even made it into Hollywood film, in a scene from Paul Mazursky's *An Unmarried Woman* (1978), a film described as "feminist" by most of its reviewers and critics.[26] In this scene, Erica (Jill Clayburgh) and her "club" of women friends are at a gallery opening, when a young European man asks them what their "club" is about. One of Erica's friends replies by asking him whether he knows what consciousness raising is; he says no. She laughs and says, "Neither do we, we just like to drink and complain a lot." The joke here depends on the audience's ability to recognize that "drinking and complaining" both is and is not an adequate description of CR—that Erica and her friends both do and do not have real problems, that their problems both are and are not political. Importantly, by 1978, audiences for mainstream Hollywood film were expected to get the joke, and indeed to see *An Unmarried Woman* itself as a CR narrative—as a film "version" of the CR novel.

In order to lay out the "overplot" and some of the important issues of the CR novel, I want to look carefully at Dorothy Bryant's *Ella Price's Journal* (1972), for Bryant's novel follows the overplot so carefully that it seems to have been written from Kathie Sarachild's consciousness raising outline, and thus makes a useful exemplary text.[27] Bryant's novel differs from more explicitly political novels, such as Marge Piercy's *Woman on the Edge of Time* (1976) and Rita Mae Brown's *Rubyfruit Jungle* (1973); comparisons with these novels help clarify just how "soft" the CR novel can be. At the same time that the novel's CR is depoliticized in crucial ways, *Ella Price's Journal* nonetheless is clearly recognizable as a feminist novel, as a novel shaped at its core by consciousness raising.

Written in journal form as an assignment for Ella's junior college English class, Bryant's novel charts Ella's consciousness raising process. A returning student who is also a housewife, Ella understands herself at the beginning of her journal as "an average person with a nice home, a good husband and a lovely daughter" (18). As Ella becomes progressively more honest in her journal, she confesses to finding "something wrong with me" (27), a confession readers recognize as Friedan's "problem that has no name":

> I was driving down El Alma Boulevard and all of a sudden I was lost. I mean, it all looked the same—the used-car lots with little flags flapping on a string, the hamburger stands, the four-rooms-of-furniture stores. I couldn't locate myself. I didn't know if I was near home or miles from home, and I had the feeling that I could go on and on, up and down El Alma, and never be able to recognize where to turn off to get home. It was like a bad dream, but I knew I was awake.
> Then I started aiming at the parked cars. I'd come closer and closer, then I'd realize what I was doing and swerve away from them, but then all at once I'd find myself going toward one again, as if I wanted to hit it. I pulled over to the curb and stopped the car. Then I started to cry. But I didn't feel it—didn't feel as if it was me crying—I just listened to the sobbing and felt water running down my face, but I didn't seem to be doing it and didn't understand it. After a few minutes I was all right. I saw I was just a block from my turnoff, and I went home. (28)

It was this experience of "reflexive perceptions" (in Kolodny's term), that led Ella back to school. She went to her doctor, but was unable to tell him what was wrong. His vague suggestion about "new interests" (28) is what brought Ella to take courses at the junior college. Six days after the entry quoted above, Ella writes,

> Suppose a person has the feeling she's done everything just the right way, and hasn't made any mistakes to speak of, and that her life should feel like a great success. But every morning she wakes up feeling uneasy. And then one day, she wakes up in the morning and she says, "Oh, no, this was not the way to do it at all. My whole life has been a mistake." But it's her whole life, and it's over, so wouldn't it be better not to know? (36)

Ella's journal traces her discovering not only that is it better to know that her life has been a mistake, but that it is better still to do something about it. At the end of the novel, Ella has dropped out and then re-enrolled in school, left her husband on Christmas Eve, and is in the hospital on Christmas night, being prepped for an abortion. Having another child, Ella comes to understand, will not solve her marital problems.

In between Ella's initial feeling that something is wrong with her and her rejecting her marriage and another child as solutions to the problem that has no name, she works through a series of confrontations with individuals and institutions that try to keep her in her place. Ella's suburban friends accuse her of neglecting her family and taking "classroom space away from some young person" (73). Ella's husband wants to stay married, but needs Ella to "be sick and neurotic" for the marriage to work (223). Ella's professor, with whom she has a brief but unsatisfying affair, says that he needs her for his own "survival" (155), but Ella discovers that he has had affairs with many of his students, and always with older, returning women students. Ella's Catholic mother-in-law calls her a murderer for wanting an abortion (200), and Ella's mother lectures her about "Shirking [her] responsibility" (203). It is not a surprise, and is in fact crucial to the CR novel form, that Ella comes to see everyone—"Well, almost everyone" (220)—as working together to thwart her efforts to change. If, as Bartky argues, feminist consciousness is experienced as something like paranoia, then the protagonist of a novel about feminist consciousness is also likely to seem paranoid.

The institutions that Ella must confront in order to change her life include marriage, motherhood, junior college, the government and the police at an anti-war march, and psychiatry. Ella needs to figure out how each of these institutions have shaped her life, and what role each should play as she changes her life. Ella decides that marriage and motherhood are no longer solutions for her:

I had realized that I had to make a change. But I saw that change as a change of men, as if I don't exist except as part of a man. But I'm not Joe and I'm not Dan, and I'm not defined by my relation to either of them. They're just part of my life. I'm myself, although I'm not too sure who that is yet. But I know who it isn't. And what I need to do has to happen in myself. Everything else is just a detour—falling in love, getting pregnant, whatever—just detours away from doing the real job, whatever that is. (208-9)

Bryant's critique of marriage and motherhood here is rather mild; it is not a particularly political critique of the institution, and it certainly does not spill over into a critique of heterosexuality. Ella learns that marriage is simply too limited to rely on for happiness or identity, but not that it is inherently oppressive to women, as many feminist analyses argued. However limited the critique, though, the result is the same: Ella leaves her husband, and leaves him in order to assert her independence. Her affair with her professor does not break up her marriage, and she doesn't leave her husband for another relationship. At the end of the novel, Ella is alone—and this ending may be an implicit critique of heterosexual relationships to the extent that Ella's freedom depends on not being in one, but it is not a critique that Bryant makes explicit.

The mildness of the critique in Bryant's novel may be because Ella does not participate in any organized feminist activities; her consciousness raising process is almost entirely solitary, "soft" in both its practice and its politics.[28] Such mildness is typical of CR novels; only rarely do critiques of marriage and motherhood in these novels develop a political edge anything like that in the radical feminist analyses being published at the same time. The science fiction novels and the lesbian novels are far more sweeping in their critiques of marriage, motherhood, heterosexuality, and monogamous sexual relationships in general; the realist novels about heterosexual women tend to critique individual marriages and relationships rather than institutions. More than genre is at stake in this difference: the mildness of the realist novels' critiques of marriage is entirely in keeping with their tendency to use "soft" rather than "hard" CR.

Ella Price's Journal's critique of psychiatry is far more sweeping than its critique of marriage. Ella begins seeing a psychiatrist because she is filled with guilt over her affair with the college professor. She drops out of school and takes a job to afford to pay for the sessions. The sessions "take the place of writing in [her] journal," and the entries through this period are very brief and choppy, some of them quite similar to her earliest entries before she began taking the exercise seriously. Ella learns that her "overseriousness," her "guilt about sex," and her "undeveloped maternal feelings" are all her mother's fault: "It all goes back to my mother" (180). The doctor tells Ella that "to some degree every woman has the same problem, recapturing the feminine side of her nature" (182). Feminist readers cannot help but hear an echo of de Beauvoir's famous formulation, "One is not born a woman, one becomes one"; Ella's psychiatrist's job is to make sure that she becomes one properly.[29]

After she discovers that the psychiatrist lied to her about needing his permission to obtain an abortion, Ella concludes, "I must have wanted to punish myself terribly to have gone to him for so long without seeing what he was" (195).[30] Consciousness-raising novels often equate women's submission to psychiatry with self-hatred, just as they establish psychiatry itself as a form of social control over women. Consciousness raising provides Ella with the ability to refuse to go to the psychiatrist any more, to refuse to be controlled in that way any longer. Piercy's *Woman on the Edge of Time* is more explicit in depicting these dynamics, in keeping with its greater political explicitness overall. Connie signs herself into the psychiatric hospital the first time, filled with "self-pity and self-hatred like a hot sulfur spring, scalding herself" (60). When Connie's consciousness has been raised, she is no longer willing to submit, no longer willing to consent to giving the machinery of psychiatry that kind of power over her. Connie sees the entire systems of psychiatry, law, and medicine lined up against her:

All those experts lined up against her in a jury dressed in medical white and judicial black—social workers, caseworkers, child guidance counselors, psychiatrists, doctors, nurses, clinical psychologists, probation officers—all those cool knowing faces had caught her and bound her in their nets of jargon hung all with tiny barbed hooks that stuck in her flesh and leaked a slow weakening poison. (60)

Similar systems are lined up against Molly Bolt, the protagonist of Brown's *Rubyfruit Jungle*. The correct behavior that these systems enforce in Brown's novel is heterosexuality. When the university administration discovers that Molly and her roommate are lesbians, for example, Molly is sent to the school psychiatrist, and her roommate to a private hospital (129–30). The administrator who later puts Molly in the hospital is herself a lesbian, and Brown points out through this narrative that institutional forces disrupt possibilities for lesbian solidarity.

In *Woman on the Edge of Time*, Connie's sense of being oppressed by the interlocking systems of psychiatry, law, and medicine may seem paranoid, especially early in the novel, but the novel makes it clear that she's right to be paranoid, for "they"—and the "they" in Piercy's novel is composed of precisely these interlocking systems—really are out to get her. By the end of the novel, "they" have designed an experiment in consciousness control, and Connie must find a way to stop it, or the utopian future may never come to be. In that utopian future, people can still be "mad," but madness is understood to be temporary, a way to recharge one's energies, something that requires healing, rather than a category used to enforce correct behavior, especially correct female behavior. Here again we see the link between madness and women's freedom, a link that figures importantly in the science fiction CR novels, as the link between psychiatry and the social control of women figures in virtually all the novels.

As their differently nuanced treatments of psychiatry suggest, Bryant's novel differs from Piercy's in the explicitness of its politics. Unlike *Woman on the Edge of Time*, *Ella Price's Journal* belongs to a category of feminist fiction that Rosalind Coward identifies as novels that do not make "explicit their allegiance to the women's liberation movement," even though "the encounter with the milieu and aspirations of feminism often forms a central element of the narrative" and "the practice of consciousness-raising . . . sometimes forms the structure of the novel" (231). Despite its CR narrative, Bryant's novel nowhere makes explicit its allegiance to the Movement, and indeed does not mention Women's Liberation at all. Ella nowhere names the process she undergoes in her journal as CR, yet it is clearly more than a structural device in the novel. The echoes of Friedan and de Beauvoir suggest that Bryant knows feminist writings, but chooses not to show Ella reading them. How are we to understand the politics of a feminist novel that deliberately does not identify itself as such? One effect of not identifying *Ella Price's Journal* as a feminist novel—by not making explicit its relation to Women's Liberation—is that CR is naturalized. That is, the process of CR is seen as natural and logical, rather than as a deliberate, conscious strategy to make social change. Here again it is important that Ella's CR is depicted as individual and private, rather than a group process. For consciousness raising becomes in this reading of the novel what women do—not (only) what feminist women do—when the contradictions in their lives become too extreme. Like Spender's argument that consciousness raising emerges from women's conversational style, Bryant's novel, and others like it, suggest that CR is fundamentally based in gender rather than in politics. Politically, this suggestion serves to naturalize feminism itself, to focus the central method of feminism on women's personal change, personal growth, rather than on social change, and certainly rather than on the early revolutionary project of radical feminism. Even if the novel is clear that power relations are at work in creating Ella's oppression, it is also clear that the solution to that oppression is personal change rather than revolution.

This contradictory reading of *Ella Price's Journal* turns on a series of slippery distinctions: between "hard" and "soft" CR (itself tied to a distinction between personal and political change), and between the CR novel and what Richard Ohmann has called the "illness story." In making CR and feminism into organic extensions of femaleness, Bryant may be participating in the important project of helping to "popularize" feminism, and indeed, a great deal of work designed to garner a broad audience for Movement ideas has tended to focus on the personal aspects of feminism.[31] But such versions of the CR novel emphasize not only the personal or "internal" dimensions of women's oppression, as Register suggested feminist fiction should, but also personal solutions to that oppression; novels like Bryant's thus side-step the *political* aspects of CR. The widespread popularity of "soft" CR helped make novels like *Ella Price's Journal* readable and recognizable as feminist novels even without any explicit discussion of feminism, just as "soft" CR insists on the political implications of personal change without directly engaging politics.

Bryant's novel tests the boundaries between the CR novel and the "illness story" that, according to Richard Ohmann, dominated the fiction "eligible for canonical status" in the period 1969–1975:

these novels told stories of people trying to live a decent life in contemporary social settings, people represented as analogous to "us," rather than as "cases" to be examined and understood from a clinical distance, as in an older realistic convention. . . . A premise of this fiction—nothing new to American literature but particularly salient in this period—is that individual consciousness, not the social or historical field, is the locus of significant happening. (80) [32]

Ohmann names a particular version of this fiction "the illness story," and suggests that it takes shape in am ambiguous balance between individual craziness and a sick society: "I seem to be crazy, but again, possibly it's *society* that's crazy" (84). We can see this idea in Fay Weldon's *Praxis*, as the "madness" Praxis identifies as part of her feminism: "the madness of believing that I was right, and society wrong" (20–21). Ohmann argues that "for the people who wrote, read, promoted, and preserved fiction, social contradictions were easily displaced into images of personal illness" (83). Despite the feminist critique of psychiatry in *Ella Price's Journal*, the novel's refusal to engage explicitly feminist politics opens it up to a reading as an "illness story." Moreover, readers familiar with CR, especially in its "soft" version, could read out any gender-specific version of the "illness story" as a feminist novel. Thus the novel invites its women readers to use it as a guide for performing their own isolated acts of self-transformation—this is the way that it transacts CR among author, reader, and character. But by isolating Ella from the Movement, and thus locating feminism so completely "in your mind" in Robin Morgan's terms, Bryant's popularizing effect shifts the burden of feminist work onto individual women rather than groups of women—exemplifying the "change yourself line" of "soft" CR. [33]

Bryant's not explicitly identifying Ella's CR as feminist has another effect as well. Consciousness raising becomes *novelized* in *Ella Price's Journal*—not just, that is, the structural device of a novel, but also a process Ella undergoes by reading novels and measuring her life against them. An explicitly feminist version of *Ella Price's Journal* might give us Ella's readings of Friedan and de Beauvoir, rather than echoes of these books Ella hasn't read; an explicitly feminist CR novel more generally might depict women's encounters with feminist theory and other Movement writing rather than focusing on women's encounters with fiction. Coward notes that the literary bias of many feminist publishing houses may be a problem for feminism, in that theoretical and political writing is often left to commercial publishers who are less committed to it (236–38); the CR novel generally, and *Ella Price's Journal* specifically, reproduce that literary bias.

Alison Lurie's *Real People* (1969) is a particularly interesting example of the difficulties in setting absolute boundaries between the CR novel, the "illness story," and the *Kunstlerroman*, and may be read as an oddly clear example of the novelization of consciousness raising. Lurie's novel is the journal of Janet Belle Smith, a short story writer on a summer retreat to a writers' and artists' colony in New England. Janet's journal traces her growing awareness that her writing suffers from her reluctance to embarrass herself, her friends, and her family by telling the truth about their lives. While *Real People* is not explicitly about feminist consciousness per se, Janet's understanding of her writing and her decision to change her life at the end of the novel parallel exactly the overplot of the CR novel. In examining nineteenth- and twentieth-century artist novels by women writers, DuPlessis describes the plot of the women's *Kunstlerroman* as exploring "the ethical role of the artist by making her imaginatively depict and try to change the life in which she is also immersed" (101). For twentieth-century women writers in particular, DuPlessis argues, the "fictional art work" described or portrayed in the artist novels "begins with its ethics, not its aesthetics; it has its source in human ties and its end in human change." The woman artist in these novels "comes into her own" by being saturated "in buried, even taboo emotions, first resisted, then sought, and finally claimed" (103). The similarities between the overplots of the *Kunstlerroman* and the CR novel are striking; in *Real People* in particular, Janet's changing understanding of her work as a "lady writer" mirrors so exactly the process of consciousness raising that the artist plot resonates with feminist politics, even though Lurie never makes such politics explicit.

Coward poses two questions to get at the political content of feminist popular fiction:

Is it that these novels are carrying out subversive politicization, drawing women into structures of consciousness-raising without their knowing it? Or is it that the accounts of women's experiences they offer in fact correspond more closely to popular sentiment than they do to feminist aspirations? (226)

In the case of *Ella Price's Journal* (and, arguably, *Real People* as well), the answer to both these questions is yes: the novel both draws us into CR and offers us an account closer to popular sentiment than to (at least radical) feminist aspirations. But Coward's opposition between "popular" and "feminist" is problematic, for the popularity of "soft" CR and of the CR novel itself demonstrates the blurring of such a distinction. The version of feminism presented in *Ella Price's Journal* and available to a feminist reader of *Real People* is both popular and feminist. This version of feminism more closely resembles the "personal conversion stories" that made up a good portion of mainstream media coverage of Women's Liberation than it does the modernist experimental fiction Coward opposes to the "popular" in the guise of the "feminist."[34]

M. M. Bakhtin provides us with a different model for locating feminist fiction. We can see the CR novel as similar to the "low genres" from which the novel emerged, as Bakhtin describes that historical process in "Discourse in the Novel" (272–73). The CR novels were written at a time when the production of literature in the United States virtually completed its movement into academic institutions, a movement that was a "centralizing, centripetalizing force of verbal-ideological life," in Bakhtin's terms. Because the academy was male-dominated and masculinist, feminist novelists responded with "a heteroglossia consciously opposed to [the] literary language" coming out of it. The particular form of the CR novel is "low" in Bakhtin's sense especially because it is comic: its heteroglossia is "parodic and aimed sharply and polemically against the official language of its given time" (273), using the same strategies of parodic humor that Kalčik identified in women's rap groups.

One place we can locate the CR novel's heteroglossia is in the sheer numbers of other novels referred to in it. Ella's reading in Bryant's novel — *Madame Bovary, Anna Karenina, Main Street, Antigone, A Doll's House, The Autobiography of Malcolm X,* and *The Golden Notebook,* among other works — is largely in "great" literature, and "great" literature that is relatively widely read. While Bryant's novel shares the qualities that Coward identifies as constituting popular literature — a confessional mode and an emphasis on sexuality — it also refers to these other novels in order to participate in a dialogue about the fate of women characters in literature, in "high" as well as "low" literature. And while the CR novels are not often stylistically experimental in the ways that Coward prescribes, they are fundamentally concerned with representation, with ways that women are represented in literary discourses.

Ella Price's Journal, like most of the CR novels, has literary designs on its readers as well as political ones. Whether the protagonist is a reader, as Bryant's is, or a writer, as Lurie's is, the effect of such an emphasis on the importance of literature to CR is to position the novels somewhere in between the popular and the literary. This in-betweenness is evident in Bryant's novel's politics as well. While Coward's two questions may be opposed politically, in counterposing the popular and the feminist, they need not be opposed within the genre of the CR novel; the tension between the questions is precisely the terrain the CR novel maps out, alongside the tension between the literary and the popular.

Ella Price's Journal ends just as Ella has begun to act according to her newly raised consciousness, and just as Ella has been prepared for the abortion. Bryant ends the novel mid-sentence, partly to suggest that Ella has just received the anesthetic, partly to suggest that her process of consciousness raising and change is not over. The unfinished ending of the novel is another way it typifies the form; these novels usually end, as Ellen Morgan argued in "Humanbecoming: Form and Focus in the Neo-Feminist Novel," with "the doubt, uncertainty, and inconclusiveness which are the experience of many women in this era" (Brown and Olson 274). The CR novel ends on the verge of changes, or in the early stages of changes, in the protagonist's life. These endings reflect the widespread sense in the seventies that the Women's Liberation Movement's effects were only beginning to be felt. Bryant's mid-sentence ending serves as well to invite readers to "read in" their own changes to finish the narrative, to complete Ella's "I feel" with their own feelings, and thus to participate in her process of consciousness raising and personal transformation. This ending is an important way Bryant draws readers into the CR process without their being aware of it.

This kind of ending, the unfinished ending, is an example of what DuPlessis calls "writing beyond the ending": "the transgressive invention of narrative strategies, strategies that express critical dissent from dominant narrative" (5). In discussing speculative fiction, DuPlessis writes,

Raising the issue of the future is another tactic for writing beyond the ending, especially as that ending has functioned in the classic novel: as closure of historical movement and therefore as the end of development. Having been posed as an experiment in change and choice, a novel typically ends by asserting that choice is over and that the growth of character or the capacity for defining action has ceased. (178)

The case that DuPlessis makes for speculative fiction applies as well to the CR novel, for these novels also refuse the "pleasurable illusion of stasis" achieved by a "happily ever after" ending. Not only do they disrupt the marriage-or-death options for female protagonists, but they also make demands on a future beyond the events of the novel. The CR novels make their demands by asking us to envision what happens after the novel, by asking us to participate, through our own newly-raised consciousness, in creating their unfinished futures. "If a novel travels through the present into the future," DuPlessis writes, "then social or character development can no longer be felt as complete, or our space as readers perceived as untrammeled" (178). These unfinished endings are one way that the CR novel makes clear the designs it has on its readers.[35]

Our space as readers is deliberately trammeled in the CR novels because these are novels with designs on us, "in the sense," as Jane Tompkins puts it, discussing the sensational designs of earlier American fiction, "of wanting to make people think and act in a particular way" (xi). What we might call, paraphrasing Tompkins, the (counter) cultural work of feminist fiction becomes clear when we explicate the ways these novels interpellate their readers as feminist readers.[36] One technique that the CR novelists use to interpellate their readers as feminist readers is the use of a specific kind of heteroglossia, one which works in precisely the same way that Kalčik argues humor does in CR groups. The authorial voice interrupts the narrative to present an ironic pseudo-critique of the novel, a criticism that encapsulates and parodies centuries of men's criticism of women's writing, men's criticism of women themselves. Joanna Russ devotes an entire chapter of *The Female Man* (1975) to this technique; here is only part of it:

Shrill . . . vituperative . . . no concern for the future of society . . . maunderings of antiquated feminism . . . selfish femlib . . . needs a good lay . . . this shapeless book . . . of course a calm and objective discussion is beyond . . . twisted, neurotic . . . some truth buried in a largely hysterical . . . of very limited interest, I should . . . another tract for the trash-can . . . burned her bra and thought that . . . no characterization, no plot . . . really important issues are neglected while . . . hermetically sealed . . . women's limited experience . . . another of the screaming sisterhood . . . a not very appealing aggressiveness . . . could have been done with wit if the author had . . . deflowering the pretentious male . . . a man would have given his right arm to . . . hardly girlish . . . a woman's book . . . another shrill polemic which the . . . a mere male like myself can hardly . . . a brilliant but basically confused study of feminine hysteria which . . . feminine lack of objectivity . . . this pretense at a novel . . . (140–41)

This technique appears as well in non-literary feminist works in the seventies, most notably in Firestone's *The Dialectic of Sex*:

But our revolutionary demands are likely to meet anything from mild balking ("utopian . . . unrealistic . . . farfetched . . . too far in the future . . . impossible . . . well, it may stink, but you haven't got anything better . . .") to hysteria ("inhuman . . . unnatural . . . sick . . . perverted . . . communistic . . . 1984 . . . what? creative motherhood destroyed for babies in glass tubes, monsters made by scientists? etc."). (237)

Both Firestone and Russ rule out by incorporating the most negative reactions to their work. Firestone's use of "hysterical" is particularly important, for "hysterical," as Russ points out in her passage, is likely to be one of the major terms employed to reject her work. Russ takes this technique to an extreme, turning it into a torrent of abuse, and using that torrent to exorcise the patriarchal critical responses it contains. Russ pours these fragments of masculinist discourse, masculinist literary criticism, on her readers, who will be sure to recognize the whole discourse in recognizing any or all of its parts. For the most part, the speakers of this torrent of abuse are male, though one immasculated female voice also appears: "we 'dear ladies,' whom Russ would do away with, unfortunately just don't *feel* . . ." (141; emphasis original). Russ makes it virtually impossible to assent to these criticisms, even the ones regarding the literary qualities of the novel that may be arguable, by setting all of them together in this way. By incorporating this discourse, Russ not only disallows it, she also establishes her readers as readers who read otherwise, who resist these discourses. This either-or choice of reading otherwise that Russ makes for us is the same kind of us-them humor, us-them heteroglossia, that CR groups rely on to preserve their harmony, to unite their members against male experts like doctors and gynecologists. Here the (mostly) male experts are literary critics.

Russ uses the same technique elsewhere in *The Female Man*, with a less direct reference to male literary critics. In this passage, the parodic references to stereotypical femininity work to unite her readers against that reading:

You will notice that even my diction is becoming feminine, thus revealing my true nature; I am not saying "Damn" any more, or "Blast"; I am putting in lots of qualifiers like "rather," I am writing in these breathless little feminine tags, she threw herself down on the bed, I have no structure (she thought), my thoughts seep out shapelessly like menstrual fluid, it is all very female and deep and full of essences, it is very primitive and full of "and's," it is called "run-on sentences." (137)

The reference to "run-on sentences" at the end of this passage underlines Russ's point that femininity is, from the perspective of masculinist literary critics, "incorrect" right down to its grammatical structure. Her heteroglossia in both these passages works to position her readers as united members of a CR group.

Other writers use a similar technique for different ends. When Alison Lurie's writer-protagonist in *Real People* begins to feel uncomfortable with her work, she decides that it deserves, "in the worst sense," the adjectives that were used to describe her earlier book:

charming
feminine
witty
sensitive
subtle
original (58)

Lurie's use of this technique differs from Russ's in precisely the way that the politics of the two novels differ. That is, Janet Belle Smith turns out to be right in her judgment of her writing; the stereotypes of feminine writing do indeed apply to her work, and her task in the novel is to find a way to write differently, to learn not to be a "feminine" writer. Russ inserts the stereotypes to disallow these categories entirely, while Lurie uses this list of qualities—not all of which are negative—in order to set out Janet's own struggle with the limitations of feminine style. Where Russ poses the struggle with femininity as women's struggle against a role created and imposed by men, Lurie poses that struggle as an internal one that individual women must undergo. Thus Russ's novel poses CR as a collective process—as "hard" CR—while Lurie's novel poses it as an individual one—as "soft" CR. Both Russ and Lurie use their lists of feminine stereotypes to duplicate their versions of the CR process for the reader.

Another strategy that CR novels use is to provide multiple, even contradictory readings, as Brown does in *Rubyfruit Jungle*. Molly Bolt's consciousness is not at issue in this novel—it is fully raised from a very early age—but few other people in the novel have sufficiently raised consciousnesses to accept Molly's lesbianism. Brown asks readers to behave differently from the characters who cannot accept Molly. To do this, Brown must depict Molly as sure, right, decided, and proud about her sexual identity—as always already a lesbian, always already a feminist, always already a heroine. I overstate this here; Brown in fact shows that Molly chooses her sexual identity, that it comes from choice rather than being imposed upon her, and thus that Molly's sexual identity represents an extension of sexual freedom for women. Molly must be irresistible—politically, personally, sexually—at the same time that others manage to resist her, so that Brown can make clear that only her lesbianism causes others to reject her. In the same way that other writers work to set aside issues of class and ethnicity, and frequently side-step the issue of race altogether, Brown here sets aside any room for doubt about the source of Molly's problems. They stem from homophobia—and only from homophobia.

The novel's central contradiction is this tension between irresistibility and rejection, and Brown provides more contradictions about the nature of lesbianism in the novel. That is, Brown makes it unclear how much of Molly's feminism comes from her cultural position as a lesbian, and how much simply from her personality. When Molly points out that advertising serves as heterosexual propaganda, Polina says, "Why the entire world must look different to you" and Molly agrees that it does (199). But Molly refuses to argue that her "perceptiveness" is a function of her lesbianism, or that the kind of critique of mass culture that she lays out for Polina is typical of lesbians. Brown has it both ways in *Rubyfruit Jungle*, arguing that Molly is so unique that prejudice against her is clearly stupid, and that Molly is so typical of lesbians that she proves lesbians' superiority to heterosexuals.

The novel's sole purpose is not, however, to present heterosexual readers with an argument about the evils of homophobia; *Rubyfruit Jungle* also works to present lesbian readers with an affirmation. Just as feminist rhetoric often shifts between contradictory strategies to elicit the persuasive power of each, so Brown shifts between contradictory strategies for presenting Molly. Lesbian readers find affirmations of the individuality and uniqueness of each lesbian when Brown emphasizes Molly's uniqueness, together with affirmations of lesbians as a group when Brown emphasizes lesbians' superiority to heterosexuals.[37] What appear to be contradictions in one reading function as affirmations in another reading, and Brown has designs on both lesbian and heterosexual readers' consciousnesses in *Rubyfruit Jungle*.

Fay Weldon brings together most of these techniques in *Praxis*. The novel alternates chapters in first-person present-tense with chapters in third-person past-tense. The first-person chapters serve as commentary, anticipating the narrative third-person chapters—when, for example, Praxis repeatedly calls herself a "murderess," though the murder itself happens near the end of the novel's penultimate chapter—and suggesting what attitudes toward events in the narrative readers should take. Praxis sees her life story as a cautionary tale, telling us in one chapter, "Watch Praxis. Watch her carefully. Look, listen, learn. Then safely, as they say to children, cross over" (109). But "cross over" what—or where? In the structure of the novel, and in the imperatives and direct addresses in the commentary chapters, Weldon asks us to cross over from the ideas and attitudes in the narrative to the feminist point of view in the commentary chapters. Like *The Female Man*, *Praxis* duplicates the process of CR for readers. Weldon describes Praxis's CR process as a "gradual thing" (262), beginning when she takes over editing a feminist newspaper. Praxis gradually comes to believe her editorials:

She wrote rousing editorials, which she half believed, and half did not. . . . Ideas which had once seemed strange now seemed commonplace, and so much to her advantage that she was surprised to remember how, in the past, she had resisted them.

She was a convert: she wished to proselytise. She wished all the women in the world to think as she thought, do as she did; to join in sisterhood in a happier family than the world had ever known. (261)

The remainder of the novel centers on that "sisterhood," and engages a series of distinctions that parallel the distinction between "soft" and "hard" CR.

However much "happier" a feminist sisterhood might be, Weldon points out that Praxis's feminist ideas do not make her "safe" or "immune" from "more distress" (262), contrary to the beliefs of the "New Women" Praxis addresses in the commentary chapters. These "New Women" are the young feminists Praxis helped create, "those lovely, lively, trampling girls" (14), whose solution to all "female pain" is to "do away with its three centres—the heart, the soul and the mind" (13–14)—whose solutions to the problems of women's oppression are wholly personal and individual. While this version of feminism is better, Praxis believes, than the "prison of shame and hypocrisy" in which her mother lived, it is not enough. Feminists instead must have responsibilities to other women, and these responsibilities come with "female sorrow" attached.

Praxis takes on her feminist responsibility by killing Mary's baby to keep Mary from abandoning her medical career and spending the rest of her life tending a "semi-vegetable" (273). Praxis kills the baby because Mary wants to, and cannot. For Praxis, feminism does not mean an end to women's sacrifices. Feminism instead shifts the arena of sacrifice from the nuclear family into a broader sisterhood: she kills the baby not only for Mary but also to relieve pregnant women of their fear, "now that one baby in every twenty was born with some defect or other" (275). Praxis's murder thus has political import; when she gets out of prison, the same kind of thoughtless, careless young feminists as the one who steps on Praxis's foot in the bus also rediscover her, and take care of her.

The argument Weldon makes through the commentary chapters, the direct address, and the last part of the narrative is this: if feminism is to replace the nuclear family, if Sisterhood is to replace sisterhood, then feminists must find a way to take care of each other—and of their old women, their heroines, their martyrs. Praxis argues that "it is not so bad to be old and alone" (230) if the only alternative is betraying other women to get and keep a man, but there must be other alternatives. By addressing her readers as these "New Women," Weldon puts the onus of creating these alternatives on readers: it is our job to combat ageism in feminism and to make provisions for women like Praxis. It is our job both to be and not be the "New Women"—to make feminism into something other than individual freedoms, personal solutions, for young women. The "soft" CR of the "change yourself line" that Sarachild criticized in *Ms.* is personified by Weldon's New Women; Weldon insists that feminism must do better than that.

The CR novel need not always be "soft" CR, as *Praxis*, *The Female Man*, and *Woman on the Edge of Time* demonstrate in their various ways, though "soft" CR novels like *Ella Price's Journal* were more common. It is not coincidental that many of the CR novels that performed the "hard" version of CR were science fiction; realist fiction, as I argue in Chapter Five, has difficulty in depicting both radical political analysis and substantive political change. As feminist critics identified the task of the CR novel—exploring the "private," "internal," or "psychological" dimensions of women's oppression—the "soft" version of CR was likely to predominate in fiction, just as it came to predominate in Movement practice.

Notes

1. The epigraph is taken from Vickie Leonard, "c-r: it ain't what it used to be."

2. My discussion of the CR novel's "overplot" derives in part from Ellen Morgan's description of "the female bildungsroman" in "Humanbecoming: Form and Focus in the Neo-Feminist Novel." That form, she argued, is "admirably suited to express the emergence of women from cultural conditioning into struggle with institutional forces, their progress toward the goal of full personhood, and the effort to restructure their lives and society according to their own visions of meaning and right living" (Koppelman Cornillon 185). Morgan's essay appears in different versions in *Images of Women in Fiction* (1972) and in *Feminist Criticism: Essays on Theory, Poetry and Prose* (1978); I have quoted from both versions, and indicated which one by the volumes' editors. The CR novel makes these same moves, but need not do so in the genre of the bildungsroman; the CR overplot can be found in other genres, such as the picaresque (*Fear of Flying, Kinflicks, Rubyfruit Jungle* [also a coming-out novel]) and science fiction (*The Female Man, Woman on the Edge of Time*), among others. The term "overplot" itself comes from Nina Baym, *Woman's Fiction.*

3. See, e.g., Florence Howe, "Feminism and Literature"; Nancy Burr Evans, "The Value and Peril for Women of Reading Women Writers"; and Fraya Katz-Stoker, "The Other Criticism: Feminism vs. Formalism." The definitional question continues in feminist criticism; see, e.g., Bonnie Zimmerman's "Feminist Fiction and the Postmodern Challenge" (1986), for this definition: "texts that are closely associated with the women's movement, late 1960s to the present, either because of the author or the content of the text itself. Feminist authors are those who have publicly identified themselves with an aspect of the movement; feminist texts are those in which gender and sex roles are central, not marginal, to its meaning" (187 n. 5).

4. See Jane Gallop, *Around 1981: Academic Feminist Literary Theory*, for a discussion of critical readings of "prescriptive criticism" (102–11).

5. For a discussion both of Ellison's influence on feminist fiction in the decade and of the importance of the sex/race analogy more generally, see Chapter Six.

6. See Thom, ed., *Letters to Ms. 1972–1987*; most of the letters in this volume are personal narratives, and many describe the "click!" moment.

7. Spender is by no means unique in reading a "women's" speaking style out of evidence from a specifically "feminist" setting; Susan Kalčik's 1975 article, ". . . like Ann's gynecologist or the time I was almost raped" (which I discuss below) suggests that her evidence from women's rap groups might lead to new ways of understanding women's language use.

8. Cf. Robin Morgan's abbreviated version of Kathie Sarachild's CR outline in the Introduction to *Sisterhood Is Powerful*, xxvi–ii.

9. In her later work, *The Politics of Women's Liberation*, Freeman argues that certain tasks are appropriate for CR groups, including producing a feminist pub-

lication (one reason, she argues, "why there are so many of them"), organizing study groups, or creating and staffing specific kinds of women's services centers (118–19).

10. The quotation is from Bernice, "keeping an eye on iwy in the midwest," which sharply criticizes the "bourgeois aspirations" of International Women's Year, even while crediting its potential to raise consciousness (23). For a different view of CR's usefulness to women who might not otherwise have been exposed to Movement analysis, see Anita Shreve, *Women Together, Women Alone,* which describes CR as specifically important to white, middle-class, suburban women who never joined the Movement (especially Chapter One).

11. Los Angeles NOW produced and distributed a CR handbook in 1974; that same year, while CR was criticized as an inadequate way to deal with racial issues at NOW's annual conference (Ann, "NOW: a new perspective?" 9), it was also central to NOW's Conference on Sexuality (Gosier, Gardel, and Aldrich, "now or never").

12. One schema, however reductive, for tracing the vagaries of CR over the past two decades might suggest that political CR gave way to therapeutic CR, which in turn has given way to twelve-step and recovery groups. The continuing presence of more generally named "support groups" evidences the unevenness and ambiguity of this development; nonetheless, a quick check of the scheduled group meetings at your local Women's Center will likely demonstrate the almost total disappearance of anything *called* CR, no matter how often feminist theorists claim it as feminism's central practice. My thanks to the Crazy Ladies Center in Cincinnati, whose newsletter and calendar helped me think through this argument; see also calendar listings for the Boston-based feminist newspaper *Sojourner.*

13. For an account of CR as theory-building, see King's reading of Celestine Ware's book in *Theory in Its Feminist Travels,* 127–28.

14. For a history of Redstockings, including the group's reconstitution, see Echols, 139–58.

15. It is tempting to see the "change yourself line" as Sarachild names it, as an early figuration of "postfeminism"; it may be the case, however, that "postfeminism" represents less a discrete break from earlier forms of feminism than the emergence into a hegemonic position of a particular strain of feminism. For a brilliant discussion of "postfeminism," see Bonnie J. Dow's chapter on *Designing Women* in her *Prime-Time Feminism.*

16. Feminists tended to use Laing's work approvingly in the seventies—the epigraph to Joanna Russ's *The Female Man* is from Laing, for example—but traditional (especially orthodox Freudian) psychiatry more often came in for condemnation.

17. In *Gyn/Ecology: The Metaethics of Radical Feminism* (1978), Mary Daly argued similarly that "psychiatry and other forms of psychotherapy" were "directly related to the rise of radical feminism in the twentieth century" (228); one of Daly's neologistic moves in her analysis was to split *therapist* into *the/rapist.* For a range of discussion of madness in the decade, see Phyllis Chesler, *Women and Madness* (1973); Shoshana Felman, "Women and Madness: The Critical Phallacy" (1975); and Barbara Hill Rigney, *Madness and Sexual Politics in the Feminist Novel: Studies in Bronte, Woolf, Lessing, and Atwood* (1978).

18. "Study groups" and "campaigning groups" may in fact represent the continued importance of CR. Coward, I think rightly, points out that these groups no longer referred to themselves as CR groups by the early 1980s. There is

evidence that some feminists began calling the practice of CR "criticism/self-criticism" at mid-decade, perhaps as a way of distinguishing their practice from the perceived dead-endedness of CR (see Carol Anne Douglas, rev. of *Feminist Revolution* by Redstockings).

19. In part, we can attribute this disjunction to the peculiar history of MacKinnon's essay: it was begun in 1973 and revised biannually until its publication in 1981. But it is unfair, both to MacKinnon and to *Signs*, simply to suggest that the essay's arguments are outdated.

20. Campbell's discussions of CR itself waver between the "soft" and "hard" in this article, perhaps in part because of her use of the Kempton essay as a crucial example. See especially 79–81.

21. Showalter neglected to note, as she described the struggle between "minority" and "professor" in her experience, that there is surely a category of academic men—and academic women of color—who have a very particular claim to the experience (and whose job she'd taken). Feminist notions of women's split, double or dual consciousness ultimately derive, of course, from W.E.B. DuBois's notion of Black Americans' dual consciousness; see *The Souls of Black Folk* (1903). That feminists would appropriate African-American theorizations—even sometimes without being aware that they did so—is not surprising; I discuss the centrality and rhetorical power of the sex/race analogy in Chapter Six.

22. My argument here derives from Bakhtin's discussion in "Discourse in the Novel" of the role of impersonating discourses in individuals' ideological development, 342ff.

23. At the same time, CR techniques have proven effective in focusing attention on racial and other differences among women, when they are employed specifically to that end. See Tia Cross, Freada Klein, Barbara Smith, and Beverly Smith, "Face-to-Face, Day-to-Day—Racism CR." It was perhaps less the practice of CR, the technique of politicizing the personal in a small group, that led to the erasure of differences than its use in the service of a strictly gender-based exploration. That is, CR was (and is) deeply affected in its practice by its theoretical agenda: when the theory works against difference, so will the practice.

24. The conference was structured to reflect the original vision of CR in radical feminism, following the CR and workshop sessions of the first day with a focus on the second day on organizing strategies (Williams, "porn again" 26).

25. Arguably, WAP's deployment of such a contained version of CR led to the so-called sex-wars of the early 1980s; such a practice certainly reinforced, even perhaps created, what Amber Hollibaugh and Cherríe Moraga called "sexual silences in feminism" in the subtitle of their influential essay, "What We're Rollin Around in Bed With" (1981). Anti-anti-porn feminists, many of whom called themselves or their positions "sex-radical," "sex-outlaw," or simply "pro-sex," have never, to my knowledge, accused anti-porn feminists of manipulating CR, but the frequent calls in their work for *more* CR are suggestive. The term "sex-wars" stands in for a complicated history and debate, in part sparked by the events surrounding the 1982 Barnard conference, "The Scholar and the Feminist," where sex-radical and anti-porn feminists came into conflict.

26. See Charlotte Brunsdon for a discussion of the film's ambiguity (23–25); rave reviews of the film include Marjorie Rosen's in *Ms.*, Roger Ebert's in *Film Comment*, and Molly Haskell's in *New York* magazine. Critical reviews, especially of the function of class as a containment of the film's politics, include David Ehrenstein's in *Film Comment*, and Todd Gitlin and Carol S. Wolman's in *Film Quarterly*.

27. Interestingly, Bryant herself has claimed that her novel was not influenced

directly by Women's Liberation Movement writings (letter to Mary Frances Pipino, cited in Pipino's "'I Have Found My Voice': The Italian-American Woman Writer").

28. Mary Frances Pipino suggests that Ella's relationship with her best friend is more important than I have suggested; Pipino persuasively reads the novel as a veiled immigrant narrative. See her "Subm/Ver/ersions of Identity: Dorothy Calvetti Bryant," in her dissertation, "'I Have Found My Voice.'"

29. One of Isadora's psychiatrists in *Fear of Flying* similarly urges her to "Ackzept being a vohman" (157).

30. I discuss Ella's abortion in greater detail in Chapter Three.

31. Echols' critique of cultural feminism as a lifestyle rather than a politics is relevant here; for contemporary versions of this argument, see the debates over Naomi Wolf's *Fire with Fire: The New Female Power and How It Will Change the Twenty-First Century* (1993).

32. The novels eligible for canonical status, in Ohmann's terms, were novels that negotiated an "interaction between large audiences and gatekeeper intellectuals" (77) — novels that sold well, were widely reviewed, and were discussed in academic journals. Many of the CR novels I discuss qualify as precanonical in this sense.

33. It may be arguable that Bryant's choice of the mock-journal form drives the individualism of the novel's politics, but one need only look at Alix Kates Schulman's use of the mock-autobiography in *Burning Questions* (1978), a form equally individualistic, to see how such a form can be re-visioned for political ends.

34. I discuss the impact of the "conversion stories" in Chapter One; see Freeman, *The Politics of Women's Liberation*, 114–15, for an account of these narratives. For a critique of Coward's argument about modernist experimental fiction as "feminist," see Felski, 156–64.

35. Unfinished endings may not always, of course, be gestures of futurity in the way that DuPlessis describes. Kathy Acker's *Kathy Goes to Haiti* (1978), for example, ends with the sentences, "Kathy turns around and walks outside into the sun. She's more dazed than before" (170); this ending is arbitrary and unsatisfying in some of the ways that the CR novels' endings are, but it suggests the radical closure of futurity (in repetition) rather than its openness (in difference or change). Kathy here is not differently dazed, only more so; the voodoo doctor performing the ceremony that is supposed to be "the most important thing in your life" (169) only leaves her confused.

36. My use of "interpellation" here is derived from Louis Althusser's "Ideology and Ideological State Apparatuses," though I apply Althusser's notion of interpellation specifically to ways that readers are addressed (or "hailed" in his term) by texts.

37. Leslie Brody has reminded me of Evelyn Torton Beck's response to this problem of affirmation. In her introduction to *Nice Jewish Girls: A Lesbian Anthology*, Beck describes her ability to affirm herself as a lesbian reader of *Rubyfruit Jungle*, thwarted by the novel's depiction of its lone Jewish character: "In 1974, as an emerging lesbian, I didn't want to admit that the movement's leading fiction writer was basing her humor on age-old anti-Semitic stereotypes. I simply couldn't afford to take it in. So I kept silent. In those early years of struggle it seemed unworthy to make a fuss. And worse — it seemed divisive. I could not yet claim my anger. I wanted too much to belong" (xxiv). Beck also critiques works by Bertha Harris, Noretta Koertge, and Jan Clausen (xxiv–xxix).

Chapter Three
Sexuality

In the beginning there was sex. Sex as in male and female sexes, sex as in sex drives, and sex as in reproduction. Sex was biology as destiny. That was patriarchy's version.
Then along came feminists.

—Kathleen Barry

Think clitoris.

—Alix Kates Shulman[1]

This chapter examines the interplay of discourses about sexuality in Women's Liberation writings and fiction; both the junctures and disjunctures between Women's Liberation and changing discourses about women's sexuality have, as Barbara Ehrenreich, Elizabeth Hess, and Gloria Jacobs argue in *Re-making Love: The Feminization of Sex*, created nothing less than a "women's sexual revolution" (1–9), and fiction was a crucial arena of that revolution. There are a wide range of reasons that sexuality should be central to the CR novel; popular fiction's emphasis on sexuality generally, the CR novel's focus on what Cheri Register called the " 'private' or 'internal' consequences of sexism" (22), and the importance of sexuality to Women's Liberation politics and discourses together overdetermine its role in the CR novels of the 1970s.

The novels were an important part of the movement of radical feminist ideas and practices into the mainstream: both into mainstream feminism, as issues of sexual politics and consciousness raising itself filtered into reformist organizations like NOW, and into the mainstream of U.S. politics, as abortion, for example, became an issue in electoral politics. For the most part (and the exceptions are notable), the CR novels moderated the radical feminist issues of sexuality they addressed, in part, as I will argue about *Fear of Flying*, simply by providing contradictory arguments about sexuality. In part, though, that moderating of radical feminist analyses in CR novels was a function of the logical contradiction between radical oppositional politics and the arena of popular fiction (a contradiction eased to some extent by the slippage from "hard" to "soft" CR).[2]

In "Are Women's Novels Feminist Novels?" (1980), Rosalind Coward argues that popular fiction—the so-called women's novel, or "the novel that changes lives"—was problematic for feminists precisely because its radical potential could be undercut by its focus on sexuality. Such novels risked becoming just another way of commodifying women's sexuality; the novels' critiques of the oppressive social conditions under which women experienced sexuality could be lost in similarities to patriarchal discourses about sex. Coward argues that feminists working with the "confessional" structure of the popular novel (what I have called earlier the testimony of the absent member, here in its most explicit form), because of the "preoccupation with sexuality" typical of that confessional structure, might "never escape beyond defining women entirely by their sexuality."[3] At the same time, Coward suggests that "this preoccupation undoubtedly at a certain level represents a response to a problem: what is female sexual pleasure?" (233–35). Ehrenreich, Hess, and Jacobs, by contrast, argue that an emphasis on "sexual liberation contributed to the populist outreach that eventually brought the movement itself into the mainstream of American culture and politics" (72).

Coward's argument specifically rejected consciousness raising as a mode for feminist fiction, reflecting her sense that CR had declined in importance as a practice in the women's movement by 1980. With the decline in CR came too a decline in the importance of sexuality as a starting place for understanding women's oppression. In the early 1970s, by contrast, CR was widely understood to be central both to fiction and to the movement. Sexuality was central to CR, as Alix Kates Shulman pointed out in describing her experience in the early years of the movement in "Sex and Power: Sexual Bases of Radical Feminism" (1980). In the early consciousness raising sessions, it seemed that every woman had some kind of "sexual discontent" to offer up:

Some said they felt sexually rejected by their partners, others complained that their husbands never left them alone sexually. Some said they were afraid to tell their lovers what pleased them sexually, others said their partners resented being told. Some told about passes they had to submit to at work and on the street, others were bereft because men were intimidated by them and they, the women, were forbidden to make advances themselves. Some spoke about reprisals they feared or suffered as lesbians, others spoke of their fear of lesbians. Some shamefully confessed to having masturbated all their lives, others declared in anguish that they could not masturbate. Many complained bitterly that their men never took responsibility for birth control, for children, for the progress of their relationships. (593)

These women, Shulman argues, "used their sexual discontents to help them understand the power relations between men and women" (592).[4] The importance of sexuality to CR and to feminism followed this logic: because patriarchy defined women by their sexuality, and woman experienced that definition as playing out in particular forms of sexual oppression, every woman's experience of that sexual oppression could be mobilized through consciousness raising to build both theory and membership for the Women's Liberation Movement.

An important part of the context for feminist consciousness raising about and theories of women's sexuality was the "sexual revolution" that was well underway before the second wave of feminism began. In *Intimate Matters: A History of Sexuality in America,* John D'Emilio and Estelle Freedman argue that an urban culture of "singles" developed in the late fifties and early sixties that "embodied the unspoken fantasies of a consumer society extended to the sphere of sex" (305). The manual for the urban single woman was Helen Gurley Brown's best-selling book, *Sex and the Single Girl* (1962), which, in its instructions for entertaining, for decorating one's apartment, and for man-hunting, neatly exemplifies the extension of consumerism into women's personal lives as a feature of singles' culture. What is most striking, in fact, about Brown's "how-to" manual for women participating in the new singles culture is that it contains virtually no information about sex—there is no mention of contraception, for instance, and only one reference to pregnancy. Instead, Brown repeatedly admonishes readers that they must "enjoy sex," and refers them to psychiatrists if they don't (58). "It really is important to surround yourself with men every day to keep up your morale," Brown argued, because even the most casual approval of men is central to the single girl's self-esteem (29). The underside of Brown's cheerful and breezy tone is her repeated references to psychiatry, so that psychiatrists become the enforcers of Brown's vision of heterosexual normalcy, of sexual "freedom" and sexual pleasure, of her vision of "the rich, full life possible for the single woman today" (246).[5]

The sexual revolution had particular ramifications for women in the New Left, many of whom, as Alice Echols has argued, felt both exploited and liberated by it—they experienced both a "compulsory sex ethic" within the movement, as well as more and more varied sexual experiences at lower emotional costs (42–43). What the sexual revolution meant was hotly debated in the emergent Women's Liberation Movement. In "Independence from the Sexual Revolution" (1971), Dana Densmore described this compulsory sex ethic as "Sexual freedom that includes no freedom to decline sex, to decline to be defined at every turn by sex" (Koedt, Levine, and Rapone 111). Alix Kates Shulman describes the ways this critique of the compulsory sex ethic surfaced in her early consciousness raising sessions with younger women:

> I was surprised to hear so many women who had come of age in the sixties talk resentfully about their sexual experience, for I had believed the media version of the great sexual revolution among the young. But far from having felt freed by the so-called sexual revolution of the sixties, those young, dedicated women—many of whom had been politicized in the New Left—actually felt victimized by it. ("Sex and Power" 592)

Such objections to providing sexual services to male leftists in the guise of revolutionary behavior surfaced in the fiction as well, as Fay Weldon's 1971 novel, *Down Among the Women*, exemplifies in this passage: "Camp followers, groupies, gangsters' molls, revolutionaries' birds, what's the difference? The perks are much the same, and one is being useful to and used by those one most admires" (83). In a 1974 essay, "Toward a Definition of Literary Feminism," Agate Nesaule Krouse similarly cautions against the assumption that "the Women's Movement and the Sexual Revolution are the same thing." Krouse argues that in evaluating feminist fiction, (hetero)sexual explicitness is less important than "the author's attitudes towards a character who chooses celibacy, who has no interest in men at all, or who prefers the friendship or love of women, and yet whose choice is not implicitly criticized" (Brown and Olson 285–86). In their overview of the history of feminist discussions of sexuality in the introduction to *Powers of Desire*, Ann Snitow, Christine Stansell, and Sharon Thompson sum up such critiques of the sexual revolution: "The sexual revolution, radical women complained in retrospect, had been another male trick: the cool sex of the counterculture was a new version of men's old need to prove their property—now communal rather than private—in women" (20).

However deeply problematic the sexual revolution was for women, though, feminists were (and are) able to use its liberationist rhetoric to make their critique of sexual practices. Echols argues that "in opening up new sexual vistas, the sexual revolution made it possible for women to demand genuine sexual self-determination" (43). Ehrenreich, Hess, and Jacobs suggest that "The feminist reclamation of sex made women's liberation, at least for a brief few years in the early seventies, as much a movement for sexual liberation" (71). Snitow, Stansell, and Thompson frame a central question about sexuality this way: "Do we gain more autonomy from saying 'yes' or saying 'no' in a grossly unequal world?" (13). That self-determination, that autonomy, took on various forms in the Women's Liberation writings: celibacy, lesbianism, non-exploitative heterosexuality, and non-monogamy, among others. But all were premised on the notion that women must have sexual self-determination as part of their freedom, that sexual freedom was high on the Women's Liberation Movement's political agenda.

One possible definition of sexual freedom, of course, was freedom from sexuality entirely, a position taken by Ti-Grace Atkinson in "The Institution of Sexual Intercourse" (1968). Atkinson argued that because "our society has never known a time when sex in all its aspects was not exploitative and relations based on sex, e.g., the male-female relationship, were not extremely hostile, it is difficult to understand how sexual intercourse can even be salvaged as a *practice*" ("Institution" 19). What Atkinson proposed instead was not lesbianism (at least, not until 1970, when Atkinson came to advocate a specifically "political" lesbianism ["Lesbianism and Feminism" 131–34]), but a- or anti-sexuality; by her logic, any sexual expression for women besides masturbation was counter-revolutionary.

Given the nature of sex, once you de-institutionalize it and it has no social function, and there is no longer any need for a cooperative effort, and when the physical possibilities of this sense can be fully realized alone, on what possible grounds could you have anything remotely like what we know today as "sexual relations"? ("Institution" 21)

Atkinson was not alone in the late sixties and early seventies in arguing that women's sexual freedom was freedom from sexuality; as Echols points out, so did The Feminists and Valerie Solanis (author of "The SCUM Manifesto" [1968]) (173–74).[6]

Far more typical of radical feminism in the pre-1975 period, though, was the view that Echols identifies as "a stereographic view of sexuality— one which acknowledged that sexuality is for women a domain of both danger and pleasure"; she argues that the splitting of that double view of sexuality occurred in "the late '70s when the anti-pornography movement began to take shape" (290). Ellen Willis, responding to a paper by Catharine MacKinnon, illuminates that double view of sexuality:

. . . it is men who have the opportunity to act out dominance; men's confusion of empowerment and sexual pleasure with dominance wreaks great devastation on women. At the same time, however, it is important to realize that sex is not monolithic; it's a minefield of all these contradictions; it's an area of struggle. Sex is not entirely given over to oppression and thus women are not limited to refusing compliance. Every time women demand their own pleasure—despite the contradictions that may entail within heterosexuality—it is a moment of empowerment and liberation and a kind of wedge into struggle in other areas. ("Comment" 119)

Perhaps the most important way that sexuality became a "wedge into struggle in other areas"—and far more important to feminist discussions of sexuality in the decade than the sexual revolution—was the discrediting of the vaginal orgasm in Masters and Johnson's *Human Sexual Response* (1966). The "rediscovery" of the clitoral orgasm, as Susan Lydon points out in "The Politics of Orgasm" (1970), opened up a sweeping critique of the politics of sexuality more generally:

Before Masters and Johnson, female sexuality had been objectively defined and described by men; the subjective experience of women had had no part in defining their own sexuality. And men defined feminine sexuality in a way as favorable to themselves as possible. If woman's pleasure was obtained through the vagina, then she was totally dependent on the man's erect penis to achieve orgasm; she would receive her satisfaction only as a concomitant of man's seeking his. With the clitoral orgasm, women's sexual pleasure was independent of the male's, and she could seek her satisfaction as aggressively as the man sought his, a prospect which didn't appeal to too many men. The definition of normal feminine sexuality as vaginal, in other words, was a part of keeping women down, of making them sexually, as well as economically, socially, and politically subservient. (R. Morgan 223)

Lydon concludes by offering the hope that "woman at long last will be allowed to take the first step toward her emancipation, to define and enjoy the forms of her own sexuality" (R. Morgan 228).

Defining the forms of women's sexuality by depicting women's subjective experience of sexuality was a central project of CR novels. The critique of the vaginal orgasm—and its prescription by a male-dominated psychiatric establishment—appears in several of the novels; these examples are from Lois Gould's *Such Good Friends* (1970) and *Final Analysis* (1974).

I wonder if he's sorry he told me all that crap about two kinds of female orgasms. "The clitoral, which of course you've experienced, is very nice," he said, "but it's nothing compared to the deep fulfillment of the *vaginal*. Only the male can give you that." You were a little nutsy yourself about that, Doctor, but it only hung me up another seven or eight years, until they proved there was only one kind of female orgasm after all and we could all stop torturing ourselves about not getting Brand X. That's right, ladies, no cock can do any more for you than you can do with a finger or tongue or this handy plastic vibrator ($4.95, batteries extra; available in ivory, pink or heaven blue). (*Such* 88; emphasis original)

True orgasm was something Dr. Foxx recommended very highly. It would beat anything she had ever had with any fantasy, he could guarantee that. . . . Ah, *those*, he would say, not unkindly. Those, I'm afraid, are merely more of your little clitoral things, that's all *those* are. Shoddy goods, suitable for girls who don't have their full growth on them, and maybe neurotics who never will. Second-fiddlers. But the adult female, what she gets is your true orgasm. That would be your vaginal model, available only through authorized dealers. (*Final* 11–12; emphasis original)

Gould's psychiatrists in both these novels, like Helen Gurley Brown's in *Sex and the Single Girl*, police the boundaries of women's sexuality by insisting on what is "normal"; her characters' resistance, typical of the consciousness-raising novel (and of CR itself, as Kalčik argued), is to parody those patriarchal pronouncements.[7] For if, as both the novels and the Movement writings pointed out, psychiatrists' knowledge of women's anatomy was wrong, then surely their attempts to pronounce it women's destiny were ridiculous.

Lydon's analysis and Gould's fiction both use the discrediting of the vaginal orgasm as a wedge into struggle (in Willis's phrase) with or against the institution of psychiatry. A more radical analysis—Anne Koedt's in "The Myth of the Vaginal Orgasm" (1968–70)—challenged another institution: heterosexuality. Like Lydon, Koedt argued that it was in men's interests to suppress knowledge of the clitoral orgasm; Koedt argued further that such knowledge could potentially make men "sexually expendable." Making men sexually expendable would have important political implications:

Aside from the strictly anatomical reasons why women might equally seek other women as lovers, there is a fear on men's part that women will seek the company of other women on a full, human basis. The recognition of clitoral orgasm as fact would threaten the heterosexual *institution*. For it would indicate that sexual pleasure was obtainable from either men *or* women, thus making heterosexuality not an absolute, but an option. It would thus open up the whole question of *human* sexual relationships beyond the confines of the present male-female role system. (Koedt, Levine, and Rapone 206; emphasis original)

The discrediting of the vaginal orgasm made sexuality available to a new kind of critique: as a practice, heterosexual intercourse could now be seen as a socially constructed "norm" that was not conducive to women's pleasure, while as an institution, heterosexuality could now be perceived to represent ideological, economic, social, and political interests that were not conducive to women's freedom; this argument would be central to Adrienne Rich's 1980 essay, "Compulsory Heterosexuality and Lesbian Existence."

The political and ideological complexities at stake in Women's Liberation discourses of women's sexuality in the 1970s are central to the CR novel. If feminist novelists understood fiction to be a powerful arena in which to "re-vision" (in Adrienne Rich's term) patriarchal constructions of sexuality, they did so because they understood fiction's power to construct sexuality for women readers. Erica Jong's Isadora Wing makes very clear feminists' stake in fictions of sexuality as she points out the influence of literature on her sexual experience: "Until I was twenty-one, I measured my orgasms against Lady Chatterley's and wondered what was *wrong* with me. Did it ever occur to me that Lady Chatterley was a man? That she was really D. H. Lawrence?" (*Fear* 27).[8] The CR novels provided women's testimony to women's experiences of sexuality, including the experience of having sexuality defined for them by men. Orgasms and the sexual revolution were only a small part of the discourses of sexuality in which the CR novels intervened. I want to turn now to other issues, beginning with abortion, then looking at how definitions of women's sexual freedom circulated in discussions of lesbianism, and concluding with one of the most important novels about women's sexuality in the decade, Erica Jong's *Fear of Flying*.

While not all feminists in the seventies agreed about what women's sexual freedom was, there was widespread consensus about what it was not. That is, privative definitions of freedom were much easier to arrive at than affirmative ones. Radical feminists were the first to link sexual freedom with abortion rights, arguing that there could be no sexual freedom for women without reproductive freedom. This was the abortion position taken, Ginette Castro argues, by "a minority of liberal feminists and most radical feminists" by 1967 (192). The minority of feminists in NOW who favored abortion rights won their battle when NOW moved to include abortion rights in its Bill of Rights for Women for 1968. NOW's inclusion of abortion rights was not without consequences: those opposing NOW's new position on abortion left the organization to found the Women's Equity Action League (WEAL), thus dividing the membership.[9] Disruptions of legislative hearings about abortion law reform in 1969 by The Feminists and Redstockings brought greater attention to the radical feminist position, as did Redstockings' abortion speak-outs—a kind of public consciousness raising in which women spoke about their experiences of abortion (Echols 169–70, 141–42).

By 1972, abortion rights emerged as an issue in United States party politics in the fight over a pro-choice plank of the Democratic platform; this further mainstreaming of the issue by 1972 demonstrates the extent to which feminists had further consolidated their consensus on the issue (Wandersee 28–30).[10] There were important debates among radical feminists in the early 1970s about the potential for abortion (as well as birth control) to be implemented in racist and genocidal ways—by governmental enforcing of abortion on poor women, women of color, and women on welfare in particular. At the same time, feminists like the St. Louis Women's Collective insisted that "The demand for direct control over our reproductive function is a morally unassailable right of all women and accessible birth control and abortion are key to that issue."[11] But accessibility was not enough; even the legal right to abortion, as Rika Alper, Pris Hoffnung, and Barbara Solomon cautioned in *off our backs* in 1972, did not equal the right to control over abortion.[12] By 1972, abortion had become such a commonplace of women's and feminist fiction that one reviewer referred to the "obligatory abortion episode." Reviewing Sandra Hochman's novel *Walking Papers* in *off our backs*, Jody Raphael argues that

It is also about time for women writers to dispense with the obligatory abortion episode and realize that a quick description of an abortion, either legally or illegally procured, will no longer serve as a shorthand substitute for an exploration of the humiliation of women. (26)

Raphael specifically criticized Hochman's novel for its refusal to "indict the society in which [its protagonist] was conditioned for this loss of self-identity and respect" (26).[13] Clearly, the novel's gesture toward feminist concerns in its abortion scene need not evidence a serious feminist critique, especially as abortion rights became less and less identified with a radical feminist position.

Obligatory, conventional, politically suspect or not, abortion remained a central issue in the consciousness-raising novels of the decade. Nearly all the CR novels of the decade make some reference to abortions, whether as a major theme or a minor plot device; no other issue of sexual freedom is as pervasive. Even a novelist whose relationship to feminism was as problematic as Joan Didion's could be read as a feminist writer by including the abortion episode; her novel *Play It As It Lays* (1970), with its discussions of the difficulties even wealthy and well-connected women faced in obtaining abortions, problematized the question of "choice." Before her abortion, Didion's Maria dreams about having the baby; afterward, she is haunted by dreams of plumbing filled with fetal tissue. Her husband gives her the telephone number of "the only man in Los Angeles County who did clean work" (54). She agrees to call because otherwise her husband will take her daughter away from her; once she calls the number, she need only follow instructions. Maria's abortion, and the passivity with which she goes through it, exemplify the way she lives her life: she knows "what 'nothing' means, *and keep[s] on playing*" (213; emphasis original). For Maria, the abortion is one more in a series of events over which she has no control, to which she can only acquiesce.

Maria remembers what she calls "just a New York story" about a woman she worked with who had had an abortion in New York. In exchange for testifying about a prostitution ring, Maria's coworker is given "a legal D & C, arranged and paid for by the District Attorney's office." Maria cannot make "a funny story" out of her own abortion, cannot put it into "the same spirited perspective" (116–17). What happened to Maria in Encino—and she thinks about her abortion in precisely these terms, as something that happened to her in Encino, a place she does not otherwise go—seems to her entirely different from this trade-off. Maria cannot re-vision her experience into anything but nightmares; while she experiences the peculiar power relations that surround abortion, she is never able to come into any kind of power herself. In both cases, though, Didion's women do manage to arrange safe abortions; while Maria's abortion hardly represents reproductive freedom or choice, it at least does not threaten her life. That even these privileged women faced such difficulties could be read, by some radical feminist readers at least, as an argument about women's shared oppression across class lines; this reading suggests the importance of abortion episodes to the CR novel.[14]

The treatment of abortion in fiction, moreover, closely follows the political status of the issue over the decade. Dorothy Bryant's *Ella Price's Journal* (1972) presents Ella's decision to have an abortion just at the moment its legal status is changing; Ella's psychiatrist tells her that she needs "letters from two psychiatrists stating that bearing a child would be dangerous to your mental health" (194), but Ella later discovers that these letters are no longer necessary as abortion has just become available on demand while the Supreme Court is considering *Roe v. Wade*. The psychiatrist lies to her to maintain his power to decide for her:

Suddenly I was terrified. He held this power over me. He could decide whether or not I was to have a baby. I felt rage well up in me, and I swallowed it. I could see by the look on his face, the pout of his lips, that he was enjoying this power. (196)[15]

Here Ella understands the power relations that are at stake in questions about the legalization of abortion. Her "terror" and her "rage" are no match for the institutional power the psychiatrist has—the power to make her have a baby, based only on his individual whim, his "enjoying" his power, and backed up, she believes, by the full force of the law. Bryant leaves no room for doubting the rightness of Ella's decision, and indeed suggests that Ella's getting pregnant in the first place resulted from a male conspiracy on the part of her husband and her psychiatrist to control her life.

Russ, in *The Female Man* (1975), notes that abortion reforms short of legalization do not significantly affect women's access to abortion. "New Yorkers (female) have had the right to abortion for almost a year now, if you can satisfy the hospital boards that you deserve bed-room and don't mind the nurses calling you Baby Killer." Russ links this kind of access to abortion to the "perfectly free access to contraception" that women

in Toronto have "if they are willing to travel 100 miles to cross the bor-
der," and to smoking "my very own cigarette" and getting "my very own
lung cancer" (136). Nothing has changed in five years of abortion reform laws, Russ points out; regulated abortion may be little better than
illegal abortion in providing women with real choices and real reproductive freedom.[16] Russ asks us to consider precisely what constitutes
"access" here—and what kind of "right" to abortion women have under
these conditions.

Marge Piercy's *Woman on the Edge of Time* (1976) suggests that reproductive rights may never have been achieved for poor women, and for
poor women of color in particular. Legal or illegal, safe abortions cost
money, and Piercy points out that poor women cannot afford them. In
Woman on the Edge of Time, Piercy links abortion with forced sterilization,
broadening the issue of reproductive freedom. Radical feminists in the
early 1970s had repeatedly coupled the fight for abortion rights with
the fight against involuntary sterilization, as complementary parts of
the struggle for women's reproductive freedom. Even after 1974 federal
regulations prohibited doctors from sterilizing anyone under the age of
twenty-one, doctors routinely pushed sterilization on any woman with
three or more children, frequently ignoring the patient's consent, or obtaining it when women were already under anaesthesia or in the middle
of a difficult labor—conditions where "consent" is problematic at best.[17]
Connie has had abortions and been sterilized: "They had taken out her
womb at Metropolitan when she had come in bleeding after that abortion and the beating from Eddie. Unnecessarily they had done a complete hysterectomy because the residents wanted practice" (45). Piercy's
portrayal of involuntary sterilization is one of the very few times the link
is made in the CR novel, demonstrating one way that issues of reproductive freedom became moderated in the fiction, as novelists focussed on
abortion—which all women were presumed to need—rather than involuntary sterilization—which affected primarily poor women and women
of color.

The presumed universality of abortion was part of the CR novel's appeal to a presumption of women's shared oppression, which worked in
many of the novels on the level of plot as well. That is, in the same way
that the obligatory abortion episode would link readers and characters,
in the novels, an abortion, especially an illegal abortion, creates solidarity between characters in important ways. In Rita Mae Brown's *Rubyfruit Jungle* (1973), for example, the abortion that Molly's room-mate has
creates an intimacy between them that leads to their becoming lovers. In
Margaret Laurence's *The Diviners* (1974), Morag's foster father conspires
in more than one illegal abortion. Christie's secret burial of an aborted
fetus, and his refusal to tell anyone, even Morag, who the woman was,

deepens Morag's trust in him. When Morag's friend Eva "aborts herself . . . with a partly straightened-out wire clotheshanger," Christie again covers it up, convincing Eva's father that she "was anaemic and she haemmorhaged" (123, 124). *The Diviners* is unusual in presenting cross-gender solidarity about abortion; more often it is women who conspire about it, and solidarity between women that the novels emphasize.

By 1979, the obligatory abortion episode could be dispensed with; by 1982, the anti-abortion backlash had to be confronted directly. Zane, the narrator of Alix Kates Shulman's *Burning Questions* (1979), describes an argument with her husband about her participating in an abortion speak-out clearly modelled on the Redstockings speak-outs in 1969; Zane's two illegal abortions are mentioned but never described. Shulman's refusal to describe the circumstances under which Zane decided to terminate her pregnancies short-circuits readers' desire to evaluate and judge. It has the rhetorical force of insisting that any woman's choice takes place under circumstances we have no right to judge and exemplifies the Redstockings' "pro-woman line" where feminists do not judge the actions of a woman in patriarchy.[18] A later novel, Piercy's *Braided Lives* (1982), tackles the anti-abortion backlash directly, where Shulman only does so indirectly in taking the "pro-woman line." When Piercy's Jill discovers she is pregnant, her mother is too frightened of arrest to find her an abortionist. When Jill finally gets the name and number of a doctor who will do abortions, she also finds out that it will cost three hundred dollars—all the money she has earned to pay for her dorm room for the fall semester, at a school that requires its women students to live on campus. With her mother's help, Jill begins a series of attempts to abort herself, culminating in a procedure so dangerous, the authorial voice interrupts the narrative to tell us, that it cannot be described in a novel in the early eighties:

If it were even a couple of years ago I would tell you more, but if I do so now, desperate young girls, desperate middle-aged women, the victims of rape, incest, battering, far more numerous than we like to believe, all the women who simply do not believe in catching a baby as you might the flu or pneumonia, would be tempted to do as I did, just because I survived it but barely. There have to be better ways. I cannot include a recipe for action that is likely to kill you. (Braided 218)

This and similar interruptions in *Braided Lives* link the "desperate" choices of women who "need" abortions to the ideological choices of women who "want" abortions, making a case for the validity of all women's choices to terminate their pregnancies. Where Shulman takes the same position in an argument by omission, Piercy makes it explicit, engaging the resistances constructed in the anti-abortion backlash of the early eighties.

The authorial voice also describes, in later passages, a woman's near death from a botched abortion, the underground network of illegal abortion providers before *Roe v. Wade*, and efforts to legalize abortion. *"We will be free. Women will not pay in blood for love. Children will not be born unchosen, unwanted, unloved,"* Piercy tells us in describing an abortion rights march in 1970 (*Braided* 224). Piercy tells this history and interrupts the narrative in this deliberate way to emphasize the horrors of illegal abortion for readers who have forgotten or are too young to remember, to raise the consciousnesses of another generation of readers on this issue. The authorial voice in *Braided Lives* specifically uses direct address to bring the reader into that group of women who are "desperate"—to create solidarity with those women. Creating this solidarity is aimed at involving readers in reproductive rights activism—in making the direct connection between consciousness and action that lay at the heart of the consciousness-raising novel's political designs on its readers.

In all of these novels, in very different ways, abortion is never a good choice, though often a necessary one. The novelists take a position most clearly articulated by Mary Daly in *Gyn/Ecology: The Meta-Ethics of Radical Feminism* (1978):

Obviously, I am by no means advocating the position that abortion is "morally wrong." Indeed, it is preferable to the agony of unwanted pregnancy and childbirth. This does not lessen the fact that it is a degrading and painful procedure which no woman should have to endure. (278)

As Kathy Acker summarizes the issue in *Blood and Guts in High School* (1978): "Abortions are the symbol, the outer image, of sexual relations in this world" (34).[19] Putting oneself in the hands of the medical establishment, if one is poor and a woman of color like Piercy's Connie, may be little better than putting oneself in the hands of a back-alley butcher. Being called a Baby Killer by the nurses, pleading with the psychiatrist, bargaining with the D.A., being blackmailed by a husband, or, worst of all, putting one's life in danger, are the conditions under which the protagonists in these novels "choose" abortion. The novelists emphasize the limitations on women's choices not only to explore the problems of reproductive freedom for women, but also to underline the commonality of women's problems, regardless of class, race, marital status, sexual preference—and even regardless of the legal status of abortion.

The tensions within the movement about the nature and meaning of sexual self-determination for women permeated Women's Liberation debates about lesbianism, and especially about its meaning for feminism. Many of the early movement writings worked to de-sexualize lesbianism—both to make lesbianism less threatening to heterosexual feminists, and to establish it politically as the movement's vanguard. When Ti-Grace Atkinson, for example, endorses lesbianism in 1970, it is a specifically political rather than sexual lesbianism:

> It is this commitment, by choice, full-time, of one woman to others of her class, that is called lesbianism. It is this commitment, against any and all personal considerations, if necessary, that constitutes the political significance of lesbianism.
>
> There are women in the Movement who engage in sexual relations with other women, but who are married to men. These women are not lesbians in the political sense. . . .
>
> There are other women who have never had sexual relations with other women, but who have made, and live, a total commitment to this movement. These women are "lesbians" in the political sense. ("Lesbianism and Feminism" 132)

"The Woman-Identified Woman" (1970)—which many feminists saw as the first manifesto of lesbian-feminism—similarly located lesbianism as a political identity rather than a sexual practice. Radicalesbians' "The Woman-Identified Woman" opened with this statement: "What is a lesbian? A lesbian is the rage of all women condensed to the point of explosion" (Koedt, Levine, and Rapone 240).[20] Martha Shelley's essay, "Notes of a Radical Lesbian" (1969), anthologized in *Sisterhood Is Powerful* in 1970, similarly argued that lesbianism *was* feminism, that "Lesbianism is one road to freedom—freedom from oppression by men" (R. Morgan 343). Later feminists, most notably Adrienne Rich, argued that all women have lesbian potential—that lesbianism in the political sense, as Atkinson put it, was possible for all women who refuse to be immasculated. Rich wrote in 1976, "It is the lesbian in us who is creative, for the dutiful daughter of the fathers is only a hack" ("It Is the Lesbian" 201).[21] Emphasizing the political rather than the sexual aspects of lesbianism worked to de-sexualize lesbian identity, which was an important political strategy enabling radical feminists to de-emphasize differences betwen lesbian and heterosexual feminists. But these efforts were not especially successful in defusing the "gay-straight split" that rocked Women's Liberation in the early 1970s.[22]

Gene Damon's [Barbara Grier's] essay in *Sisterhood Is Powerful* blames homophobia in Women's Liberation for preventing lesbians from making common cause with feminists:

Certainly many of us [lesbians] are ardent feminists. Equally certainly many of the women's rights groups shun and fear Lesbians because of the "brand" they fear they will receive. It comes as no surprise whatever to the Lesbian civil rights worker to find that she is, among some of these brave women's groups, once again *persona non grata*. (R. Morgan 341)

In *Rubyfruit Jungle*, Brown makes a very similar political argument about homophobia in the women's movement as her protagonist, Molly Bolt, comes specifically to reject political activism:

My bitterness was reflected in the news, full of stories about people my own age raging down the street in protest. But somehow I knew my rage wasn't their rage and they'd have run me out of their movement for being a lesbian anyway. I read somewhere too that women's groups were starting but they'd trash me just the same. (246)

Molly's rejecting activism ought not to be taken too seriously, of course, because activism is not the problem, homophobia is. The rhetorical effect of this passage at the end of Brown's novel is to ask us to combat that homophobia, and to open up Women's Liberation to lesbians, just as Gene Damon had argued in 1970.[23]

The more mainstream women's organizations like NOW experienced a "purge mentality" in the early 1970s when faced with what Betty Friedan called "a lavender herring" and a "lavender menace." One group of radical lesbians mocked Friedan's and other feminists' fear, taking over the stage at the 1970 Congress to Unite Women and calling themselves "Lavender Menace." One of the resolutions proposed by Lavender Menace at the Congress linked lesbians and feminism, asserting that "Women's Liberation is a lesbian plot."[24]

Lesbian, bisexual and heterosexual women in Women's Liberation debated the meaning of lesbianism in the early seventies especially. Some argued that lesbianism was—sexually or not—feminism carried to its logical extension, that it was the "practice" for which feminism was the "theory," a formulation attributed to Ti-Grace Atkinson.[25] Sidney Abbott and Barbara Love made the argument rather modestly in an essay titled "Is Women's Liberation a Lesbian Plot?": "If women's liberation does mean liberation from the dominance of men, lesbians' opinions should be actively sought out, for in many ways the lesbian *has* freed herself from male domination" (Gornick and Moran 437; emphasis original). Leah Fritz described this thinking as the "Precocious Political Awareness theory"—the belief that lesbianism was inherently (at least proto-) feminist—which became "widespread as an adjunct to growing lesbian pride"; the effect, she argues, "was to make heterosexual feminists feel stupid by comparison" (96). Some, especially heterosexual women who perceived that the sexual revolution within oppositional movements made them sexual servants to revolutionaries, argued that lesbianism within feminism was just another form of objectification for movement women. Some argued that lesbianism offered women a more authentically female sexuality, less caught up in sexual "conquest" and more "sensual." Some argued that lesbianism offered women a temporary refuge from male dominance, strengthening the movement by providing respite for individual women in it. Still others, especially The Furies, argued that lesbianism was the bottom line marking women's commitment to feminism, the equivalent of " 'picking up the gun' " for members of Weathermen or the Black Panthers, "the barometer of one's radicalism."[26]

Echols argues that the effect of the gay-straight split was essentially to drive heterosexual women out of radical feminism: "some heterosexual radical feminists remained involved in radical feminist groups, but by 1975 the radical wing of the movement was predominantly lesbian" (240). Fritz describes the difficulties some heterosexual women experienced when "some feminists began exerting psychological pressure on other feminists to become lesbians" in the early years of the gay/straight splits, and particularly notes the ubiquity of the problem (91–92, 103–9). According to Echols, the exodus of heterosexual women led to radical feminism's ceding issues of reproductive freedom to liberal feminism, an argument that may be true within the specific micro-generational, micro-organizational history she charts. Within Women's Liberation more broadly, however, Snitow, Stansell, and Thompson describe instead "a sexual consensus," however uneasy, in which "Lesbians and heterosexual feminists theoretically accepted each other's moderated, healthy sexual proclivities—although somewhat in the same spirit that St. Paul accepted the inevitability of marriage for those weak of flesh and soul" (34–35). This consensus marked the success of arguments that sexual freedom for women required a free choice of object— that "sexual preference," under the same rubric of freedom of choice that underlay reformist feminist arguments about abortion, was important.[27]

Depictions of lesbian sexuality were far more common in science fiction novels in the decade than in realist ones. Gould, for example, in her critique of the myth of the vaginal orgasm, does not make the connection, as many radical feminists did, between a non-penis-based women's sexuality and lesbian sexuality. Such an absence may seem odd, given the importance of lesbian feminism in the seventies, but in fact the privileged genre for lesbian feminism in the seventies—with a handful of crucial exceptions such as *Rubyfruit Jungle*—was the lyric poem rather than the novel.[28] This is another instance of the moderating of Women's Liberation ideas about sexuality in the CR novel: sexual freedom in the fiction was almost exclusively heterosexual freedom. Even when some realist and mainstream novels did attempt to deal with lesbianism, as did Lisa Alther's *Kinflicks* (1975), other literary conventions subverted whatever radical politics those portrayals attempted. *Kinflicks* is instructive for precisely that reason, and I will return to it after discussing *Fear of Flying*.

No single work claimed women's heterosexual freedom as its subject as much as Erica Jong's *Fear of Flying* (1973), and Jong's famous formulation of the "zipless fuck." The scenario of the zipless fuck is based in women's sexual *un*freedom, a fantasy evolved to compensate for the fact that "It is heresy in America to embrace any way of life except as half of a couple" (*Fear* 10–11). The zipless fuck, Jong writes, is "zipless" because

the incident has all the swift compression of a dream and is seemingly free of all remorse and guilt; because there is no talk of her late husband or of his fiancee; because there is no rationalizing; because there is no talk at *all*. The zipless fuck is absolutely pure. It is free of ulterior motives. There is no power game. The man is not "taking" and the woman is not "giving." No one is attempting to cuckold a husband or humiliate a wife. No one is trying to prove anything or get anything out of anyone. The zipless fuck is the purest thing there is. (*Fear* 14)

The zipless fuck is "a platonic ideal," an impossible fantasy in a society where sex is always a power game. Only in fantasy can a woman experience sexual freedom—freedom from the social conventions of marriage, from power games, from the double standard. The conditions for a zipless fuck are "brevity" and "anonymity," values that have more usually been associated with men's sexuality than with women's (*Fear* 11, 12).

Fear of Flying uses the conventions of the male sexual picaresque and the character of the male sexual rogue, but sets a woman character into those conventions and that role. Putting a woman into that plot, however, necessarily requires some changes, and the zipless fuck marks the nature of the plot changes required. Because of the double sexual standard, because of the different social meanings of "free" sexuality for women and for men, when Isadora discovers that her sexual adventuring leaves "the men reduced to sex objects," it seems to her "very sad" rather than funny. Reversing the gender roles, making men rather than women into sex objects, only partially masks the power that men still have in Isadora's life. Isadora considers herself a "free woman," but she still finds that "our lives seem to come down to a long succession of sad songs about men." Even women writers and artists, the women she most admires, are not "free"—they are "shy, shrinking, schizoid" women, "Timid in their lives and brave only in their art" (*Fear* 109). In a world so supersaturated with gender politics, where heterosexual relationships for women are ideological minefields, even the zipless fuck is finally impossible. Jong presents the zipless fuck at the end of the novel as frightening: when a conductor on a train in France makes a pass at

Isadora, she discovers that "instead of turning me on, it had revolted me!" and "There was no longer anything romantic about strangers on trains." This last thought leads Isadora to wonder, "Perhaps there was no longer anything romantic about men at all?" (*Fear* 332). Isadora discovers the limitations of the picaresque plot for women, and even the limitations of sexual freedom for women if that freedom must take place in a grossly unequal world. Jong interrogates Plath, Lawrence, and Freud, popular songs and literary conventions (the novel's last chapter is called "A 19th Century Ending"[29]), to make them yield up some kind of truth about women's sexuality. What she finds is that "all the soupy longings that every high-school girl was awash in" are inescapable, that women are interpellated into romance plots inevitably (*Fear* 10).

When women tell the story of their interpellation into romance, it need not, and does not in the case of *Fear of Flying*, create alternatives to the romance plots, but it can and does unmask them as plots in every sense of the term. Romance plots are narrative plots, obviously. They are also cemetery plots in the sense that marriage-or-death is the same thing for women characters in the "nineteenth-century ending," and plots of land in the laws of familial inheritance in which marriage participates. They are also conspiracy plots, plots created, as Isadora comes to understand, by a wide-ranging conspiracy of men, women, institutions, texts — by everyone and everything in culture. The woman protagonist who comes to see romance as a plot, who re-visions romance into another means of the social control of women, is paranoid: she understands that everything is out to get her, and usually to get her married off.[30] Jong's "zipless fuck" is simply another romance plot, a re-visioning of the romance plot that marks the failure of everything romance is supposed to provide for women — relationality, intimacy, futurity — by replacing these things with anonymous, momentary sexual pleasure. But transforming the romance plot still cannot break its hold over Isadora; only rejecting any such plots can do that.

Both the double sexual standard and the ways that patriarchal literature has constructed and reinforced it are clearly under attack in *Fear of Flying*. But the novel makes an additional and more radical argument as well — that sexual behavior, sexuality itself, is an insufficient arena for women's freedom. Jong re-visions the sexual revolution, and finds that no revolution is possible on such narrow terrain. As Mira would in Marilyn French's *The Women's Room* (1977), Isadora decides at the end that learning to be alone is the only thing that will change her life. When Isadora goes back to her husband, she determines that either she and her husband will remake their marriage or she will be alone — but the possibility of remaking her marriage depends absolutely on her willingness to leave it. Real sexual freedom — figured in *Fear of Flying* as the freedom to choose whether to have a sexual relationship at all—thus depends on women's willingness and ability to free themselves from their dependence on sexuality.

And yet, despite this rhetorical reading of the novel's argument about the limitations of sexuality as an arena for women's freedom, *Fear of Flying*, more than any other novel of the decade, made its mark as a novel about sexuality, as a novel that defined its protagonist by her sexuality. Reviewers characterized the novel as "Erica Jong's bestselling hymn to the body electric," as a "funny, horny first novel [that] will scare any male pig who believes women 'don't think like that,'" as "mak[ing] a bold stand on sexual promiscuity," and celebrating "radical sexual experiment," as "bawdy," as a "raunchy, comical account of one summer of sex and self-discovery,"[31] and, perhaps most telling in John Updike's review in the *New Yorker*, as having "more kind words for the male body than any author since the penning of *Fanny Hill*" (149).[32] Millicent Dillon described *Fear of Flying*, together with Sandra Hochman's *Walking Papers* and Lois Gould's *Final Analysis*, as the fiction of "the new bawd," a fiction characterized by a narrator who is "a bawd in boldness, bold in the pursuit of her lovers and lustier and bolder in the telling of that pursuit" (219). This reception has influenced feminist readings of Jong, as Rita Felski's decision not to discuss her work in *Beyond Feminist Aesthetics* demonstrates:

The novels of Erica Jong, for example, which have been marketed as examples of feminist writing, do not seem to me to reveal any serious questioning of the existing basis of male-female relations or any sustained refusal of the values of male-dominated society. It can be noted in this context that some feminist ideas which might once have been considered radical (such as the critique of the sexual double standard) have filtered down to the extent that they are now relatively familiar. Consequently, these ideas have gradually become incorporated into a great deal of material which cannot be construed as consciously feminist or oppositional in any meaningful sense. (14–15)

By 1989, the novel's attack on the sexual double standard has become "familiar" enough to make Jong's novel appear banal—and indeed, to make its argument about the inadequacy of sexuality as an arena for women's freedom virtually unreadable. In part because Felski believes that Jong's critique of the sexual double standard post-dates the wide circulation of that critique, she, like other feminist critics who decide not to deal with *Fear of Flying* in the eighties and nineties,[33] comes to read the novel in precisely the same way as its reviewers did in 1973— as a wholly affirmative, celebratory account of women's sexual freedom. The later feminist critique of the politics of such fiction suggests that Jong's novel is limited by that affirmation to repeating without critiquing popular and patriarchal notions of women as carriers of sexuality. *Fear of Flying* becomes in this reading precisely the kind of fiction Coward warned against accepting in setting standards for feminist fiction: a "women's" novel that is not a "feminist" novel because its feminism is undermined by its emphasis on sexuality.[34]

These contradictory readings of *Fear of Flying*—its argument about the inadequacy of sexuality as an arena for women's freedom coupled with the centrality of sexuality in it—nicely catch the difficulties of the CR novel's focus on sexuality. While such a focus did help move the ideas and issues of radical feminism into the mainstream, it did so by moderating them. In the case of *Fear of Flying*, that moderation occurs because Jong both conflates and critiques the conflation of the sexual revolution with feminism—making its radical politics all but unreadable to contemporary critics. Radical feminism's pre-1975 stereographic view of sexuality, which has since given way to the "pro-sex" and "anti-porn" divide, was difficult to sustain at its outset in popular fiction, and is no less difficult to read back into those CR novels that managed this balance rather badly.

When compared with Alther's *Kinflicks* (as many reviewers did compare the two novels), Jong's *Fear of Flying* is hardly the most problematic novel of the decade. Like *Fear of Flying*, *Kinflicks* adapts the picaresque plot for a woman protagonist. Unlike Jong, however, Alther includes lesbianism as one of Ginny's several sexual adventures, or, more accurately, as one of many lifestyles that Ginny takes on. Alther presents Ginny's relationship with Eddie, her lesbian lover, as essentially no different from any of Ginny's other socio-sexual roles—teenage "good girl" flagtwirler, "bad girl" biker's girlfriend, asexual intellectual, small-town housewife, or mystic sexual initiate. But there is one major difference: only Ginny's lesbian relationship with Eddie ends in death.

The comparison with *Fear of Flying* is useful, for it reveals the literary-political limitations of Alther's novel. While Alther extends the woman's picaresque beyond the limits of heterosexuality and depicts her character in a lesbian relationship, which Jong does not do, Alther still preserves the marriage-or-death endings for both of the women in that relationship: Eddie dies and Ginny marries someone else. The picaresque as it is reworked in *Kinflicks* can accommodate a lesbian relationship, but only by reasserting traditional narrative strategies—narrative strategies that need not be reasserted to depict the novel's heterosexual relationships. At the end of the novel, Ginny packs up to leave, "to go where she had no idea," after failing to commit suicide (503). As in *Fear of Flying*, and in most endings of consciousness-raising novels, we do not know what the protagonist will do next.[35] Unlike *Fear of Flying*, though, it is not clear that Ginny has rejected her passivity, that Alther or Ginny have rejected the picaresque plot, or that they have re-visioned it deeply enough to "break its hold over us" in Rich's phrase.[36] The inclusion of a lesbian relationship seems at first to represent a further opening up of the picaresque plot, a radicalization of its definition of sexual freedom. But by reasserting the marriage-or-death strategies, and by hedging on whether Ginny's consciousness has been raised, Alther's re-visioning of the picaresque ends up being even more conservative than Jong's.

    Fiction, and particularly the CR novel, was a crucial part of the movement of ideas from the small groups that made up radical feminism. In the same way that sexuality served as "a wedge into struggle in other areas" for women in the small-group CR sessions—as an opening move in forming analyses of women's oppression—so too did the CR novel's emphasis on sexuality enlist the conventions of popular fiction to present feminist ideas to a wider reading public, even as those ideas were in turn circumscribed by the very conventions that made the CR novel popular. Both *Kinflicks* and *Fear of Flying* demonstrate this problematic: the former in its opening up of the picaresque to lesbian issues and then closing them off in the reassertion of marriage-or-death narrative strategies, the latter in its contradictory readings about the centrality and limitations of sexuality as an arena for women's freedom.

    Another way of understanding the contradictions of the CR novel's focus on sexuality is to see the CR novel as circumscribed by its presumption of the universality of women's experience—as a problem in feminist theory rather than in literary history. This presumption is perhaps clearest in the example of abortion, an issue so frequently treated in the CR novel that it seemed to some reviewers "obligatory" as early as 1972. The CR novel's attentive engagement with the precise political status of abortion as the decade wore on is perhaps the clearest example of its political intentionality, its attempt to engage not only with its readers' processes of CR but also with the public political debates about abortion as an issue of women's sexual freedom. That the CR novel's notion of sexual freedom was overwhelmingly constructed as heterosexual freedom demonstrates the limitations of CR itself. Conceptualized by radical feminists as a means to theorize women's commonality rather than women's differences, it was thus likely to marginalize lesbian and other issues (such as involuntary sterilization) that did not seem to apply to "all" women.[37]

    That the obligatory issue in feminist fiction in the 1970s was abortion is significant in other ways. The focus on abortion rather than rape, for example, is itself evidence of radical feminism's "stereographic" view of sexuality. That is, feminist views of abortion rested on the assertion of women's right to sexuality, a "pro-sex" stance that was coupled with the assertion of women's right to control its consequences. The CR novel described women's victimization by legal and medical systems that denied and limited reproductive freedom—regardless of class, race, marital status, age, sexual preference, and even regardless of abortion's legal status—as part of a larger argument that heterosexuality could be controlled by women, could be an arena of women's freedom. Rape and other violence against women, however central to feminist debates in the decade,[38] was less accommodating to this stereographic view of sexuality, and so less useful to the CR novel. The CR novel was more interested in women's oppression by bad sex than by sexual violence—logically so, since the former can be rectified within a novel, while the latter cannot. Since the CR novel required a vision of women's (hetero)sexual freedom in order to maintain the balanced view of sexuality, rape and other forms of sexual violence simply could not be central in it.

Contemporary feminist critics and historians have read the literary history of the 1970s selectively, dismissing or ignoring novels like *Fear of Flying*, and focussing instead on either more "literary" fiction (feminist metafiction, for example) or more comfortably "political" fiction. Such selective readings, however valuable for what they tell us about the novels they do encompass, cannot fully account for the contradictions and multiplicities of literary feminism in the 1970s, and tend to unify and simplify the range of feminisms in the decade. The CR novel, as a form that cuts across genres and includes both bestsellers and feminist metafiction, is a more useful way of understanding fiction's relationship to the Women's Liberation Movement. Nowhere do the range of the contradictions and complexities of that relationship come clearer than in its treatment of sexuality. If, as Ehrenreich, Jacobs, and Hess argue, Women's Liberation helped to create nothing less than a "women's sexual revolution," we need to see that revolution in its range and multiplicity, its contradictions and variety, and thus to see the fiction that helped to popularize feminist ideas in its diversity as well.

Notes

1. Kathleen Barry, "Deconstructing Deconstruction (or, Whatever Happened to Feminist Studies?)"; Alix Kates Shulman, "Organs and Orgasms," Gornick and Moran, 206.

2. Marge Piercy's *Woman on the Edge of Time*, with twenty-seven printings and 460,000 copies in print since its publication in 1976 (information from the publisher; my thanks to Jennifer Ridenour for tracking it down), demonstrates the continuing appeal of novels that did not moderate the issues, as does Joanna Russ's *The Female Man* (1975), which has taken on a new life as a postmodern novel since its re-publication in the Beacon Press Neglected Women Writers Series in 1986. Best-sellers like *Fear of Flying*, which did moderate the issues, have

not fared so well since their initial appearance in print (see below); in some cases, the most immediately popular novels have had the shortest shelf lives.

3. Compare Biddy Martin's reading of Foucault's "repressive hypothesis" in "Lesbian Identity and Autobiographical Difference(s)"; she argues that "Laying claim, then, to one's sexuality and the rights associated with it, insisting on the freedom to speak freely of one's sexuality, risks subjection to regulation and control" (80). In the context of the increasing commodification of sexuality in the second half of the twentieth century, the act of laying claim to one's sexuality and the freedom to speak its truth also risks having that sexuality further commodified. See also Robert Goldman, Deborah Heath, and Sharon L. Smith, "Commodity Feminism," for a description of advertising's ability during the 1980s to "choreograph a non-contradictory unification of feminism and femininity [that has] given rise to an aesthetically depoliticized feminism" (334). The authors argue that feminist claims to sexual freedom for women, detached from the feminist critique of the social conditions that make that freedom problematic, become "rerouted" in the 1980s to sell products.

4. See also Ehrenreich, Hess, and Jacobs, 65–72, for a similar view of sexuality as the centerpiece of CR.

5. To be fair, Brown makes it clear that the single girl's job and her women friends are also important in her life, but they primarily provide resources for money and happiness when her relationships with men are less than satisfying. And both job and women friends also provide additional sources of available men. See Ehrenreich, Hess, and Jacobs, 56–60, and S. Douglas, 68–69, for different readings of *Sex and the Single Girl*.

6. Echols identifies The Feminists as one of "the four most influential early radical feminist groups" (21).

7. Gould's parody here is similar to the parodic laughter Susan Kalčik identified as a major source of harmony in women's rap groups; I discuss Kalčik's analysis in Chapter Two.

8. This passage is virtually identical to one in Jong's essay, "The Artist as Housewife," 116.

9. See Castro, 62; F. Davis, 67–68; Ryan, 44; and Wandersee, 40.

10. A dissenting position on abortion can be seen in this 1970 excerpt from *Red Star*, the publication of the Red Women's Detachment: "liberal reformists posing as radicals in Women's Liberation circles are placing abortion law repeal first on their agenda to ensure the phony sexual revolution, while working class women on welfare are having birth control pills and sterilization forced on them in an increasingly compulsory manner" (quoted in "Defining the fight").

11. "Birth Control and Abortion, Some Things to Worry About," by the St. Louis Women's Collective, which summarizes the arguments about genocide and racism, was excerpted in *off our backs* in February of 1971.

12. Alper, Hoffnung, and Solomon, in their fabulously named article, "i eat your flesh plus i drink your blood (the double features of the abortion business)," specifically critique abortion provision as a male-controlled business (10–11).

13. I take up this issue in more detail in Chapter Five.

14. See, e.g., Mimi Alberts' review of *Play It As it Lays*: "That Joan Didion, among others, is writing about the realities of the woman's body is symptomatic of what is happening to all of us. We are coming out of the menstrual hut to which we have been confined" (20).

15. Some radical feminists observed that hospital policies, including interpre-

tations of regulations concerning psychiatrists' approval, created greater barriers than laws did in restricting women's access to abortions in the early 1970s; see, e.g., the critique of D.C. General's policies by Bev Fisher, Anne Hatfield, and Marie Khouri, "a house divided" (1971). See Carol Edelson, "supreme court abortion ruling" (1973), for a radical feminist critique of abortion regulation after the *Roe v. Wade* decision.

16. For a critique of abortion reforms in New York in 1970, see JGS, "money doesn't talk, it swears: abortion industry in new york."

17. Claudia Driefus, "Sterilizing the Poor" (1974), 58–66.

18. Teaching *Burning Questions* in the early 1990s, I discovered that students found Shulman's casual mention of multiple abortions disturbing, which suggests both the alienness of the "pro-woman line" to contemporary feminism, and the radical shift in discourses about abortion with the rise of the anti-abortion movement and the anti-feminist backlash. For Redstockings' "pro-woman line," see "Redstockings Manifesto" (R. Morgan, 598–601); for a stunning example of the shift in discourses about abortion in the 1990s, see Naomi Wolf, "Our Bodies, Our Souls" (1995), which argues that pro-choicers ought to reframe their positions by engaging the language of sin and atonement.

19. *Blood and Guts in High School,* while not a consciousness-raising novel on the level of plot, nonetheless exemplifies the hegemony of the form, as its conventions and discourses influence other kinds of novels in the decade. Acker's incisive depiction of the politics of abortion—"We had given ourselves up to men before. That's why we were here. All of us signed everything. Then they took our money" (32)—is strikingly similar to some of the CR novels. For another link between *Blood and Guts* and the CR novel, see the "Hello, I'm Erica Jong" passages (125–26).

20. F. Davis notes that Radicalesbians began as Lavender Menace (266).

21. The term "immasculated" comes from Judith Fetterley's *The Resisting Reader,* where she defines it as ways that women are made to identify with men and men's interests, including misogyny (xx–xxii); I find it more useful because more precise than "male-identified." See also Rich's 1980 essay, "Compulsory Heterosexuality and Lesbian Existence" (Snitow, Stansell, and Thompson 177–205), for her discussion of the "lesbian continuum."

22. Snitow, Stansell, and Thompson 33; Echols 216. Echols argues that the gay-straight split continued from 1970 to 1972 (220), but she refers specifically to that split in New York and Washington, D.C. In other places, notably the West Coast, the split came later.

23. In its original 1973 publication by Daughters, a feminist press with a Women's Liberation audience, *Rubyfruit Jungle*'s particular critique of homophobia in the movement reached its target, an effect that was lessened when *Rubyfruit Jungle* appeared in its second edition in 1977, as a mass-market paperback published by Bantam. I discuss the novel's contradictory messages to readers in Chapter Two.

24. Accounts of this event include: Sidney Abbott and Barbara Love, "Is Women's Liberation a Lesbian Plot?" in Gornick and Moran; F. Davis, 262–66 (Davis attributes "lavender herring" to Friedan, 263); D'Emilio and Freedman, 316; Echols, 215–19; Fritz, 33. Rita Mae Brown's retrospective view can be found in "Reflections of a Lavender Menace" (1995).

25. Echols 238; Koedt, "Lesbianism and Feminism," in Koedt, Levine, and Rapone, 246. In *Theory in Its Feminist Travels,* Katie King describes the "displacement of meaning" this misquotation creates; according to King, Atkinson's

formulation was, "Feminism is a theory; Lesbianism is a practice," which establishes a very different relationship between feminism and lesbianism (125).

26. Echols summarizes these views, 217–18, 239, 233. See also "Loving Another Woman," in Koedt, Levine, and Rapone, 85–93.

27. For a useful overview of the tenuousness of this consensus (and a shrewd speculation about the displacement of the gay/straight split onto the so-called sex-wars of the 1980s), see B. Ruby Rich, "Review Essay: Feminism and Sexuality in the 1980s" (1986), 525–61.

28. Bonnie Zimmerman's Select Bibliography in *The Safe Sea of Women: Lesbian Fiction, 1969–1989* lists 171 novels, of which only 25 were published in the 1970s; Zimmerman argues that the period from 1969 to 1978 marks the emergence of lesbian fiction, as writers "set out the premises of a new genre" (13). I do not mean to suggest that lesbian fiction was not important, but rather that the privileged genre of lesbian-feminism in the period—performing the cultural work needed to form, to found, and in some sense to theorize a lesbian feminist culture—was the lyric poem, exemplified in the works of Adrienne Rich, Audre Lorde, Judy Grahn, Pat Parker, and others. Why that should be so—that larger question of the relationship between genre and politics—is clearly beyond my scope here.

29. In a response to an essay about her work, Jong insists that the ending of *Fear of Flying* is a direct response to literary conventions of two centuries: "Above all, I wanted to show Isadora as a *survivor*—in opposition to all those 19th century heroines who *die* for the one sexual transgression (Bovary, Karenina, et al.) and to all those 20th century heroines who suffer madness, breakdown, the deaths of their children, imprisonment in dying marriages, and the like. (The retribution for female independence is always harsh indeed.)" "Comments on Joan Reardon's '*Fear of Flying*: Developing the Feminist Novel,' A Letter to the Author" (1978), 625, emphasis original.

30. My use of the term "paranoid" here reflects a comparison drawn by a number of feminist theorists in the 1970s; I discuss Sandra Lee Bartky's and Mary Daly's use of the term in Chapter Two.

31. Quotations are from Paul Gray, "Blue Genes" (1976), 80; Walter Clemons, "Beware of the Man" (1973), 111; "Altitude Sickness" [rev. of *Fear of Flying* by Erica Jong] (1974), 813; "Isadora & Adrian, John & Mimi" [rev. of *Fear of Flying* by Erica Jong and *John & Mimi: A Free Marriage* by John and Mimi Lobell] (1974), 125; Terry Stokes, Rev. of *Fear of Flying* by Erica Jong (1973), 41; Molly Haskell, Rev. of *Fear of Flying* by Erica Jong (1973), 27.

32. Updike's reference to *Fanny Hill* is especially appropriate given Jong's rewriting of that novel in *Fanny, Being the True History of the Adventures of Fanny Hackabout-Jones* (1980). Though *Fear of Flying* was not reviewed in the radical feminist newspaper *off our backs*, a 1971 review of Jong's volume of poems, *Fruits and Vegetables*, demonstrates a very different reading of heterosexuality in Jong's work from Updike's; Frances Chapman argues that "her bawdiness . . . is a survival mechanism to get on the good side of the male libido," and accuses Jong of "internalized sexism" and "male identification" ("The Wrong Side of the Dream" 10). See also Laura Chester's response to Chapman's review ("erica's poems"), and Chapman's reply, which goes even further to call Jong "a slave still though she waits on the master in the big house of mainstream poetry" ("Reply" 30).

33. Perhaps the most interesting dismissal of *Fear of Flying* is Gayle Greene's in *Changing the Story: Feminist Fiction and the Tradition*, where she initially defends her interest in the novel in ways similar to my own, but proceeds to argue, in the end,

that Jong's work contains a "failure to imagine otherwise," a cliched convention-ality, and a surface feminism (87–91); Greene's reading (and, I suggest, many dismissals of *Fear of Flying*) is highly colored by the sequel, which she calls "the most embarrassing novel written in recent decades by a woman with literary pre-tensions" (90). See also, among others, Joanne S. Frye, *Living Stories, Telling Lives: Women and the Novel in Contemporary Experience,* for a "faint praise" dismissal (192).

34. Still later readings of *Fear of Flying*—in the aftermath of the sex-wars—take a different attitude toward feminism's relationship to sexuality. At the 1994 Mod-ern Language Association panel celebrating the twentieth anniversary of *Fear of Flying,* for example, Debra Hotaling and Mary Munsil argued that the novel had lost popularity during the 1980s because its celebratory attitude toward hetero-sexuality was not in keeping with (hegemonic) anti-porn feminism, an argument Jong herself seemed to endorse in her response to the panel, which began with a vehement attack on anti-porn censorship. Reading *Fear of Flying* as, in essence, "prematurely pro-sex" may turn out to be a useful strategy for reclaiming it for mainstream feminism, but such a reading cannot account for the novel's com-plex and multiple attitudes toward sexuality.

35. See Chapter Two for a discussion of the unfinished endings of the CR novel.

36. See "When We Dead Awaken: Writing as Re-Vision" for Rich's argument about a radical criticism that operates "not to pass on a tradition but to break its hold over us" (35).

37. Despite originating as a search for commonality, CR techniques have proven effective in anti-racist work based in difference; see Tia Cross, Freada Klein, Barbara Smith, and Beverly Smith, "Face-to-Face, Day-to-Day—Racism CR," 52–56.

38. See Castro, 193–95, for a discussion of the centrality of rape to radical feminism.

Chapter Four
Men

> ONE-SIDED: Men used their traditional positions of power to exploit vulnerable women in the workplace. Men have been conditioned to consider women fair game.
> BALANCED: Some of the men I talked to seemed genuinely frustrated about changing definitions of sexual harassment. According to them, if the woman likes the man, advances are welcome; otherwise, the advances are unwelcome and are defined as sexual harassment. No wonder that men are confused about the role of their gender in courtship situations.
> —A strategy to avoid alienating "fair-minded readers"
> from a 1996 composition textbook[1]

The relationships between men and a movement for women's liberation, between men and individual women in that movement, between men and feminism in its varied and various manifestations, have been unevenly important concerns for the second wave from the outset. In this chapter, I examine briefly the role of men in Movement writing and then turn to the importance of men characters in setting evaluative standards for feminist fiction. In doing so, I examine reviews of CR novels in the mainstream press (the *New York Times* and its *Book Review*, *Time*, *Newsweek*, and the like), and in the feminist press, represented here by *Ms.* and by *off our backs* as exemplifying mainstream and oppositional feminism respectively. I examine specific instances of controversies over women writers' depictions of men characters, using *The Women's Room* and *The Color Purple* to discuss the differing function of men in discussions of works by white and black women writers. A central tension emerges from both the fiction reviews and the Movement writings between the Movement's focus on women, and its practical politics of setting limits on men's behavior toward women. Redstockings captured this tension in their Manifesto, arguing both that "Our chief task at present is to develop female class consciousness through sharing experience"

(R. Morgan 600), and that "We do not need to change ourselves, but to change men" (R. Morgan 599).

It is not so simple to resolve this tension into some kind of false distinction between a feminism that is "for" women versus one that is "against" men, though any number of feminist writers have attempted such a resolution, and separating the two became, over the course of the decade, an important rhetorical strategy in the fiction reviews in *Ms.* magazine. Separating the two has, in fact, enormous political meaning in terms of the limits it sets on feminism, for a feminism without advocacy for women has no political base, and a feminism without setting limits on men's behavior has no political efficacy.

In her introduction to *Sisterhood Is Powerful,* Robin Morgan wrestled briefly with the question of men's usefulness to Women's Liberation. "I haven't the faintest notion what possible revolutionary role white heterosexual men could fulfill, since they are the very embodiment of reactionary-vested-interest-power," she writes, "In addition to doing the shitwork that women have been doing for generations, possibly not exist? No, I really don't mean that. Yes, I really do. Never mind, that's another whole book" (xl). As if to emphasize Morgan's ambivalence, the book's back cover excerpts a text not otherwise included in the anthology, Jayne West's "Are Men Really the Enemy? A Questionnaire." In a series of three multiple choice questions, West provides this one about rape: "Most rapes are committed by: (a) women; (b) children; (c) men (perverts); (d) I am unable to distinguish rape from ordinary sexual relations." In terms of rape, both "perverse" and "ordinary" men seem to be "the enemy."[2]

The anthology also excerpts Valerie Solanis's "The SCUM [Society for Cutting Up Men] Manifesto,"[3] which, even as it advocates male extinction, nonetheless identifies the primary feminist struggle as taking place between two kinds of women. Solanis sets out feminist struggle between, on the one hand, the "free-wheeling arrogant females" of SCUM and, on the other, the "nice, passive, accepting, 'cultivated,' polite, dignified, subdued, dependent, scared, mindless, insecure, approval-seeking Daddy's Girls" who refuse to recognize their freedom (579–80).[4] More than what would later be called "male-identification" was at stake in Solanis's locating a version of feminism in the struggle between these different groups of women; because the Manifesto theorized an inverted version of gendered hierarchy that rendered men irrelevant at the outset, only women could be worthy adversaries. In Solanis's view, the place of "men in feminism"—to invoke the title of a 1987 anthology[5]—was, first, irrelevant and, second, extinct. In the *Sisterhood Is Powerful* anthology as a whole, the place of men in feminism was uncertain at best.

An article in *Radical Feminism*, "Man-Hating" by Pamela Kearon, confronts its title subject directly. Kearon argues that feminists who do not allow themselves to hate men—who fear the stigma of man-hating more than they want to work for their freedom—will turn that hatred toward other women and toward children. In claiming "man-hating" as "a valid and vital issue" (78), Kearon specifically argues that hatred is a genuinely human emotion that women necessarily experience, "that part which is really human and cannot submit." "If it is a choice between woman-hating and man-hating, let it be the latter," she writes, because only this enables women to "respond immediately and directly to injury instead of taking it all out on a more likely victim" (80). Because hatred is a logical and psychological human reaction to oppression, claiming the legitimacy of man-hating becomes a political strategy to resist internalized misogyny.

More than a strategy to resist horizontal violence, by the late 1970s, man-hating became in works by lesbian separatists such as Mary Daly, a crucial strategy to discover the "truth" of women's oppression. Daly argued in *Gyn/Ecology: The Meta-Ethics of Radical Feminism* (1978) "that males and males only are the originators, planners, controllers, and legitimators of patriarchy," and that feminists had been "intimidated" into denying men's responsibility for patriarchy, focusing instead on abstract notions of " 'forces,' 'roles,' 'stereotypes,' 'constraints,' 'attitudes,' 'influences'" (28–29). Daly's work, with its uncompromising vision of men as the agents of women's oppression, suffers none of the ambivalence toward men found in the earlier part of the decade.

As I have argued in Chapter Three, the CR novel's focus on heterosexual women and on abortion as the issue central to women's sexual self-determination, logically required depictions of men characters. Frequently, these characters were, in Bakhtinian terms, mouthpieces for patriarchal discourses, the speakers of ideas and ideologies about women, gender, and the world that the novels deconstructed, dismissed, and ridiculed. The men doctors and therapists in *Ella Price's Journal, Fear of Flying, Such Good Friends, Final Analysis*, and *Woman on the Edge of Time* (to name examples I have discussed in Chapters Two and Three) exemplify this textual practice: they speak parodic and hyperbolized versions of the medical and therapeutic discourses of women's oppression. Husbands and men lovers, too, serve as mouthpieces for patriarchal discourses in the CR novels, and serve the additional purpose of bringing these patriarchal discourses into the protagonists' intimate romantic and familial spaces. As carriers of these discourses into the protagonists' personal lives, husbands and men lovers are an important part of the way CR novels transact CR with readers: they serve to deny the "exceptionalism" that Irene Peslikis identified as one of several "Resistances to

Consciousness" ("Thinking that our man is the exception" is her word-ing [R. Morgan 379]), and to reinforce the personal-political linkage so central to the practice of consciousness-raising.

Alix Kates Shulman's *Burning Questions* exemplifies this strategy. Zane describes repeatedly her lover's insistence that she not think so much. "Later, catching my eyes wandering during a kiss, he said again, 'Can't you ever stop thinking?' I stopped my eyes obligingly, but the truth was, with my fate in his hands, I didn't dare stop thinking" (77). Her sense of dependence, a condition she recognizes as political, is thus linked pre-cisely with her tendency to think too much. Her friendship with Nina comes about in part because of Marshall's inability to see beyond sex as the basis for a relationship. "But as he held himself above my mundane interests and did nothing to discover my spiritual ones either ('Come on baby, forget about the want-ads. Stop thinking so much and come over here, will you?'), I had to find appreciation elsewhere" (81). In both these passages, Shulman brings Marshall's voice into Zane's recol-lections, emphasizing that the famous beatnik poet speaks only banal clichés when it comes to sex and relationships, and that, as is clear throughout this section of the novel, the celebrated unconventionality of 1950s bohemia did not extend to women.[6]

Reviewers fastened onto the depictions of men characters, and used this focus as a way to set particular agendas for feminism itself. Evalua-tions of feminist fiction implicitly or explicitly set standards for femi-nism, define it as a movement, and legitimate or critique its perceived political agendas. What feminist fiction can legitimately represent, in other words, bears a direct relationship to what the reviewers believe feminism itself can legitimately claim. Reviews of feminist fiction in the decade were thus sites of contestation for the nature and meaning of feminism; they were, in effect, sites of theorizing, even if not recogniz-able as theory itself.[7]

The contrast between the following two reviews—one of Margaret Atwood's *Lady Oracle* (1976) in *Newsweek* and one of Shulman's *Burning Questions* (1978) in the feminist journal *Chrysalis*—suggest the range of claims reviewers in different arenas allowed to feminist fiction and thus to feminism itself. Peter S. Prescott, writing in *Newsweek*, defined the ap-propriate subject for feminist fiction to be women's psychology:

Anyone who reads contemporary fiction is by now familiar with the heroine who, in the course of a novel, graduates from the role of victim to that of guer-rilla warrior. The aggressor forces may be played by oppressive parents, insen-sitive men and malicious fellow females, but in the better novels the principal enemy is not these—it is the heroine herself. Battling her neuroses and repell-ing boarders, she fights covertly to become her own self, even before she can determine what that self is. (62)

The proper subject for feminist fiction in "the better novels" was an individual woman's "covert" struggle with herself rather than with other possible "enemies." Fictional representation cannot be "political" in the meaning that term takes on in CR, "shared" and resulting from a system of women's oppression; it must be pre-feminist, "resulting from an individual's idiosyncratic history and behavior," to return to the language of the CR outline in *Radical Feminism*.[8] Beverly Tannenhaus made quite the opposite argument in her review in *Chrysalis*, insisting than if a writer "explicitly identifies her characters and themes as feminist . . . we do not expect her to attribute symptoms and consequences of patriarchy to character flaw, coincidence of plot, or no-fault inevitability" (104–5). A feminist novel in Tannenhaus's terms, because it must perform a systemic critique of patriarchy rather than merely depict individual character flaws, could never be one of "the better novels" in Prescott's terms. Similarly, "the better novels," because wholly focussed on the heroine's "neuroses," could never be feminist. Feminism itself, by implication, would be for Prescott essentially a women's self-help movement, for Tannenhaus a movement with total social transformation as its goal.

As a self-help movement for women, feminism was perfectly acceptable to the mainstream press. When feminism was perceived to impinge on, to set limits to, or to critique men's behavior, however, its claims had to be delegitimated, even in the fiction reviews in *Ms.* by the end of the decade. Parallels between this dynamic in the fiction reviews of the 1970s and controversies in the early 1990s over, for instance, the Thomas-Hill hearings and the film *Thelma & Louise* suggest that cries of "men can't be that bad" continue to be used to establish the legitimacy of feminist credibility in arenas other than feminist fiction.[9]

Prescott's position in his *Newsweek* review was by no means unique or idiosyncratic. "Men can't be that bad," reviewer Christopher Lehmann-Haupt describes himself as "wanting to shout at the narrator" of Marilyn French's *The Women's Room* (1977): "There must be room for accommodation between the sexes that you've somehow overlooked" (C20). Anatole Broyard, also writing in the *New York Times*, proposed "a program of civil rights for characters in novels" because it seemed to him "[un]fair for authors to push them around or malign them just to make a point or put across a message" ("Two Heroines"). While Broyard's language suggests a non-gendered standard for "fairness" in realist fiction, his specific "program" was to defend men characters against their feminist novelist oppressors. To depict men characters as "dull and feckless, demanding but not giving, interested in women only so long as they will bear children, run households and service sexual needs" (T. Schwartz, "Woman as Pinball"), as "oppressive, lethargic, and sexually incompetent" (Duffy 81), as "exploitative brutes" (Lehmann-Haupt, *High Cost of Living*), or even simply as "lifeless or fall guys" (Stokes 41)—just to give a sampling of reviewers' complaints—was necessarily to "push them around" in Broyard's terms.

These and other reviewers did not mean to suggest, I think, that men were *never* oppressive, let alone dull, but rather that a fictional depiction of a boring man character had a particular political weight within the confines of realist fiction's presumed neutrality. Such depictions of men characters had the force for some reviewers of transforming fiction into what Lehmann-Haupt called, reviewing Margaret Atwood's *Surfaces*, "mere anti-masculine propaganda" ("Novels"); even minor men characters depicted as oppressive could "destroy the credibility of the entire story," as he argued in reviewing Lois Gould's *Final Analysis* ("Old Point of View"). What is particularly striking in these reviews is that none of the reviewers attempted to argue that some men were oppressive (or dull) and that most men or men in general were not. Instead, any negative or shallow depiction of any man character was made to stand in for all men. Even the most minor of such depictions, in other words, signaled to reviewers the eruption of "ideology" into "objective" or "fair" realist fiction.

The presumption that realist fiction was "objective" was never argued in the reviews, but clearly underpinned the evaluative criteria at stake. A novel that was not "objective" could not be "good"; reviewers' repeated invocations of "bias" worked to dismiss the literary quality of novels that could be so described. The presumption that realist fiction was "objective" also worked politically: it enabled reviewers to dismiss the (counter) cultural work of feminist realist fiction as "ideological," a dismissal that worked to foreclose political debate, since the reviewers did not need to articulate their own (competing) ideological stance. This foreclosure in turn situated feminism, but not anti-feminism, as a "special interest group," and facilitated the imaging of feminism as "man-hating" (and, again, not of anti-feminism as misogyny).

Of course, the assertion that negative depctions were "ideological"— that men can't be that bad in fiction—rested on the belief that men could not be that bad in real life. The credibility of realist fiction was measured by its upholding a presumed commonsensical understanding that violence against women, for instance, simply did not exist—or if it did exist, could be explained or explored in fiction only within the women characters' psychology (as Prescott's "better novels" would have it). By extension, then, feminist realist fiction could only be credible insofar as it critiqued women and not men, only insofar as it upheld a prefeminist understanding of women's oppression as personal and not political and participated in antifeminist victim-blaming. The "change yourself line" that Kathie Sarachild attacked in *Ms.* in 1975—the notion that women's problems rest solely with women—was central not only in the transformation of "hard" CR into its "soft" version, but central as well in evaluating feminist realist fiction; reviewers' moves to delegitimate critiques of men's behavior worked to contain feminism's critique of the political relations between men and women.[10]

This sequence of arguments about men and realism was most clearly articulated in the fiction reviews in *Ms.*, as this passage from Karen Durbin's review of Fay Weldon's *Female Friends* (1974) evidences:

> What we are shown is the bad stuff, convincingly portrayed, but standing alone, a vision of punishment and torture, and one-sided torture at that, the relationship of monsters and victims. At some point, we stop believing. Life is more complicated than that, the war between men and women is more complicated than that (if it weren't, women would have walked off the battlefield by now), and novels have to be more complicated than that. There is a good novel here, but it's caught inside a tract. (34)

Durbin's notion of "complexity" gets at the burden realist fiction was presumed to carry: however "convincingly portrayed," any depiction of women's oppression by men must be balanced, made "fair," in order to be credible. A novel about sexual politics must account, for example, for most women being heterosexual (more accurately, for most women not being lesbian separatists), or else it's not a novel at all, but a "tract." Besides its obvious heterosexism, making "lesbian fiction" an oxymoron, this review and others in *Ms.* participated in the same containment of feminism's critique of men's behavior as the mainstream press reviews.[11]

One might argue that Durbin's sense of "complexity" in fact attempted to hold depictions of sexual politics to the radical feminist "stereographic" view of sexuality as doubly the site of women's oppression and women's freedom, as I discussed in Chapter Three. But such an argument would require reviewers to articulate an ideological view—to say that Weldon's novel, for instance, did not reflect the understanding of women's experiences as those experiences were described in feminist theory and CR. That is, rather than critiquing the novel as unrealistic, a reviewer would have to critique it as unfeminist. Instead, Durbin and other reviewers in *Ms.* appealed to commonsensical notions of "complexity" that depend ultimately on finding "truth" in some kind of "middle ground"—an appeal to the "middle ground" that Ellen Willis has neatly satirized: "the feminist bias is that women are equal to men and the male chauvinist bias is that women are inferior. The unbiased view is that truth lies somewhere in between" (in Rubin "Thinking Sex" 38).

It may seem surprising to see this containment of feminism in *Ms.*, but this and other similar strategies were central to the notion of hegemonic liberal-cultural feminism that the magazine developed over the 1970s. In 1972, when *Ms.* was founded, its notion of feminism was counterhegemonic, oppositional. It understood itself and feminism to be opposed to majority views and opposed to a range of mainstream and commonsensical understandings of women's oppression—either, for instance, that such oppression did not exist, or else that it was necessary, inevitable, or good. Many radical feminists, of course, immediately attacked the magazine, even before the reconstituted Redstockings did so in 1975; Ellen Willis, for example, defined "*Ms.*-ism" as a new liberal feminism that co-opted the "sexual and emotional issues radical feminists were raising" by ignoring "the existence of power relations" ("Radical Feminism" 108).[12] Nonetheless, in its first few years of publication, *Ms.*'s particular version of feminism did represent itself as an oppositional stance within U.S. politics and culture; over the decade, however, this political stance changed significantly.

Catharine Stimpson's *Ms.* essay on Joan Didion's work in 1973 demonstrates how the magazine's initial oppositional stance played out in its discussions of fiction. Stimpson characterizes Didion's position as "a woman who critics said told men and women what the modern woman's experience was" (36), a characterization that accurately reflected reviews of Didion's work in the early 1970s.[13] While she discusses Didion's novels and essays, Stimpson also focuses on the article Didion published in the *New York Times Book Review* in 1972, called "The Women's Movement." There Didion attacked feminists as "women too 'sensitive' for the difficulties and ambiguities of adult life, women unequipped for reality and grasping at the movement as a rationale for denying that reality" (14), neatly playing out the slippage from politics to psychology that we see in the fiction reviews. Stimpson argues in response that Didion's "attitudes pose a problem to us all," not only because she rejected feminism, but especially because her prominence as a woman writer enabled her to do so on the front page of the *New York Times Book Review*; Didion's view of feminism-as-adolescence was, Stimpson argued, "too inaccurate, too obvious when it was accurate, and too smug to be taken seriously." Moreover, such a "woman's anathema of a Woman's Movement," Stimpson pointed out, was a familiar antifeminist strategy (38).[14]

Stimpson's essay marks a precise moment both in the development of *Ms.*'s politics and in the political definition of feminist fiction. Because, Stimpson argues, the world of Didion's work (what she calls "Didion world") is fundamentally antipolitical, quietistic, and patriarchal, we must understand the real dangers she poses to the movement.[15] Stimpson's analysis here is similar to radical feminist analyses of Anaïs Nin's work, which attacked not only the work itself, but also the politics of any feminism that would value it.[16] Didion's attack on the women's movement, based on notions of "maturity" and "ambiguity," is strikingly similar to Durbin's "complexity" and to Prescott's argument that the "better novels" be concerned with psychological rather than political issues: all three work to shift feminism's terrain from the political to the personal. For Stimpson, importantly, all women writers could not be claimed for feminism; feminist and women's fiction were distinct and different categories; and feminist fiction was defined by its systemic critique of patriarchy, to reinvoke the terms of Tannenhaus's review, rather than by its feminine signature or female protagonist.[17] Even *Ms.* shares this view—or, perhaps more accurately, prints it—in the early 1970s.

By the late 1970s, though, Didion's status in *Ms.* had changed considerably. In 1977, *Ms.* published an essay-interview with Didion by Susan Braudy called "A Day in the Life of Joan Didion." Braudy accounted for Didion's earlier antifeminist diatribe in this passage from the essay-interview's prologue: " 'I never understood that piece too well,' I answered. 'But I think she was saying she's not a joiner, a political person, a utopist, that she's a loner, a Western writer, sort of a John Wayne character. She's against political cures for terror, loneliness, or pain. It's her art to describe the pain, not to cure it' " (66). Braudy transforms Didion's essay from an attack on a political movement into a personal statement of her feelings about politics, thus following the shift from politics to psychology that typifies mainstream-press fiction reviews. Too, Braudy's distinction between "describing" and "curing" pain implicitly invokes the presumed political neutrality of realist fiction; a novelist who presented "cures" for pain—especially political cures—would not be writing fiction at all, but rather "tracts," in Durbin's term.

Near the end of the interview, Braudy describes herself as finally asking "the feminist question": "Why does she write about women in despair who believe in nothing and do nothing, when Didion herself is a strong woman who does a major thing—her writing? Why doesn't she write about women more like herself?" (108). Braudy gets her answer from Didion's husband, as she does most of the answers to her questions in the interview: "Whoever asks that question doesn't know a goddamn thing about the questions of literature. Joan writes because she writes" (108). Braudy notes but does not address Dunne's tendency to answer the questions she puts to Didion, allowing the problem of Didion's not speaking for herself to sit unexamined beside the problem of the kinds of women for whom her fiction speaks. By 1977, Didion had become one of "Your Favorite Authors," along with such unambiguously feminist writers as Kate Millett, Marge Piercy, and Alix Kates Shulman, as her inclusion in an essay called "What Your Favorite Authors Are Working On . . ." indicates (Turner 58).

By the late 1970s, Didion could be claimed for feminism simply because she was a woman writer; this change in *Ms.*'s reading of Didion exemplifies changes in the magazine's definition of feminism itself. *Ms.* increasingly conflated "women's" and "feminist" fiction, which enabled the magazine to claim Didion as important to, even as a "Favorite Author" of its readers, regardless of the political content of her work, or her earlier antifeminist essay. Feminist critics and scholars have generally characterized *Ms.* as a liberal feminist magazine, but I suggest that this conflation of "women's" and "feminist" fiction implicitly claims *all* women writers as representing (some kind of) feminism. Thus it exemplifies less liberal feminism (public-sphere reform efforts) than it does cultural feminism (the production of women's/feminist culture). As Echols argues in her critique of cultural feminism in *Daring to be BAD*, one of its strongest appeals lay in its promise to leverage women out of "the vicissitudes of political struggle" (269). The specifically literary equivalent of radical feminism's "political struggle" was the attempt to define and to evaluate feminist fiction by its politics; *Ms.*'s move to conflate "women's" and "feminist" fiction marks a cultural-feminist escape from that literary-political struggle.

Ms.'s move toward cultural feminism in its discussions of fiction was based in its significantly reconceiving the nature and position of feminism itself. By the middle of the decade, *Ms.* had come (unevenly) to understand feminism as a hegemonic rather than a counterhegemonic ideological and political position. The opposition to feminism no longer comprised most people, most men, or social institutions; rather the opposition to feminism was increasingly portrayed in *Ms.* as comprising right-wing lunatics, the emergent institutions of the New Right like the Moral Majority, and hypocritical women like Phyllis Schlafly. *Ms.* took on the struggle for the center and the putative "middle ground" between being "for women" and "against men." In struggling to occupy a hegemonic position, the magazine fought the Moral Majority precisely on the basis of its claim to represent a majority position. "Guess Who's For the ERA?" became a semi-regular feature, commencing with an essay by Howard Cosell discussing his support for the Amendment in the first Special Issue on Men in October 1975.[18] The political claims of hegemonic feminism required an uncritical and unquestioning inclusiveness: everyone must be a feminist, whether they know it or not, in this line of argument, and everyone must be claimed for feminism. The task of a feminist movement, as *Ms.* conceptualized it, was to publicize unlikely feminists as a part of its task to persuade people that any inkling of vaguely feminist thought—any hint of feminist literacy—*was* feminism. Rather than articles denouncing prominent women like Didion for their antifeminism, *Ms.* increasingly included articles on prominent women—and men—who could be seen to be feminist. Not only did *Ms.*'s hegemonic feminism establish itself as not anti-male, but it also came to be actively pro-male, as the (always controversial) Special Issues on Men demonstrated.

In the shift from an oppositional to a hegemonic feminism, *Ms.* necessarily had to count and count on men to make up—both numerically and ideologically—the majoritarian position. Men became central, more than a men's auxiliary to a women's feminist movement and more than "feminist sympathizers," to use one popular term describing men's position in feminism. Men feminists evidenced the centrality of feminism itself: feminism could not be a "special interest group" or even "ideological" if it could claim to represent everbody. Not only, in other words, are (all) men not that bad, but *no* men are really all that bad: all men can and must be saved for feminism. Any overstepping of the bounds of feminist realism—any negative or shallow portrayals of men characters—threatened the claims to centrality of *Ms.*'s cultural feminism. Any eruption of political (definitional) debate—of who was and was not a feminist in the case of Didion—threatened the consensus that, like Howard Cosell, we are all feminists in our own way. Feminism itself thus became individualized, psychologized, and apoliticized in *Ms.* in precisely the same ways that the mainstream-press reviews suggested were appropriate to the "better novels."

Perhaps no other novel from the 1970s occasioned the playing out of these issues so clearly as did Marilyn French's *The Women's Room* (1977). Reviewers in the mainstream press agonized over their own unfairness to the novel in relation to French's perceived unfairness to men.[19] Lehmann-Haupt, for example, wrestles with the question of the novel's realism, admitting that perhaps his "insistence that *The Women's Room* is finally only make-believe has less to do with critical judgment than it does with a desire for self-protection and comfort"; his review alternates claims that the novel is "right" and "true" for women with claims that it is flawed and manipulative about men. Anne Tyler makes a very careful set of distinctions to argue that

what victimizes Mira is not men, but the chasm that she perceives between men and women—the mistrust, incomprehension, and exploitation. Whether we agree that this chasm exists, it exists for her; it affects her whole life. With a narrator like Mira, a certain bias in the telling is not merely forgivable; it serves a clear purpose. (38)

Tyler's insistence that one need not "agree that this chasm exists" allows her to claim the text as an ideological text by locating that ideology in the narrator's bias rather than in realism's truth claims. We believe *that* Mira believes, rather than believing *what* Mira believes—a move that enables Tyler to accord the novel psychological realism rather than political realism.

The reviews in the feminist press—both in *Ms.* and in *off our backs*—similarly characterize the novel's realism in relation to its men characters. These reviews differ from those of the mainstream press, though, by introducing another issue: the need to defend the women's movement against writers like French and novels like *The Women's Room.* Sara Sanborn's review in *Ms.* characterizes the novel as "soap opera, and low-budget soap opera at that," because "the book has all the complexity of a sentence diagram. Subject-verb-object: he kicks her." [20] The "impression of richness and reality" French's sheer number of characters provides at first glance collapses, according to Sanborn, into "melodrama" because of French's "single-mindedness in the pursuit of malefactors"—because French's narrator insists on blaming men for women's oppression. Such a system of blaming men, she argues, creates a world in which "women are not responsible" for their own lives, precisely the lack of responsibility that "some men [presumably sexists] have ascribed to women" (34).

Sanborn's references to soap opera and melodrama—the title of the review is "A Feminist Jacqueline Susann?" work to equate French's novel with mass culture directed at women, an equation Lindsy Van Gelder took up in her 1979 essay in *Ms.* called "A Year Later: The Lure of 'The Women's Room.' " Van Gelder suggests that readers of *The Women's Room* are like the characters French depicts, "suburban housewives, women over 40, and women who never went to college" (43), precisely the consumers of women's mass culture and precisely the kind of woman Van Gelder claims to have been before she became a feminist. She identifies the novel as immature and pre- or proto-feminist, reflecting a common attitude in *Ms.* in the late 1970s that feminism had outgrown its earlier radicalism. Two *Ms.* reviews in 1978 similarly argued that feminism had "matured"; reviewing *Some Do* and *Burning Questions*, Susan Dworkin and Lynne Sharon Schwartz (respectively) asserted what they saw as feminism's move to "a quieter, more individualized search for fulfillment" in contrast to the novels' less mature visions of feminism (Schwartz 41).

Where Stimpson used Didion to establish a boundary between "women" and "feminist" writers in 1973, Van Gelder used French to establish a boundary between "feminist" and "anti-male" writers in 1979. The purpose of Stimpson's distinction in the early 1970s was to define feminism as an emergent oppositional movement; the purpose of Van Gelder's distinction in the late 1970s was to protect that movement's hegemony—which leads Van Gelder to employ the same "men can't be that bad" strategy as the mainstream-press reviews. Van Gelder insists on distinguishing readers of *The Women's Room* from "Movement activist[s]" and "Movement spokeswomen":

The unequivocal antimale tone of the book, I suspect, explains its lukewarm popularity among Movement spokeswomen. (If you had been going on TV talk shows for years and patiently explaining that no, we don't hate *men*, we just hate oppression, how would you deal with a heroine who says that men "were not to be trusted, being members of the inferior gender"?) In fact, at the time that *The Women's Room* was first sweeping the best-seller charts in 16 countries, feminists I know were reading Dorothy Dinnerstein's *The Mermaid and the Minotaur . . .* a very positive futuristic vision of equal support and respect between women and men. (42–43)

Despite the novel's admitted emotional power, Van Gelder insists that French's desire to "start a revolution" with her novel will not succeed because feminist revolution is not possible without men. At stake in Sanborn's review and Van Gelder's essay is the novel's credibility as a representation of feminism's investment in men: only "immature" feminists believe that men can be that bad.

This is where *Ms.*'s uncritical inclusiveness breaks down: we can all be feminists in our own ways, so long as those ways do not alienate or criticize the men we need in order to demonstrate our hegemonic position. Here, "The Rule of Niceness" that Brooke Williams identified as central to "soft" CR in her review of Dreifus's *Woman's Fate* becomes a central tenet not only of how women are to treat other women, but also of how women are to write about men. "Mature" feminism thus became *polite* feminism in the pages of *Ms.* More specifically, the rule of niceness toward men applied to *white* women writing about *white* men; *Ms.*'s coverage of the controversies over Alice Walker's novel *The Color Purple* (1982), and especially over Steven Spielberg's film version (1985), demonstrates that the rule of niceness was entirely set aside in the early 1980s when it might have applied to *black* men. I will return to this argument later in the chapter.

The radical feminist press, here represented primarily by *off our backs*, was just as interested as *Ms.* was in protecting the movement from *The Women's Room*, but from a different aspect of its politics. The fiction reviews in *off our backs* focussed not only on novels' depictions of men, but also on their depictions of feminist activist politics. Wendy Stevens in *off our backs*, like Van Gelder in *Ms.*, disavowed *The Women's Room* as a feminist novel. Stevens suggests that the attention the novel received "in the straight press" indicated "how little reading of women's books . . . they do" (18), arguing that French's novel represents neither women's nor feminist fiction. The basis for the novel's unrepresentativeness was not, however, its depictions of men, as Stevens points out that French "has shown us how victimized women are and how hateful men are toward women" (19). Instead, Stevens's dismissal of the novel comes from its rejection of feminist activist politics as the solution to that "hatefulness." Despite French's accurate portrayals of men, Stevens writes that she herself "remain[s] distrustful of [French] and her present ability to continue on with her life as if her 'women's movement' was something passed through like puberty" (19). Where *Ms.* defended the movement from the novel's political immaturity in its "unequivocal antimale tone," *off our backs* defended the movement from the novel's pretense of maturity in rejecting activism as merely a stage. Such a novel cannot be feminist in the radical feminist press because it offers a personal solution to the political problem of men's oppressive behavior.

Stevens's review of *The Women's Room* typifies the fiction reviews in *off our backs*, both in its insistence that feminist fiction critique men's behavior and in its attention to the novel's alignment with feminist politics. Like Tannenhaus, who insisted that women's "character flaw" was an insufficient vision of the cause of women's oppression, reviewers in *off our backs* argued that feminist novels must "move beyond a sympathetic description of the character to indict the society in which [the protagnist] was conditioned for this loss of self-identity and waste," as Jody Raphael wrote in reviewing *Walking Papers* in 1972. Without such systemic analyses, novels merely repeat, without clearly critiquing, patriarchal ideas about women.

Reviewers in *off our backs* were deeply concerned with novels' depictions of feminist politics. In some instances, that concern was manifested in questions of historical accuracy. Terri Poppe, for instance, found "a major incongruity [in] the place/time setting" of Rita Mae Brown's *In Her Day*, arguing, "I find it very hard to believe that radical women in New York City in 1976 are mostly into consciousness-raising groups and only beginning to be activists. That feels more like 1972 or 1973." Other reviewers wrestled with the absence of depictions of activist politics from feminist novels. Carol Anne Douglas, reviewing *Small Changes*, granted that "changes in lifestyle are political in themselves," but also suggested that a novel that "almost completely ignores the more overtly political aspects of the women's movement" was "disturbing." Margie Crew, reviewing Elana Nachman's *Riverfinger Women*, works out this question at some length:

> *Riverfinger Women* is not obviously political—there is very little rhetoric, and political actions and movements are barely mentioned. But Nachman seems to be saying that all this *is* political, that Inez has come to an understanding that it is, and she is honing her ability to resist and defy. Her lifestyle is a resistance and she is engaging on some level in tactical practice for greater battles. (22; emphasis original)

Crew suggests that the novel itself makes the connections between lifestyle and resistance, rather than requiring the reader to supply them.

Her reading of *Riverfinger Woman* differs from Stevens's of *The Women's Room* or Douglas's of *Small Changes* by locating the novel's thematization of these connections, thus granting that novel both greater political explicitness and greater political sophistication.

Another of the accuracy questions for fiction reviewers in *off our backs* did revolve around depictions of men characters; reviewers argued that the same depictions of men that both the mainstream press and *Ms.* found objectionable were both "realistic" and politically necessary. Whatever problems Douglas found with *Small Changes*, she also insisted that "some male critics have complained that the men in the book are too obnoxious to be believable; few women will find anything unbelievable about them." Men critics were not only mistaken about the realism of such men characters, Douglas argued, but their misreadings—both of women's lives and of women's fiction—were motivated by bad faith, by an insistence on finding men heroes in all literary works. Men characters are indeed "that bad" in this analysis—and men reviewers are possibly worse.

One reviewer in *off our backs* criticized two of Piercy's novels for being insufficiently anti-male to be useful or realistic. Vickie Leonard, in separate reviews of *Braided Lives* and *Vida*, argued that Piercy's "special contribution" to feminist fiction "continues to be portrayal of the subtle battles between men and women" ("She"); Piercy "holds back showing how they [men] operate," and this was "regrettable since no one can write these scenes the way Piercy can" (rev. of *Braided Lives*). Leonard speculated that Piercy "may have refrained from writing such scenes out of personal unease or fear of being labelled anti-male," but concluded, "it's too bad there weren't more" ("She"). Negative depictions of men characters serve an important consciousness-raising purpose, as Leonard argued: "we women need to have explicit examples of how our everyday relationships with men can eat at our self-respect" (Rev. of *Braided Lives*). That is, feminist fictional representations of men who are "that bad" better enable women readers to critique men's oppressive behavior in their own lives.

Reviewers in *off our backs* were clearly opposed to the polite, pro-male feminism of *Ms.*'s fiction reviews; the reality to which realist fiction referred differed quite radically between these two feminist publications, as even their titles suggest. At its founding, as Echols points out, *off our backs* was "highly politico, its pages filled with reports of women in third-world liberation struggles" (221), where *Ms.* had no such alliances with other movements for social change. Even during its early years, when *Ms.* understood feminism as an oppositional movement, it avoided other radical causes and issues, unwilling to risk either its advertisers or its subscribers. As *Ms.* moved toward its later vision of hegemonic feminism, it studiously avoided the kinds of political and definitional debates that erupted with some frequency in *off our backs*—debates over separatism, over the usefulness of liberal feminism, even over the desirability of recruitment.[21] In short, the political reality of feminism for *Ms.* was that the movement needed the support of white men, while the political reality of feminism for *off our backs* was that the movement needed to make common cause with men of color in the U.S. and in the third world.[22]

Ms. treated Alice Walker's portrayals of black men in *The Color Purple* (1982) in just the same way that *off our backs* treated white feminist novelists' portrayals of white men: the rule of niceness simply did not apply. The controversy over *The Color Purple* differs significantly from the earlier controversy over *The Women's Room*, not least because the former has been throroughly discussed by scholars; so much fine work has been done on the novel, the film, and the controversies surrounding both of them that my arguments here rely largely on scholarly sources, rather than on the reviews themselves. Walker's two essays defending her work ("Finding Celie's Voice" [1985] and "In the Closet of the Soul" [1986]) may have come about because of her affiliation with the magazine;[23] nonetheless, the effect of the magazine's defense of *The Color Purple* was to establish a different standard for white and black feminist novelists, and thus for white and black men's relation to feminism. In the context of this double standard, the suspicions articulated by a number of African-American critics that the novel appealed to white women and feminist readers in particular because of its "verification of all the racist stereotypes [they] have grown up on" (Harris 158) make a certain kind of sense, especially if one were suspicious of white feminists' politics about race generally.[24] On the other hand, *Ms.*'s defense of Walker's work can be seen as a response to those suspicions, as an act of solidarity with black feminists, even as a kind of mimicry of the intense sense of loyalty to a black woman novelist that Trudier Harris describes this way:

To complain about the novel is to commit treason against black women writers, yet there is much in it that deserves complaint, and there are many black women critics in this country who would rather have their wisdom teeth pulled than be accused of objecting to it. (155)[25]

By the mid-1980s, it may be the case that *Ms.*'s particular brand of cultural feminism was more concerned with the need to exhibit cross-racial solidarity with an African-American woman novelist than with its earlier need to exhibit cross-gender solidarity with men by policing the boundaries of acceptable depictions of them in feminist fiction. Since Walker's novel lends itself to being read within the conventions of the CR novel, that solidarity was not especially difficult to achieve.

Walker's novel uses virtually every convention and device of the CR novel; critical analyses of the novel have tended to focus on its relation to African-American literary traditions, and thus have not attended to its additional grounding in white feminist fiction of the 1970s.[26] Celie's story in the novel follows the "overplot" of the CR novel, as I discussed it in Chapter Two; Celie moves into sexual self-determination, into increasingly complex self-awareness, and into increasingly politicized understandings of her history. Like Dorothy Bryant's Ella Price, Celie also demonstrates a growing articulateness in her writing, a developing style, over the course of the novel, which further links her to the "amateur" writer-protagonists of the CR novel; Alison Light links Celie's personal development with the novel's "first-person narrative which invited the mechanism of identification and needed it in order to be read" (107).[27] The novel also uses two of the crucial devices of the CR novel that I discuss in Chapter Five: multiple characters to represent different aspects of women's situation, and daughters to represent futurity. The inclusion of Nettie's letters underlines Walker's use of the multiple characters device, as does her use of Sophia and Shug as models for Celie, "feminist models daring to assert autonomy, challenge patriarchy, and shed feminine decorum," as King-Kok Cheung argues (168). Similarly, the ending, where the entire extended family is reunited, emphasizes the daughter device, though here, in keeping with Walker's "womanism," it is daughter and son (and daughter-in-law).[28] Like many of the science fiction versions of the CR novel, *The Color Purple* is, as Light argues, "utopian in its form: Celie gets it all at the end of the story, and through her we are offered this dream of full achievement, of a world in which all conflicts and contradictions are resolved" (111).[29]

The Color Purple shares with the CR novel its focus on sexuality—on sexuality as a site of women's oppression, and on sexuality as a privileged site of women's self-determination. I argued in Chapter Three that the CR novels of the 1970s typically focussed on abortion as a central issue that encapsulated both views of sexuality, both freedom and victimage, a focus that posits women's control of the consequences of sexuality as the tension holding together this double view. *The Color Purple*, by contrast, maintains the earlier radical feminist double view of sexuality by splitting it: incest is the site of Celie's oppression, and lesbianism her site of freedom. This splitting reflects the emergence of the anti-pornography movement's analysis of the interrelations of sex and gender, in which, as Snitow, Stansell, and Thompson argue, male sexuality was figured as "violent and lustful" and female sexuality as "tender and gentle" (38). Pornography was the organizing tool of the anti-porn movement, but its analysis of male sexuality as essentially predatory helped focus attention on other issues of violence and sexual violence against women and

girls, especially incest and childhood sexual abuse.[30] *The Color Purple* engages the anti-porn movement's emphasis on sexual victimage while still
maintaining a vision of sexual self-determination that is not wholly privative, a combination that may help account for the novel's popularity
with a wide range of feminist readers.

The Color Purple's happy ending underlines its departure from realism,
its move into romance, fantasy, or fairy tale.[31] A similar departure from
realism lies in the novel's depiction of lesbianism, which is not named
as such and carries no negative consequences. Bonnie Zimmerman's
discussion of incest in lesbian fiction is illuminating here: "incest has
become the paradigm of patriarchal power, the ultimate abuse by the
Father" (*Safe Sea* 213), especially, she points out, in lesbian novels after
1986.[32] *The Color Purple* marks the emergence of this trope in feminist
fiction; it bridges the focus of 1970s fiction on sexuality as an arena of
women's self-determination with the focus of 1980s feminist fiction on
sexuality as an arena of women's oppression.

The controversy over *The Color Purple's* portrayals of men is particularly interesting because it so entirely ignored any history of similar debates surrounding white feminists' depictions of men. The mainstream
(white) press loved this controversy as a window into division in African-
American communities; "the conflict," as Jacqueline Bobo sums up in
her insightful essay on the controversy over both novel and film, "was
framed as an in-house fight between black women and black men"
(335). Entirely forgotten were earlier debates about whether novels like
The Women's Room unfairly or unrealistically treated its men characters—
even though the controversy over French's novel had taken place only
five years before. The controversy about men in *The Color Purple* replayed these debates in ways that were specifically racialized; rather than
staging their arguments as a question of realism or credibility, most critics of Walker's depictions of her men characters argued that critiques of
black men's behavior formed a political rhetoric that divided the (presumably unified) African-American community. In this analysis, a black
feminist could not be responding to gendered divisions and problems
within the black community, but could only be creating those divisions
and problems—and, moreover, could only be doing so in ways that were
inevitably complicitous with white racism.

Such critics managed to overlook both the novel's and the film's insistence on the recuperation of black men characters; indeed, one might
argue that Walker's depiction of Mr. ____'s transformation into Albert is
another instance of her use of the multiple-character device, given his
own process of consciousness-raising. Differently from women characters in CR novels, though, Mr. ____'s movement from "male oppressor to
enlightened being" requires his being "completely desexualized as part

of the transformative process" (hooks "Writing" 460), again suggesting the novel's engagement with notions of male sexuality constructed by the anti-porn movement in the late 1970s. Mr. ____'s desexualization as recuperation is, on the one hand, entirely in keeping with this view of men's sexuality, and thus likely to appeal to feminist readers and viewers grounded in feminist discourses. On the other hand, the insistent desexualization of an African-American man cannot help but resonate with what Angela Davis has called "The Myth of the Black Male Rapist," and thus be taken far too comfortably by white readers and viewers as confirmation of that stereotype.

The Color Purple's grounding in the CR novel may help account for its popularity, especially among white women readers, for it is one of the very few novels by and about a black woman to use these conventions and devices that had become so widespread by the early 1980s. Trudier Harris argued in 1984 that black and white women's reactions to the novel were very different; "most" white women she spoke to "loved the novel," while "most" black women had a "feeling of uneasiness with the novel" (155). Harris locates the crux of these different responses in the women's understandings of traditions of resistance, and she then points to a wide range of black women's resistance, historical and literary, to suggest that Celie's near-total victimage through much of the novel was "unimaginable" (157). Harris identifies the novel's adoring white readers as "spectator readers . . . who do not identify with the characters and who do not feel the intensity of their pain," who "stand back and view the events of the novel as a circus of black human interactions" confirming "racist sterotypes" (155). Without denying the existence of such spectator readers, especially among white critics and reviewers, I want to suggest that adoring white readers also included feminist readers grounded in the CR novel, who read *The Color Purple* as an authentically African-American feminist CR novel. Such readers did identify with Celie—as a woman, as a CR protagonist, as a victim who learns to stand up for herself, as a bourgening businesswoman, as a sister, as an incest survivor, and for some, as a lesbian.

These white feminist readers whose readings of *The Color Purple* were shaped by the CR novel may not have identified *with* Celie as African American, though they certainly did identify her as African American. In that sense, such readers were spectators in Harris' sense—in reading Walker's novel from within a different literary and historical tradition, and making of the novel's African-American elements something of a fetish, a "quintessential statement on Afro-American women and a certain kind of black lifestyle in these United States," as Harris puts it (155), or a part of the "occult of true black womanhood," in the title of Ann duCille's important article. The white readers grounded in the CR novel were by no means the only readers of Walker's novel to overlook even while fetishizing the African-American specificity of the novel: this is a common critique of the film version in particular.

In their persuasive article on the film adaptation (or "appropriation") of the novel, Wayne J. McMullen and Martha Solomon argue that the film version shifts the novel's focus in ways that create an entirely different (set of) rhetorical meaning(s) for the story. The film's narrative erasure of Celie's voice, together with its evisceration of the specifically lesbian elements of the novel, led viewers to focus on Celie's eventual success within the comforting structures of melodrama. As McMullen and Solomon summarize their argument:

Walker's affirming narrative concerns a black woman's self-creation and self-empowerment through her relationships (especially with other women) and community. Spielberg's film displaces key issues of gender, race, and sexuality with a tale that emphasizes personal fulfillment through American ideals of persistence and capitalistic savvy. (171)

In short, the film "reassures the viewer that even subjugated African-American women can succeed and find happiness in American capitalistic society" (170). As persuasive as I find this reading of the film's "normalization and containment of difference" (171), I want nonetheless to note that even viewers who are not critical of the terms of the film's transformation may still understand it as a feminist film, if we connect it with the institutionalization of the feminist public sphere I discussed in Chapter One. In the context of the importance of feminist businesses and institutions as the material outgrowth of feminist literacy in the 1970s, the film's recasting of Celie's struggle for self-determination into the terms of American entrepreneurship may not seem to contradict its CR narrative.[33]

The Color Purple's use of the strategies of the CR novel—strategies that had become so visible and entrenched by the early 1980s—may account for the novel's availability to this transformation into film. When the CR novel's narrative strategies became, by the early 1980s, ubiquitous, it became possible to recognize little other than those conventions at work—and thus possible to tell "the story" of Walker's novel without relying on its specifically black and specifically lesbian elements. The CR aspect of the narrative, the CR "overplot," became by the early eighties so recognizable that it could be reproduced in film—even while the film eviscerated much of the novel's specific political context.

The film version of *The Color Purple* was recognizable as a CR narrative in part because a number of films from the late 1970s and early 1980s similarly contained elements of the CR narrative—usually deploying those elements in storylines not specifically feminist. Films such as

Coming Home (1978), for example, used such feminist-inflected devices as the housewife's coming to consciousness and sexual awakening as political awakening in the famous orgasm scene; these devices were in the service of a story about the Vietnam war. Similarly, *Norma Rae* (1979) looks like a CR narrative and attends to some extent to gender issues, but stops short of a feminist analysis of the labor issues that are its focus. Perhaps the most simply feminist film of this period, and another in a spate of films focusing on working-class women, was *Heart like a Wheel* (1983), the story of Shirley Muldowney's career in auto racing.[34]

Walker's is, in many respects, the last of the important CR novels. Because of the ways that its surrounding controversies were so specifically racialized, critics have not read it as a CR novel, nor has the film been read in relation to this narrative form. The questions that surrounded Walker's depictions of black men take on a different dimension when compared to earlier controversies about the depictions of men characters in feminist fiction by white women. Critics of white women's fiction policed the boundaries of white feminist credibility; their insistence that men can't be that bad worked as a strategy in the mainstream press to contain feminist politics and as a strategy in *Ms.* to protect the alliance between white women and white men required by the magazine's vision of cultural feminism. Critics in *off our backs* policed a different boundary of feminist credibility, protecting the legitimacy of activist politics. None of these questions applied to Walker's novel: *The Color Purple* generated a different kind of debate, suggesting that black women writers faced a different credibility standard from the one established for white women.

In fact, *The Color Purple* was nearly always read as a rhetorical statement about African-American politics rather than as a realist novel depicting African-American people. It is not, I suggest, the novel's move away from realism, its fairy-tale quality, that produced overwhelmingly rhetorical readings of it. Instead, I would point to the debates about racism in feminism in the early 1980s. As Susan Stanford Friedman points out, a central dynamic in the racism debates was white women's "performance of guilt whose very display tends to displace and thereby reconstitute the other as other"—a "fetishization of women of color that once again reconstitutes them as other caught in the gaze of white feminist desire" (11). The credibility question of realist fiction—including its "men can't be that bad" versions that *Ms.* applied so stringently to white women writers—did not apply to black women writers, whose work was simply too "other" to be evaluated by the same standards. Because *The Color Purple* was expected to be ideological rather than presumed to be neutral, the questions raised about it took shape in defining *which kind* of tract it was ("pro-black woman" or "anti-black men") rather than whether it was one at all. Like feminists who cross the boundaries of neutral depictions of men, a black woman writer could only be "one-sided," to invoke the terms of my epigraph for this chapter; the difference, however, is that fiction by white women feminists had to be shown to cross that line in the 1970s, while fiction by black women feminists was already presumed to be beyond it.

As the reviews of feminist fiction in the mainstream press demonstrate, the strategy of "developing female class consciousness" could be a far more acceptable vision of feminism than the strategy of "changing men," to return to the language of Redstockings' Manifesto. The former could be depoliticized into a vision of feminism as women's self-improvement,[35] so that feminist fiction's emphasis on women's struggles for self-determination, designed to transact CR with readers, could be read within dominant assumptions about realist fiction as dramatizing the needs of its women protagonists for self-improvement rather than for political change. The slippage from the political to the psychological constituted a strategy of containment in the mainstream press: feminism's demands on men to change their behavior toward women could be ruled out of bounds as "unfair." The slippage in the fiction reviews in *Ms.* served much the same purpose, and it could do so in the name of feminism because of the slippage from "hard" to "soft" CR that I discussed in Chapter Two.

So long as reviewers in the mainstream press read feminist fiction as focused specifically on women (and not on white men), they could perceive it as credible and realistic; when reviewers perceived novels to be critical of white men as the agents of women's oppression, they saw that critique as an eruption of "ideology," a violation of realist fiction's presumed neutrality. This dynamic, however, played differently for black women writers, as *The Color Purple* demonstrates, since black women's work was never granted the neutrality of realism in the first place. White men can't be that bad, even reviewers in *Ms.* argued—but that presumption was never granted to black men.

Notes

1. This passage appears in the Introduction to Dolores laGuardia and Hans P. Guth, eds., *American Voices: Multicultural Literacy and Critical Thinking* (17)—a 1996 composition textbook. The example is supposed to demonstrate the improvement made by "listening to the other side." Thanks to Mike Mitchell of Miami University for sharing his outrage over the textbook with me.

2. West's third question, however, shifts the focus from men to institutions, as well as insists on women's biology as a legitimate political issue: "If I could do away with anything I wanted, the first thing I would do away with is: (a)

the family; (b) the state; (c) private property; (d) menstrual periods; (e) all of the above."

3. Solanis's text has become a stand-in for a debate about Women's Studies, as Elayne Rapping's account of the 1995 conference sponsored by the Women's Freedom Network evidences; Rapping cites a lecture by Daphne Patai which claimed "The SCUM Manifesto" was being widely taught in Women's Studies classes "as serious feminist theory"—a "fact" Rapping disputes by claiming that "No one I know reads, or even talks about, Valerie Solanis these days" ("The Ladies Who Lynch" 9). Rapping's statement predates release of the film *I Shot Andy Warhol*; for different views of Solanis's and her Manifesto's importance to second-wave feminism, see two reviews of the film: Jennifer Baumgardner, "*Who Shot Andy Warhol?*" (in *Ms.*); and Kathi Maio, "I Shot Andy Warhol" (in *Sojourner*). For yet another view, see Castro's reading of "The SCUM Manifesto" as parody, 72–74. I teach the *Sisterhood Is Powerful* excerpt from the manifesto in my Feminist Theory course to exemplify what Meaghan Morris has called the "forgotten and ignoble," "disgraced and disqualified" texts of second-wave feminism (Morris 68–69).

4. See also Joreen [Jo Freeman], "The BITCH Manifesto" (1970), for an account of conflicts between women. Joreen argues that "bitches," because of their unorthodox gender styles, have particular difficulties with women.

5. Interestingly, nowhere in *Men in Feminism* do any of the authors refer to these or similar gestures from feminism's early second wave, in large part because the "feminism" the anthology claims as its terrain is specifically identified as poststructuralist feminist theory. Since non-academic works like Morgan's anthology do not count as "theory," neither do they count as "feminism."

6. For a nonfictional account of the Beats that emphasizes precisely this point, see Joyce Johnson's wonderful memoir, *Minor Characters*.

7. See King, "Producing Sex, Theory, and Culture: Gay/Straight Remappings in Contemporary Feminism," for a meditation on the varieties of feminist activities that one might properly count as "theory" (*Theory in Its Feminist Travels* 143–47; see also Chapter One of that book, "What Counts as Theory?").

8. For other examples, see Lehmann-Haupt, rev. of *The High Cost of Living*, which describes the ending as "the incongruous imposition of an ideological solution on a psychological problem" (C18); and "The Waiting Game" (rev. of *Down Among the Women*), which argues that "the only honest answer to Kate Millett" is a novel's insistence that "the blame for empty female lives is not laid at anyone's door" (1075).

9. Indeed, many of the controversies about feminism in the first half of the 1990s revolve around issues of feminist credibility. It is no accident, for example, that one response to the Thomas-Hill hearings about Thomas's alleged sexual harrassment was the widespread appearance of bumper stickers and buttons reading "I believe Anita Hill"; that Roiphe's *The Day After*, like most recent works of anti-feminist feminism, argues that claims for the ubiquity of date-rape are simply not believable; or that Phyllis Chesler's essay collection, *Patriarchy*, is subtitled *Notes of an Expert Witness*. I return to this issue in my discussion of *Thelma & Louise* in the Conclusion.

10. Dow discusses the move of CR into women's magazines in the middle 1970s; the CR depicted in places like *Mademoiselle* was resolutely "soft," and very much in keeping with the focus on the personal. See especially 67–68.

11. For other examples, see Lucy Rosenthal, who argues that *Small Changes*

upsets the "delicate balance" between fiction and ideology (29); Susan Braudy, who critiques the shallowness of the men characters in *Making Ends Meet* ("She Only" 96); and Susan Dworkin, who critiques the shortsightedness of the depictions of men characters in her review of *Some Do* as "stupid, callous, brutal" and sexist (41).

12. For other radical feminist criticism of *Ms.*, see Echols, 265–69; "*Ms.* Politics and Editing: An Interview"; and Willis, "Conservatism."

13. See, e.g., Gerrity, who identifies Didion as a "ranking dramatic muse" of "the new feminist wave," comparing her to Kate Millett; and Segal, who names the publication of *Play It As It Lays* "an event" (6).

14. Stimpson compares Didion to Midge Dechter. I want to point out that the "woman's anathema of a woman's movement" remains a familiar strategy today, though frequently in recent years such anthemas have been couched as feminist critiques of the "extremes" of certain kinds of feminisms. See, among others, Sommers, *Who Stole Feminism?*; Roiphe, *The Morning After*; and Wolf's recanting of pro-choice politics in "Our Bodies, Our Souls." See also Patrice McDermott's wonderful reading of the controversies over some of these texts in "On Cultural Authority: Women's Studies, Feminist Politics, and the Popular Press."

15. For a similar view of Didion, see Doris Ribera's "Women in Women's Eyes," a 1971 essay for the Los Angeles feminist periodical *Everywoman*; Ribera accuses Didion (and Anais Nin, among others) of presenting "mutilated, neurotic, burned-out" women characters, neither "free" nor "satisfied" (9). See also Nin's reply. In Chapter Three, I note a dissenting view, in which a reviewer of *Play It As It Lays* in *off our backs* specifically claimed the novel's treatment of abortion as feminist; see Alberts.

16. See Estelle Jelinek, for example, for an argument that "the cult surrounding Anais Nin is a regressive aspect of the women's liberation movement" because Nin's work is elitist, male-identified, essentialist, apolitical, and self-indulgent (19).

17. See Coward, "Are Women's Novels Feminist Novels?" for a similar argument.

18. I do not mean to suggest that *Ms.* was ever particularly anti-male, but rather that the magazine's emphasis on including men as a feature of its changing vision of feminism did increase over the course of the decade. As the inclusion of a section called "Humanized Men" in *The First* Ms. *Reader* in 1973 (an anthology of articles reprinted from 1972 and 1973) suggests, *Ms.* had some investment in bringing men to feminism from the outset.

19. As early as 1970, some men reviewers expressed concern that they would be "dismissed as male chauvinists" for disliking feminist fiction (see, e.g., John Leonard, "Ugliness and Expertise"); for the most part, though, this concern in the early part of the decade was disingenuous, a strategy used to disarm opposition to reviewers' antifeminism.

20. The parallel here to MacKinnon's formulation in "Feminism, Marxism, Method and the State," "Man fucks woman; subject verb object" (27), marks the depth of the difference between Sanborn's liberal-cultural feminism and MacKinnon's radical feminism. For a more recent history of *Ms.*, and one that could provide a complex sense of the magazine's changes since its "ad-free" reconstitution, one might trace the changing status of MacKinnon's work in the magazine over the late 1980s and into the 1990s.

21. On separatism, see Echols 226; on liberal feminism, see the opening of

Ellen Willis's "Feminism without Freedom," which summarizes questions about the relationships between feminism and liberalism (151); on recruitment, see Williams and Darby, "business vs. revolution."

22. For a history of *off our backs*, see Jennie Ruby, "*Off Our Backs*."

23. Walker was a Contributing Editor for *Ms.* from December 1974 to January 1987; my thanks to Tracy Davis for reading the masthead for me.

24. By the early to mid-1980s, after the publication of several enormously popular and influential anthologies devoted to the feminism of women of color (which I discuss in Chapter Six)—and to debates about racism in the women's movement—the arguments about white feminism's racism were ubiquitous in the movement.

25. See also Cheryl B. Butler's description of the black women students' response to a seminar discussion of *The Color Purple* in "The Color Purple Controversy: Black Woman Spectatorship."

26. Even the novel's harshest critics find Walker's use of voice and style compelling; see, e.g., Trudier Harris, "On *The Color Purple*, Stereotypes, and Silence."

27. For discussions of Walker's revisioning of the epistolary form, see, among others, Mae G. Henderson, "*The Color Purple*: Revisions and Redefinitions"; and Lindsey Tucker, "*The Color Purple*: Emergent Woman, Emergent Text."

28. Walker specifically defines womanism as a non-separatist politics that includes men, in contrast to feminism, which may not include them. See *In Search of Our Mothers' Gardens*, xi.

29. This is one source of bell hooks's criticism of the novel; as she argues in "Writing the Subject, Reading *The Color Purple*": "Walker creates a fiction wherein an oppressed black woman can experience self-recovery without a dialectical process; without collective political effort; without radical change in society. To make Celie happy she creates a fiction where struggle—the arduous and painful process by which the oppressed work for liberation—has no place. This fantasy of change without effort is a dangerous one for both oppressed and oppressor. It is a brand of false consciousness that keeps everyone in place and oppressive structures intact" (469). *The Color Purple*'s version of CR is, to shift the terms, "soft" rather than "hard," more invested in happiness than in social change.

30. In "Notes of a Post-Sex Wars Theorizer," Carla Freccero makes this argument (308), and cites Rosalind Coward's "Sexual Violence and Sexuality" in doing so.

31. For a discussion of the novel as a romance, see Molly Hite, "Romance, Marginality, Matrilineage: Alice Walker's *The Color Purple* and Zora Neale Hurston's *Their Eyes Were Watching God*"; for a discussion of its "fairy tale" and "fantasy" elements, see Lauren Berlant, "Race, Gender, and Nation in *The Color Purple*."

32. Zimmerman nowhere discusses *The Color Purple* in *The Safe Sea of Women*, even while she notes repeatedly the absence of lesbian fiction by women of color; her definition of lesbian fiction requires that the central lesbian character "[understand] herself to be a lesbian" (15), which excludes Celie, who does not evidence any such understanding. Nonetheless, *The Color Purple* was wildly popular among lesbian readers, and does address the themes Zimmerman identifies as conventional in lesbian fiction. Moreover, Walker's novel anticipates in some sense the move to mystery and recovery narratives that Zimmerman sees as central to lesbian fiction in the late 1980s. It is just plain silly to fault a scholarly book that discusses 167 novels for a single omission, and that is not my intent here. Rather, I want to suggest that just as *The Color Purple* adapts the CR

novel form and conventions, and thus can be read in my specific literary history, so too could it be read productively in Zimmerman's.

33. Another important recasting of the CR novel into the terms of entrepreneurial triumphalism can be seen in the made-for-television version of Marilyn French's *The Women's Room*, which concludes not with Mira's isolation and meditation, but rather with a lengthy scene of her giving a lecture on feminism and receiving a standing ovation. The television film seems to establish teaching Women's Studies as the feminist version of the American dream, or as some kind of an academic equivalent to Celie's Folkspants Limited. Linda M. Blum compares the endings of the novel and the TV movie in "Feminism and the Mass Media: A Case Study of *The Women's Room* as Novel and Television Film," 15–20.

34. The films that focus on working-class women at the turn of the decade include *Coal Miner's Daughter* (1980), and *Silkwood* (1984), with *Alice Doesn't Live Here Anymore* (1975) as an important influence on these films; one might also include the ambiguously classed clerical workers of *Nine To Five* (1980). The success of the "women's films" of 1978 (*The Turning Point, An Unmarried Woman, Julia*, and *Girlfriends*), which focused on middle- and upper-class women, may have been a factor in generating a remarkable number of films about women in that period; the number seems remarkable especially in relation to the near total absence of films about women coming out of Hollywood in the past few years. For a reading of films made for television in the same period, see Rapping, *The Movie of the Week*, especially her meticulous reading of class issues in *The Burning Bed* (1984), 69–87.

35. The relationship between feminism and women's self-help—and especially between feminism and the recovery movement—has been a controversial one. For a smart and careful reading of the controversy that addresses precisely the question of politics vs. psychology, see Cynthia Schrager's fine review of two books devoted to this subject, "Self-Help or Self-Harm?"; see also Elayne Rapping, *The Culture of Recovery*.

Chapter Five
Strategies of Futurity

The King was pregnant.
—Ursula K. Le Guin[1]

Imagining a specifically feminist future was a crucial way for the CR novel to raise consciousness, to show the limits of patriarchy by imagining its alternatives, to demonstrate and theorize the kinds and processes of change that could liberate women (and sometimes men), and to forward specific political agendas for the women's movement. This chapter examines visions of feminist futures in the CR novel, and the range of narrative strategies and devices the novels used to forward their visions. While the emergence in the 1970s of a specifically feminist body of science fiction provided novelists with a useful set of conventions for imagining futurity, realist novels also use many of the strategies and devices I examine here, including unfinished or suspended endings, daughters, historical mothers, and multiple characters.

In her afterword to *Feminist Literary Criticism: Explorations in Theory* (1975), Josephine Donovan explains the double nature of feminist criticism, in a formulation that parallels the double nature of feminist fiction:

Thus, as feminist critics, our sensitivities must be negative in that we are saying no to a whole series of oppressive ways, images, and falsehoods that have been perpetrated against women both in literature and in literary criticism. But, on the other hand, we must be sensitive, too, to the new imaginative perceptions, to the new shapes that are beginning to take form—partly as a result of our negations. (76)

The practice of CR asked women to compile narratives of their oppression, to list out the "oppressive ways, images, and falsehoods" found in their experience, and in the group's collective knowledge. This "negation," in Donovan's term, provides motivation for change, while the "new imaginative perceptions" to which she urges us also to attend provide evidence of the possibility of change. At stake in the strategies of futurity forwarded by the CR novels was not only this sense that change was possible, but also the novels' speculations about ways such changes might happen.

Given the CR novel's interest in representing (at least the need for) social change, and the wide range of organized feminist political activity in the decade, it is surprising how few realist CR novels actually do represent activism; when they do so, these representations frequently help locate the novels' political designs. Marilyn French's *The Women's Room* (1977) represents failed activism—specifically, the failure of violence to "liberate" even one woman. Mira's friend Val is killed by police while she is trying to rescue a young black woman from jail. That young woman, Anita, has been convicted of murder because she stabbed a man who tried to rape her. The logic of Anita's conviction is important. Despite pleading self-defense, Anita is convicted of murder, rather than freed, because the prosecutor "proved" that she was not a legitimate student, and thus had no legitimate reason to be out on the street at night. A woman on the street at night for no good reason, especially a black woman, must be a prostitute; since prostitutes cannot be raped, Anita's stabbing cannot be self-defense. Thus "Anita Morrow was found guilty of murder on the grounds of illiteracy" (674–75). Val's group of women shows up with guns when Anita is being transferred to prison; tipped off by FBI infiltrators, the police kill Val and all the members of her group. French's argument is that violence, however tempting for women, however righteous and even legal it may be, results only in more oppression, more violence and deaths. The price for women is too high. "Nothing really changes," one of Val's friends says at her funeral. Mira responds, "It does, it does. It just takes longer than we do" (677). As Val had pointed out repeatedly in the novel, institutions "get you in the end" (673); individuals cannot escape their social conditions, and remaking social conditions takes longer than one lifetime.

The argument that feminist social change requires generations occurs again and again in the CR novel, as part of the problem of the individual solution. Mira makes decisions about how she'll live, under what conditions she'll survive, but she does not believe that such individual decisions themselves constitute social change. Meanwhile—that is, while we await the revolution or whatever it is that Mira believes can or will make real social change—Mira presents her story, and the stories of her women friends, as bearing witness to these women's struggles.

The parallel between such feminist notions of witnessing and the Christian practice is deliberate here, for I want to emphasize again the way that feminist consciousness-raising works as a conversion experi-

ence. Mira's emphasis on bearing witness is similar to Weldon's imperative in *Praxis*: "Watch Praxis. Watch her carefully. Look, listen, learn.
Then safely, as they say to children, cross over." The model of social
change at issue here requires faith—not faith in the power of prayer to
effect social change, as was the case, for instance, in Harriet Beecher
Stowe's "Concluding Remarks" to *Uncle Tom's Cabin*, with its imperative
to "feel right in your heart" as a means to ending slavery.[2] Instead, the
model of social change at work in *The Women's Room* and some other
CR novels requires faith in the cumulative, long-term effectivity of individual conversions: at some point, these individual conversions reach
critical mass, and somehow, things change. Of course, this version of
feminist social change prioritizes the problems of women's oppression
that are attributable to men's sexism (and women's internalization of
it), rather than to institutions; individual change in this model *is* social
change, at least implicitly, at least cumulatively.

Alix Kates Shulman's *Burning Questions*, published one year after *The
Women's Room* and one year before *Praxis*, also comes to the conclusion
that remaking social conditions takes longer than one lifetime, but with
a radically different tone. Zane IndiAnna's autobiography, *My Life as a
Rebel*, presents feminist activism as pleasurable, even joyous. Shulman
depicts a "zap action" (spray-painting slogans on the walls) at the Harvard Club; a women's history project; and the August 26, 1970 Women's
March, all of which give Zane a tremendous feeling of accomplishment:
"By will and work and vision we had altered the course of history, we
had affected the consciousness of the world, and now no one in it, not
one of us, would ever be the same" (291). Writing in the mid-seventies,
Zane decides that even though the feminist revolution of the early
seventies may have failed—though she will not grant that it has—participating in that revolution has given her a sense of the value of her
life: "I am now a veteran of the passion of my time—never again can my
life be discounted" (301). Zane's connection to the passion of her time
links her to the revolutionary women of the past. She discovers while
working on the women's history project that "almost every idea we were
now exploring in the movement, even the most outrageously radical,
had been delved by our predecessors" (274), and understands that both
backlashes and subsequent waves of feminism will come after her.

Zane entertains the notion that feminism has brought about only surface changes:

These days it was hard to fathom who had really changed. On the surface, at
least, everyone had: rulers, liberals, and misogynists alike all claimed to have
come around. Those who'd denied us our rights in the old days by saying we
didn't need them could now deny us our rights by pretending we already had
them. (304)

But Zane insists, in the "Dialectical Epilogue," that "Some things were different because we passed this way" (358). She cites the legalization of abortion, the criminalization of domestic violence, and the increased prosecutability of rape cases among her examples, recognizing in each case that gains are temporary, and in some instances very small. At the end of her autobiography, she quotes one of the Moscow Amazons' asking, "how can you count all the circles made by a stone when you toss it into the water?" (361). Shulman's Zane ends her story sitting in a women's cafe, continuing to debate feminist questions—an ending that suggests at least as strongly as anything else in the novel that feminism itself continues. Shulman's futurity here is the survival of struggle; the movement continues, and its longevity is more important than individual conversions.

French's Mira is alone at the end of *The Women's Room,* corresponding with her friends; the women's community of that novel is a friendship network that becomes diffused. Shulman's Zane is in the coffeehouse, talking all night with her friends, and thus the women's community is institutionalized, so that the diffusion of friendship networks need not result in Zane's isolation—other women will find and join Zane's network, as indeed happens in *Burning Questions.* The difference in tone in these novels results at least in part from this difference: feminist political and cultural institutions like the women's coffeehouse, institutions that do not appear in *The Women's Room,* nurture the important friendship networks, and continue a sense of feminist political connectedness. Feminism for Shulman is not lonely as it seems to be for French, because Zane's feminism becomes housed within the institution-building of the first half of the decade, as I discussed in Chapter One.

The CR novel relies on representing personal change within a political context—on representing individual women's consciousness-raising processes. While realist fiction can easily encompass such individual change, representing substantive political change presents more of a problem. Realist fiction, as Marilyn Hacker pointed out in an essay on Joanna Russ, demands "the individual solution, or, failing that, the individual defeat." But, Hacker argued, a feminist solution "is, by definition, *not* individual," and since the demands of realist fiction make "a denouement of growing political awareness and subsequent activity" difficult, "the writer is left with a pessimistic conclusion" (67–68). The demands of realist fiction, in other words, preclude depicting feminist revolutionary change. *Burning Questions* is an exception to this formulation and may escape this realist problematic by presenting itself as an autobiography, one within a tradition of autobiographies by revolutionary women. Novels like *The Women's Room,* however, clearly exemplify Hacker's problematic. Hacker's argument helps us understand why the CR novels end in such unfinished, and indeed often unsatisfying ways, but she does not suggest that such endings themselves serve feminist political ends, an argument that DuPlessis's work draws out. Hacker suggests instead that science fiction is the generic solution to the realist problematic—not surprisingly, science fiction is a solution chosen by many feminist writers, and by writers using the CR form as well.

Before I go on to lay out a typology of science fiction CR novels, I want to suggest that "feminist science fiction" and "the consciousness-raising novel" perform the same (counter) cultural work, to return to my earlier paraphrase of Jane Tompkins: both have "designs" on their readers. Not all feminist science-fiction novels depict their protagonist's CR process as she (sometimes he) confronts the extrapolated, alternate, or possible future, though certainly many do; such depictions of CR mark the clearest relationship between the two kinds of novels. Perhaps less clearly, extrapolation itself is a fundamental part of the CR process, just as it is of science fiction, as Joanna Russ points out in her essays on feminism and science fiction in the early 1970s.[3] That is, asking "what if?" is a central project for consciousness-raising. What if, to cite again the examples of feminist self-speculation that Sandra Lee Bartky forwarded in "Toward a Phenomenology of Feminist Consciousness" (1977), my suggestion is *not* inherently unintelligent—but is ignored because I am a woman? What if "attractiveness" does *not* inevitably mark my acquiescence to gender roles—but is a way to express healthy self-love? Indeed, the central question of CR is a "what if" question: what if individual actions are not isolated, but supersaturated with political meanings?[4] Science fiction, above all other fictional genres, explores these "what if" questions: this is its cultural work, its designs on its readers. Whether the novels depict CR explicitly or not, their project *is* CR.

In addition to providing a generic solution to the problem of representing revolutionary political change, science fiction offered another possibility to feminists in the 1970s: the possibility of radically rethinking gender itself. Feminist science-fiction novels in the 1970s can be divided into these three types: the extra-terrestrial gender system discovery, the eco-fantasy, and the post-apocalyptic utopia/dystopia. Obviously, any such typology is arbitrary, as perhaps any attempt to make generic distinctions working from a small number of texts must be, but it does help account for the political differences between these novels, differences that reflect major debates within feminism.[5]

The most important example of the extra-terrestrial gender-system discovery novel was Ursula K. Le Guin's *The Left Hand of Darkness* (1969). Le Guin sets her novel on the only one of the eighty known, inhabited worlds in which the people have no gender, in which even biological sex is temporary. When the inhabitants of Gethen go into "kemmer," their mating cycle, each of the two partners takes on either male or female sex; afterward, both partners will return to their unsexed state. Anyone may take on either sex in any kemmer; the temporarily female partner may conceive and bear a child. In an essay called "Is Gender Necessary?" (1979), Le Guin explained her reasons for this experiment with gender: "I eliminated gender, to find out what was left. Whatever was left would be, presumably, simply human. It would define the area that is shared by men and women alike" (163–64). Le Guin distinguished her novel from utopian fiction, arguing that *The Left Hand of Darkness* "poses no *practicable* alternative to contemporary society, since it is based on an imaginary, radical change in human anatomy" (168; emphasis original).

At first glance, Le Guin's emphasis on the commonality of human experience, on "whatever was left," would seem to align the extra-terrestrial gender-system discovery novel with certain strands of reformist feminism emphasizing women's access to the public sphere on the same terms as men's.[6] However, it is largely Le Guin's admitted areas of failure in the novel that leads to this reading. Le Guin writes,

the plot and structure that arose as I worked the book out cast the Gethenian protagonist, Estraven, almost exclusively into roles which we are culturally conditioned to perceive as "male." . . . One does not see Estraven as a mother, with his children, in any role in which we automatically perceive as "female": and therefore, we tend to see him as a man. ("Is Gender Necessary?" 168)

Even though Le Guin does include the king's pregnancy in the novel, she sets the action of the book so much in the public rather than the private sphere that her Gethenian "men-women" seem more like men with wombs than radically unsexed and ungendered people. Not a polemic but an exploration, a "thought-experiment," she calls it (163), Le Guin's novel asks a crucial question for second-wave feminism: just how foundational is gender? In this sense, the novel enables a reading aligned with a strand of radical feminism that identified itself as "radical" by arguing that its attention to sex/gender as the "primary contradiction" positioned its analysis to lead to a more thorough-going, foundational social change than could be produced by any other oppositional movement.[7] The novel opens up the possibility of radically reshaping human society by eliminating gender altogether, even though it fails in some sense to deliver that possibility because it so insistently sets its genderless characters into the public sphere.[8] For all its failures, however, *The Left Hand of Darkness* was a tremendously important novel, for whether and in what way gender was "necessary" continued to be a central concern of feminist science fiction throughout the 1970s, and indeed continues to be so into the 1990s.[9]

While the extra-terrestrial gender-system discovery novels tend to be aligned with strands of radical feminism, the eco-fantasy novels correspond politically most closely to varieties of cultural or separatist feminism. Any of the terms used to typologize feminism are, of course, highly contested terms, and I mean here less to reify the terms than to enlist their limited explanatory power; there are real differences in the visions of social change forwarded by the eco-fantasy novels from those by other kinds of feminist science fiction. Charlotte Perkins Gilman's *Herland* (1915), which depicts a woman-only utopia stumbled upon by three male explorers, is generally considered to be the intellectual ancestor of contemporary eco-feminist fiction. Originally serialized in Gilman's magazine *The Forerunner*, *Herland* was first published in novel form in the 1970s. This peculiar publishing history makes it both an ancestor and a contemporary of the later novels. Gilman's eco-fantasy is based in early twentieth-century feminist values, primary among which is social motherhood: "A motherliness which dominated society, which influenced every art and industry, which absolutely protected all childhood, and gave to it the most perfect care and training" (73). All the children of Herland, Gilman writes, grow up in conditions of "Peace, Beauty, Order, Safety, Love, Wisdom, Justice, Patience, and Plenty" (100). Like the later eco-fantasy novels, Gilman's utopia is non-hierarchical in its social organization, which puzzles the explorers a great deal, since they expect to find women fighting among themselves.

Like *Herland*, the feminist eco-fantasy novels of the 1970s frequently focus on women-only communities, in which traditionally or conventionally "feminine" virtues such as cooperation, communication, gentleness, and care-taking govern both individuals and the group as a whole. The later novels do not so explicitly rely on women's capacity to mother as the basis for their notions of women's moral superiority on which their utopias are based, though, of course, motherhood always lurks in the shadows of any such argument.[10] *Herland* differs, though, from the later eco-fantasy novels in two important ways: in the asexuality of its women, and in the tameness of its nature. When Gilman's three male explorers marry three of the Herland women, the men are completely unable to convince their wives that sexual intercourse has any meaning, any necessity, beyond those few occasions when conception will occur. Furious at what he perceives to be an utter lack of sexual "submission," one of the men tries to rape his wife; he is thwarted by Alima's physical strength and by a group of women who hear her scream. The Herland women, individually and collectively, simply do not understand—and will not tolerate—any non-procreative sexuality, whether violent or not. Procreation in Herland is non-sexual: "before a child comes to one of us there is a period of utter exaltation—the whole being is uplifted and filled with a concentrated desire for that child" which the women either accept or repress depending on whether the community is able materially to sustain another child (70).

The absence of sexuality, of what comes to be figured after the "sexual revolution" of the 1960s as a kind of wildness, is similar to the absence of literal wilderness in the country of Herland itself. Herland is "a land in a state of perfect cultivation, where even the forests looked as if they were cared for; a land that looked like an enormous park, only it was even more evidently an enormous garden" (11). Even the roads in Herland are "as dustless as a swept floor" (43). There are no wild animals and no weeds.[11] Gilman is careful to differentiate this tameness, this conservation, from conservatism: the women of Herland continue to experiment with and refine every aspect of their society and culture, including their human nature and nature itself. But the Herlanders live in a park rather than a wilderness, and value reason and order far more highly than women living in the eco-fantasy novels of the 1970s.

The later eco-fantasies emphasize both wildness and wilderness: both nature and women in the later novels are explicitly *untamed*. Sally Miller Gearhart's *The Wanderground* (1979) is the best example of the later eco-fantasy. Gearhart's "Hill Women" live in a post-apocalyptic, women-only community with perfect communion between women, plants, and animals. The Hill Women communicate telepathically with plants and animals, which is possible because the women understand themselves to be "sister" to everything in nature.[12] Sisterhood with the natural world in this sense goes beyond a sort of Earth Day awareness that human beings depend on nature: it requires that one understand oneself *as* nature. The ecstatic conclusion of Susan Griffin's *Woman and Nature: The Roaring Inside Her* (1978) exemplifies this understanding:

> And she wrote, when I let this bird fly to her own purpose, when this bird flies in the path of his own will, the light from this bird enters my body, when I see, the arc of her flight, I fly with her, enter her with my mind, leave myself, die for an instant, live in the body of this bird whom I cannot live without; as part of the body of the bird will enter my daughter's body, because I know I am made from this earth, as my mother's hands were made from this earth, as her dreams came from this earth and all that I know, I know in this earth, the body of the bird, this pen, this paper, these hands, this tongue speaking, all that I know speaks to me through this earth and I long to tell you, you who are earth too, and listen *as we speak to each other of what we know: the light is in us.* (227; emphasis original)

Griffin fuses here four sets of images: "nature" (in the figures of the bird and earth), matrilineal feminist inheritance (in the chain of mother, daughter, self), art (paper and pen), and consciousness (in knowledge and enlightenment). Her address to "you who are earth too" claims a "sisterhood" that is organicized and naturalized rather than one specifically created out of political interests.[13] The organic sisterhood here works as a kind of magical sign, in Katie King's sense: an evocation of (the possibility for) identification that leaps over the difficult political work it would take to make real political coalition possible.[14]

In Gearhart's *The Wanderground*, such a sisterhood is indeed powerful: the apocalypse that made possible and necessary the founding of the Hill Women's community came about when "there was one rape too many," and "The earth finally said 'no'" (158). Animals refused to work for men any longer, technologies and machinery failed, and men became sexually impotent outside the city limits. The apocalypse results from precisely this mystical union of women and nature—and not from a revolution or some other political intervention. After the apocalypse, the Hill Women replace technology with psychic energy; their telepathic communication enables them to manipulate the natural world with its consent. Nature cooperates without being tamed. In *Herland*, science and scientific interventions in nature are necessary ecological management techniques enabling the community to survive; in *The Wanderground*, such interventions are seen by the Hill Women as one cause of the apocalypse. The Hill Women live in a wilderness, a wilderness linked in the novel to the women's sexual freedom and to their mental or spiritual freedom as well.

An important argument in Gearhart's novel is the lesson of the apocalypse: "the essential fundamental knowledge: women and men cannot yet, may not ever, love one another without violence; they are no longer of the same species" (115). Science-fiction writers tend to make this argument more literally than the realist writers do, but the *alienness* of men appears everywhere in the feminist fiction of the 1970s. Christa Wolf, in "*Selbstversuch: Traktat zu einem Protokoll*" (1973), makes a similar argument as her protagonist comes to discover that "Mann und Frau leben auf verschieden Planeten" (235; "Men and women live on different planets"). One way the larger Women's Liberation debate about the significance of gender difference works in the science fiction novels is as a debate about whether and how a sex-integrated utopia might be possible. Some eco-fantasy novels are sex-integrated, or "bi-sexual" as Gilman calls it (*Herland* 88), though these communities are also based on values that are perceived to be feminine or feminist.

Dorothy Bryant's *The Kin of Ata Are Waiting for You* (1976; originally published as *The Comforter* in 1971) is one such sex-integrated utopia. Like *The Wanderground*, Bryant's fictional society has a strong mystical component, and strong ecological values. Like *Herland*, Bryant's novel brings a dangerous and sexist man into a utopia where sexual danger and sexism have been abolished. Bryant's novel, though, is ultimately more centered in mysticism than in any kind of recognizable political feminism. While there is no pronoun denoting gender (or number) for people, and while Atan society is egalitarian, the Atans live entirely for, in, and by their dreams—which they may neither question nor interpret. Such obedience and absence of conflict are unusual in a utopian novel from the early 1970s, at a time when radical feminists were envisioning utopia as an extension of political activity, as one long meeting—at a time when activism itself seemed likely not only to bring about utopia, but to be the lifestyle one would find there.[15] In Bryant's novel, activism is what one does when one leaves utopia; Augustine dreams she leaves Ata, and then surfaces in the United States as a political organizer.

Like the extra-terrestrial gender-system discovery novels, the eco-fantasies focus on alternative societies that are found rather than made. These novels extrapolate from reality as does all science fiction, but along different political lines and political choices from those in the post-apocalyptic utopian/dystopian novels. The "foundness" of their societies is one way we can see the novels' alignment with the particular vision of cultural feminism that Alice Echols has defined: these novels take as their project the articulation of a post-revolutionary women's and/or feminist and/or lesbian *culture*, leaving aside the revolutionary processes and practices that would lead us to such a culture. Or, in an even clearer distinction, these novels understand their cultural work, the act of imaging or imagining those futures *as* the revolutionary process and practice that will enable such a culture to come into being.[16] Like Bryant's Ata, they provide respite from political struggle, promising, as Echols argues that cultural feminism did, a refuge from "the vicissitudes of political struggle" and "a conduit out of subordination" (269). The eco-fantasy novels were both based in and constitutive of this strand of feminism that Echols names cultural feminism.

The post-apocalyptic utopian/dystopian novels often offer similar kinds of post-revolutionary culture and are often based in similar kinds of eco-feminism, but these novels emphasize to a much greater extent the ways that the societies arise. In some cases, these novels are virtually textbooks for revolution. The post-apocalyptic novels focus on a relationship between the present world and the future world or worlds represented. Examples of this category of feminist science fiction include *Woman on the Edge of Time*, *The Female Man*, Zoe Fairbairns's *Benefits* (1979), Suzy McKee Charnas's *Walk to the End of the World* (1974), and *Motherlines* (1978).[17] These novels emphasize the political choices in the present moment that are necessary to bring about the utopian or prevent the dystopian future, and this link highlights the political messages of the novels. By making their futures contingent on present political acts, these novels lay out agendas for organized feminist political activities.

In *Woman on the Edge of Time*, Piercy creates a feminist utopia that is sex-integrated, racially-integrated, and culturally diverse. Her attention to race and culture along with gender is extremely rare in the utopian fiction of the decade. The utopias in *Motherlines* and *The Female Man* are women-only and pay much less attention to racial and cultural diversity. Charnas describes the Riding Women in *Motherlines* as having a variety of skin colors, but her language in these descriptions is so horse-like (and horses play a major role in reproduction in the novel) that this variety loses its connection to human diversity. Similarly, Russ uses a wide range of names—European, African, Asian—for the women in Whileaway, but we meet only white women in the scenes that take place there. Moreover, both the Riding Women and Whileaway are monocultural, so that whatever racial or ethnic diversity Charnas and Russ imply exists in their utopias is purely cosmetic. What these three utopias have in common is the centrality of ecological values, and non-hierarchical forms of social organization.

Piercy's and Russ's novels focus on the ways their utopias—contingent utopias—come into being. In *Woman on the Edge of Time*, Connie helps make the future possible by poisoning the doctors who design and perform experiments in controlling consciousness. Piercy depicts each stage in Connie's process of consciousness raising. Connie begins by feeling that the oppression she experiences results from her personal failings; she checks herself into the hospital the first time. She submits to the psychiatric system; she submits to her own oppression.[18] Moving back and forth between the utopian future and the present helps Connie understand the institutional forces ranged against her. She moves to take action against these forces after a brief encounter with the dystopian future; this encounter clarifies the contingency of Mattapoisett, the extent to which it depends on her to come into being. Luciente tells Connie, "the past is a disputed area" (267), and Connie decides that "she was enlisted" in "Luciente's war" (301). Consciousness raising thus not only enables Connie radically to re-think her role in the mental-health system, but also to take action. Connie understands—even if the system does not, as Piercy makes clear in the documents from Connie's file which she appends to the novel—that her actions are political, and only this understanding makes her actions possible.

The Female Man both depicts CR in its characters and transacts it with its readers. In Russ's novel, the J's who live in 1969, Joanna and Jeannine, must balance out the alternative futures represented by Janet and Jael. Joanna casts her lot with Janet and becomes a lesbian; Jeannine casts her lot with Jael and opens up her world to the Womanlander bases. Each of these characters has her consciousness raised by one of the characters from the two futures. At the same time, though, an important argument in *The Female Man* is that all four Js represent fragments of the female self, that all four must be brought together and allowed to exist in all their contradictions and "contrarieties." Only by recognizing the contradictory elements that make up the female self, and the contradictory conditions under which women live, is it possible to imagine the day when "we will all be free" (213). Russ ends her novel with that promise—its last line is, "on that day, we will all be free." Our freedom in Russ's novel depends on both Janet and Jael—on both imagining the utopian future and committing ourselves to the struggle to bring it about. Our freedom depends as well on accepting the duality that Joanna and Jeannine represent—on balancing Joanna's fantasies of power with Jeannine's fantasies of romance and powerlessness. The Js raise each other's consciousnesses in the novel, and this leads them to action; they also raise our consciousness as readers, enabling us to envision women's freedom.[19]

Fairbairns's *Benefits* is a dystopian novel with a utopian promise at the end; it, too, like *Woman on the Edge of Time* and *The Female Man*, makes its imagined future contingent on present actions. Fairbairns depicts the rise in Great Britain of a Moral-Majority-style, radical right-wing, political movement called FAMILY. FAMILY enlists the support of (some) feminists through its campaign to pay "benefit"—a wage based on the number of children—to all mothers. Once FAMILY's benefit policy is in place, FAMILY increases its power until, acting in concert with a world wide neo-facist right, it introduces contraceptives into the water supply in order to control the fertility of Great Britain. To receive the antidote, women must pass racial, genetic, and ideological tests. Fairbairns emphasizes FAMILY's racism and the relationship between population policies and genocide; like Piercy's utopian novel, Fairbairns's dystopian novel pays significant attention to race. When the combination of the contraceptive, the antidote, and the pollutants already in the water turns out to cause massive damage to the babies born to women who passed FAMILY's tests, the government falls, FAMILY falls apart, and the few feminists left in Britain after years of persecution step forward to insist on radical change. At the end of the novel, feminists are in a position to dictate terms—the only terms under which women in Britain will ever again decide to reproduce.[20]

Fairbairns's novel inserts itself into critical political debates about the possibility of making alliances with the right: such alliances (as some U.S. feminists made in order to outlaw pornography[21]) will ultimately lead to the right's control and suppression of feminism—to re-education camps for feminists in *Benefits*. The novel also warns of the danger that the feminist debate over wages for housework—an important debate in British feminism—could easily be co-opted by the right and turned into government control of women's reproduction and thus women's lives.

The utopian promise at the end of the novel—that British women "are going to be the first to find a style of life that isn't determined by men having power over us because we have children" (213)—is only a possibility; the political meetings for Women's Day are chaotic CR groups, not yet ready to face the government with lists of demands. Our faith in that utopian promise in fact depends on our faith in CR as an organizing and strategic tool for making political change. Different readers—and different feminist readers—will see the ending differently, depending on their view of the political efficacy of consciousness raising, a political efficacy that was hotly debated in the early 1970s, as I discuss in Chapter Two.

All three of these post-apocalyptic utopian/dystopian novels emphasize the contingency of the future. Piercy's Mattapoisett depends on Connie's realizing that, as Bee tells her,

> There's always a thing you can deny an oppressor, if only your allegiance. Your belief. Your co-oping. Often with vastly unequal power, you can find or force an opening to fight back. In your time many without power found ways to fight. (328)

The revolution that brings Mattapoisett into being depends on "the people," Connie is told—on "all the people who changed how people bought food, raised children, went to school," and who "made new unions, withheld rent, refused to go to wars, wrote and educated and made speeches" (198). Russ's Whileaway may or may not depend on the Womanlanders' ultimate victory over the Manlanders, but clearly the day when "we will be free" depends on feminism's ability to make itself obsolete—on work done to make Joanna's anger, Jeannine's romanticism, Janet's strangeness, and Jael's violence "quaint and old-fashioned" (213). The utopian promise at the end of *Benefits* depends on feminism's ability to ride out periods of extreme reaction, and on feminists' refusing to make common cause with the radical right, no matter what the temptation. All of these utopias depend on individual and collective acts, on consciousness raising and action. The future in these novels is not extra-terrestrial, as in the gender-system discovery novels that show us a gender equality somewhere radically other than here. Nor is the future in these novels accidental, as in the eco-fantasy novels that depict small pockets of utopia created in the fringes of major ecological disasters. These are *made* futures, and the novelists emphasize how these futures are being made right now, in the present moment. The contingent utopias and dystopias, more clearly than any other category of the science fiction CR novel, make explicit their political agendas.

The made future is not limited to science-fiction versions of the CR novel. Both science-fiction and realist CR novels rely on three strategies of futurity to represent social change: the figures of daughters, multiple characters, and historical mothers. Daughters and historical mothers represent change over time, the movement toward a future or the movement away from a past. CR novels vary in how deliberate these changes are, how much they are products of planning and agency, and how much they are historical changes beyond the reach of specific political movements. Using multiple or parallel characters represents a range of alternatives, successful or not, toward some forms of liberation for women. This strategy tends to emphasize individual agency, individual life-choices, though in some cases (most notably, in *The Female Man*), it may also hinge upon historical accident.

The daughter device is central to Connie's process of CR in *Woman on the Edge of Time*. Connie repeatedly sees her daughter Angelina as a "small dose of herself" (61), and comes to understand that she is better off in significant ways in the utopian alternative future. Tom Moylan argues in *Demand the Impossible* that it is Luciente, Connie's double, "the person she could be in a better social structure" (205), who makes Connie's change possible, but he minimizes Connie's moment of assent to the future, which centers on Angelina. Connie sees Luciente's daughter, Dawn, while she is touring the children's house in Mattapoisett. Dawn looks like Angelina, like "any brown-skinned girl child of seven or so with golden-brown eyes" (141). "Suddenly," Piercy writes,

she assented with all her soul to Angelina in Mattapoisett, to Angelina hidden forever one hundred fifty years into the future, even if she should never see her again. For the first time her heart assented to Luciente, to Bee, to Magdalena. Yes you can have my child, you can keep my child. . . . She will be strong there, well fed, well housed, well taught, she will grow up much better and stronger and smarter than I. I assent. . . . She will never be broken as I was. She will be strange, but she will be glad and strong and she will not be afraid. She will have enough. She will have pride. She will love her own brown skin and be loved for her strength and her good work. She will walk in strength like a man and never sell her body and she will nurse her babies like a woman and live in love like a garden, like that children's house of many colors. (141)

Many of the people in Mattapoisett are doubles of people Connie knows; seeing these doubles helps her sharpen her critique of the present. But Dawn is the most important first double, and Connie must assent to this possible future, to Angelina in Mattapoisett, before she can enlist in the fight to make it possible.

Daughters in CR novels always represent the future; they provide the protagonists with one way of thinking into possible futures, and the daughter device is an authorial strategy for writing beyond the ending, in DuPlessis's terms. In *Benefits* the feminist protagonist's daughter joins FAMILY, but cannot pass the tests to receive the antidote. She then reconciles with her mother in order to have access to the underground feminist network so that she can have a baby. Jane's joining FAMILY is her way of rebelling against her mother, but the political situation effects a reconciliation between mother and daughter, just as it leads later in the novel to a new unity among women. At the end of the novel, Jane represents an ambiguous future; she is "one of the lucky ones, being the mother of one of the youngest and healthiest babies in Britain" (201), but how she will fit into the novel's utopian possibility is unclear, for she already has a baby and thus cannot exercise blackmail against the state. Fairbairns asks us to consider what possibilities feminism can create for women who have babies: this is the futurity, the debate beyond the ending, that Jane represents.[22]

Weldon's *Down Among the Women* (1971) combines the daughter device with the use of multiple characters. Weldon's novel traces the lives of several different women to show a range of women's problems and their attempts at solutions; the final alternative, the one that structures the novel's ending, is the daughter device. Byzantia, daughter of one of the major characters, explains at the novel's end that she is simply not interested in the older generation's "trivial" way of "seeing success in terms of men" (233). Byzantia identifies this way of measuring success as symptomatic "of a fearful disease from which you all suffered. One of you even died on the way. I think the mortality rate is too high" (233). Jocelyn, who overhears this conversation, understands that Byzantia's disease metaphor represents the end of the "old order" of relations between women and men; she and the novel conclude, "We are the last of the women" (234). The daughter figure in *Down Among the Women,* and in other novels as well, stands for the problem of representing substantive social change. Byzantia assures readers that women will be—even are— different from the generation of women whose stories are presented as cautionary tales. While the writers may not detail ways they are or will be different, feminist readers who believe in the transformative power of consciousness raising assent to the daughters' difference from their mothers: we take it on faith, precisely to the extent that we believe we differ from our own mothers, or our daughters differ from us.

The daughter device in the CR novel can be read to represent a fundamental tension in feminism itself, one that Ann Snitow historicizes in "Feminism and Motherhood: An American Reading." Snitow draws a three-stage timeline of feminist work in the United States on motherhood, locating the critiques of motherhood between 1962 and 1974, the major work on motherhood as institution between 1975 and 1979, and the emergence of pro-natalist feminism around 1979. A feminism based in a logic that grants authority to women specifically as mothers—such as Gilman's in *Herland,* for instance, or as the daughter device may be seen implicitly to deploy—may have fundamentally conservative overtones, as Snitow points out. At the same time, the daughter device and the political weight it carries is crucial to the CR novel, precisely because of the realist novel's relationship to individualism and its difficulty in representing social change without enlisting the familial. That even science fiction CR novels used this device suggests its indispensability to feminists, and the centrality of the tensions between feminism and maternalism more generally.

Rather than daughters, *The Female Man* uses a different device to pose alternatives—multiple or parallel characters. Russ posits each of the four "Js" as versions of each other—Joanna, Jeannine, Janet, and the assassin Jael are the same woman in parallel universes, the same "genotype, modified by age, by circumstances, by education, by diet, by learning, by God knows what" (161). Historical accident makes these women very different from each other. They are also versions of the authorial voice's self, as Russ makes clear at the end of the novel. Joanna lives in the possible universe that her readers inhabit, "our" 1969; Jeannine in a universe shaped by Hitler's death in 1936, in which World War II never happened and the Depression is still going on; Janet in Whileaway, a future possible universe in which all the men on Earth were killed in a plague some nine hundred years before; and Jael in a universe she identifies as having led to Janet's, in which the men were killed not by a plague but by a war between the women and the men, a war Jael is fighting.

Each of the Js represents a different attitude toward feminism, created in the different ways each of their universes plays out the war between women and men. Both Joanna and Jeannine have their consciousnesses raised in the novel. Joanna is the female man of the title, a woman who tires of pleading with men to "*Let me in, Love me, Approve me, Define me, Regulate me, Validate me, Support me,*" and decides instead that her attitude toward men will be "*Move over*" (140; emphasis original). The party games in Joanna's universe define the relations between the sexes: "His Little Girl" and "I Must Impress This Woman," for example, are games exhibiting men's "dominance behavior" (93–94). Joanna's feminism has the style of some kinds of radical feminisms of the late sixties and early seventies—vulgar, threatening, and angry. Janet is her mentor, and Joanna becomes a lesbian. In the "other" 1969, Jeannine loves her cat, watches the tree outside her window for hours, dreams endlessly of romance and marriage, and hates being called "Jeannie." In her universe, romance rules the relations between the sexes. Jael's murder of the Manlander startles Jeannine out of her romantic fantasies. The possibility of vengeance that Jael represents radically changes Jeannine's life: she is "out on the town on a Saturday afternoon saying goodbye, goodbye, goodbye to all that" (209), a clear reference to Robin Morgan's essay ("Goodbye to All That" [1970]) that links Jeannine as well to the discourse of feminism in the 1970s. Jeannine is the first to permit Jael to use her world as a base for the war, and is "surprised" that any of the Js "could hesitate to do business with Womanland" (211).

Living in the utopian, woman-only future, Janet simply cannot understand what all the fuss is about. Janet won't play the party games she finds in Joanna's world, and takes the teenage Laura Rose as her lover (a double of the "Laur" who becomes Joanna's lover). Janet refuses Jael's request to use Whileaway as a base, and also refuses to believe Jael's story that the plague was actually a war. At the end of the novel, the authorial voice tells us that Janet is "in secret our savior from utter despair, who appears . . . in our dreams" (213). Russ here suggests that the found woman-only utopian future Janet represents, however important and necessary a vision, is not possible—is "a blessedness none of us will ever know" (213). Jael is no less impossible as an alternative than Janet, though she too represents an important and empowering vision. Russ's Js represent the contradictory identities, inspirations, and aspirations that make up "Everywoman" (212), a range of women we could be in extremely different universes, a range of women whose potential exists in us regardless.

The alternate-universe convention of science fiction enables Russ to play out the dividedness of feminist consciousness in an extraordinarily vivid way by dividing up "Everywoman" into the Js; the device of time traveling enables Piercy to populate her utopian future with doubles of Connie, her daughter, and her lovers, to demonstrate how they are oppressed and thwarted by the social conditions of the present. Realist writers also use the device of multiple or parallel characters to illustrate a range of women's options in the present. In *The Women's Room*, for example, French's Mira has her circle of friends, whose stories she tells. "I sometimes think I have swallowed every woman I ever knew," French writes, and suggests that telling the stories will "help me understand how they ended as they did, how I ended here feeling engulfed and isolated at the same time" (18). French suggests here that all the stories together contribute to each one—that, by extension, any woman's story can only be told in a context of the range of possibilities available to her. Mary Gordon's *Final Payments* (1974) uses this device in a more limited way, just as her novel makes far more limited claims to representativeness in general. Gordon focuses on Isabel's friendships with Liz and Eleanor, who represent to Isabel the things she has missed while providing care for her invalid father. Liz and Eleanor do not stand for women's lives in any broad sense—they do not represent all, or even a very wide range of, women. But they do represent other possibilities for

Isabel. The multiple-character device works differently in realist and science fiction novels: realist novels use the multiple-character device to demonstrate the range of the presently possible, where science fiction novels use the same device to demonstrate the range of alternatives that are *not*—or *not yet*—possible.

In a 1974 essay, Agate Nesaule Krouse identified the use of "paired or multiple complementary characters" as a characteristic of literary feminism (287–88). E. M. Broner uses the multiple character device in *A Weave of Women* (1978), and both multiple characters and the daughter device in *Her Mothers* (1975).[23] In *Her Mothers*, the multiple characters are the narrator's imagined mothers—and these mothers include historical, biological, and mythical mothers, as well as mothering friends. Beatrix, the protagonist, searches the lives and works of Margaret Fuller, Louisa May Alcott, Emily Dickinson, and Charlotte Forten, initially to compile an anthology called *Unafraid Women*, but also to find "her inheritance" from each (103). Broner tells stories about these historical mothers and alternates them with stories about Beatrix's childhood friends, her family, her missing daughter, and her research for the book. Beatrix is herself one of the multiple mothers, since a major theme in the novel is her search for her daughter Lena, but she is also a daughter of these multiple mothers, learning from their examples what an unafraid woman might be. The novel ends with Beatrix and Lena reunited, and with Beatrix's understanding that Lena is that unafraid woman. Broner argues that "It is the final generosity to embrace one's mother" (116), a generosity that, by the end of the novel, both Beatrix and Lena share.

Historical mothers are important in the consciousness-raising novel, as they are throughout feminist literary works more generally. Historical mothers represent, in some instances, a heroic past to which the protagonist aspires, those "unafraid women" who achieved some victory within the system of male dominance. In Shulman's *Burning Questions*, the novel-within-a-novel called *My Life as a Rebel* begins by invoking "all the other brave, single-minded women who devoted their lives to the revolution" ("Preface" 7). Zane IndiAnna, the author of this *Life*, argues that "No matter how far short of their achievements mine may fall, our lives are intimately connected by history" because "for one glorious moment some of us did manage to find each other and launch our rebellion" (9). "The revolution" to which Zane's historical mothers devoted their lives is the Russian Revolution; "our" rebellion, as Zane's autobiography goes on to make clear, is Women's Liberation. Linking her struggle to her historical mothers' struggles, as I've pointed out, gives Zane an empowering sense of her own historical agency.

In other novels, the historical mother device represents the damage done to women by a system of male dominance. Erica Jong's Isadora, for example, searches the lives and works of women writers and artists, the women she admires most, and cannot find role models:

Emily Dickinson, the Brontes, Virginia Woolf, Carson McCullers . . . Flannery O'Connor raising peacocks and living with her mother. Sylvia Plath sticking her head into an oven of myth. Georgia O'Keefe alone in the desert, apparently a survivor. What a group! Severe, suicidal, strange. (*Fear* 101)

Isadora is searching for a particular kind of role model—"the female Chaucer"—a woman writer able to combine "juice and joy and love and talent too" (110). Isadora wants proof that women artists need not be "spinsters or suicides," but she cannot find it. By the end of the novel, Isadora has changed her criteria: survival is still paramount, but her new understanding of what survival means leads to her willingness to take on spinsterhood if her marriage cannot be reworked. Isadora comes to assert her similarity to rather than her difference from her historical literary mothers. Her willingness to embrace singleness shifts the terrain of her analysis of these earlier writers—their being "severe, suicidal, strange" is no longer a matter of their personal, individual failings, and Isadora cannot find an individual solution to the problems they faced. Instead, Isadora discovers that she must engage in a personal struggle with her husband to re-make their marriage; this personal struggle very clearly has political dimensions since it involves power relations, and since it is connected to a larger struggle to re-make an institution.

In their strategies of futurity, both the science-fiction and the realist consciousness-raising novels attempted to resist the limitations of the individual solution. Despite the feminist-critical privileging of "personalized polemic" which would emphasize "the private or psychic effects of discrimination," in Cheri Register's terms (23), or the popular press' insistence that "the better novels" would focus on internalized oppression ("the heroine herself" as "the principal enemy," as Peter Prescott put it, reviewing Atwood's *Lady Oracle*), women and feminist writers in the decade were deeply concerned with ways of representing (at least the potential for) the reverberations of individual changes in consciousness beyond the individual. The CR novels play out the tensions between the demand for authenticity and realism and the competing need for strategies of futurity. These tensions demonstrate the CR novel's contradictory nature, based in the contradictions of CR itself, as the novel is caught between the competing imperatives of "negation" and "alternative possibilities," to return to Donovan's terms.

The realist CR novels, which cannot show us their imagined political futures, bring their strategies of futurity to rest on nothing less than faith: a faith in a notion of (political) feminist progress that the novels ground specifically in (personal) generational change—in our difference from our mothers, our mothers' difference from their mothers, our daughters' difference from us. Such a faith in "our" generational difference relies upon the Women's Liberation Movement's overwhelming sense of its uniqueness and urgency. Even the historical-mother device, which ought logically to cross-cut that sense of historical newness, worked to suggest instead that the women protagonists had remarkably new opportunities to make changes that earlier generations of women could not—to be "unafraid women" able to link daughters with the past, to create a rebellion that could last beyond a revolution, to be women poets without committing suicide.

The impact of individual acts, an individual's ability to change the course of history, has long been a convention of science fiction. Feminist science fiction in the decade used that convention to trace out fantasies of individual and collective women's power and to create alternative visions of social and sexual organization. And yet, even the post-apocalyptic utopian/dystopian novels, the most overtly "political" of my categories of feminist science fiction, personalized those strategies of futurity in their use of the daughter device; this strategy worked to bring the revolution home in a very intimate way, and to remind us that the relationship between the personal and the political moved both directions.

Both realist and science-fiction CR novels struggled toward futurity, struggled toward imagining futures the women's movement could or should create. However much some feminist theorists argued that patriarchy was a "closed system based on [women's] powerlessness" (A. Dworkin 33), the novelists worked to imagine openings in that system—or, at the very least, they ended their novels on the brink of such openings, suspending both the system's and the novel's closure. Whether the novels detailed the practices that would lead to their visions of futurity or not, then, they took seriously the double imperative of feminist fiction, of feminist criticism, of CR itself: the imperative both to critique patriarchy and to begin to imagine its alternatives.

Notes

1. The epigraph comes from *The Left Hand of Darkness*; in "Is Gender Necessary?" Le Guin notes that this sentence was in some sense generative of the novel (163).
2. Tompkins's important chapter on *Uncle Tom's Cabin* in *Sensational Designs* establishes ways that such a model of social change is associated with women;

the critical mass model, I suggest, is a twentieth-century version of this earlier "sentimental" model. I am indebted to my students in Feminist Theory for helping me to work out this argument.

3. See, e.g., Russ's discussion of SF as "what if?" literature in "Images of Women in Science Fiction." Marleen S. Barr, among many contemporary critics of feminist SF, takes up this question in *Feminist Fabulations: Space/Postmodernism/ Fiction* (1992).

4. Importantly, the distinction between "soft" and "hard" CR that I draw in Chapter Two affects the *answer* to the "what if" question, and not the question itself.

5. One novel this schema cannot account for is Ursula K. Le Guin's *The Dispossessed*, which has elements of all three types. *The Dispossessed* is an important novel in utopian fiction in the seventies, as Tom Moylan points out in his chapter on it in *Demand the Impossible* (91–92). Although Le Guin's novel helped establish the questions and concerns of feminist (and other oppositional) utopian fiction, she addresses these questions in strikingly different ways from other feminist writers. See Moylan's chapter for a discussion of political critiques of the novel, especially Samuel R. Delany's (91–120).

6. I am deliberately avoiding the term "liberal feminism" here because of its limited explanatory power. "Reformist" is the more accurate term in this specific context.

7. I discuss this position and its use of the sex/race analogy in Chapter Six, particularly as exemplified in Shulamith Firestone's *The Dialectic of Sex* (1970), where I identify it as a feminist domino theory of oppressions.

8. It may also be the case that science fiction visions of the radical elimination of gender anticipate contemporary queer theoretical and political emphases on gender transgression. On one hand, the radicality of gender-bending as transgression depends on a sex-gender system that is 'commonsensical'; on the other, how better to interrogate its status as commonsensical than imagine its elimination? A good example of contemporary queer theory is Eve Kosofsky Sedgwick's "Queer and Now."

9. An example of a more recent extra-terrestrial gender-system discovery novel is Joan Slonczewski's *Door into Ocean* (1987), which also bears an interesting relation to *The Dispossessed* in its contrast of two planets, the utopian and dystopian.

10. In "Antifeminism," Andrea Dworkin makes this argument in examining a range of what she calls woman-superior models of antifeminism: "Being good or moral is viewed as a particular biological capacity of women and as a result women are the natural guardians of morality: a moral vanguard as it were. . . . Motherhood is especially invoked as biological proof that women have a special relationship to life, a special sensitivity to its meaning, a special, intuitive knowledge of what is right" (14).

11. It is difficult while reading Herland not to think of Louise Bogan's opening line in the poem "Women": "Women have no wilderness in them," for the Herlanders fit this description exactly. The Herlanders are not, however, the frustrated, isolated women of the rest of the poem, "Content in the tight hot cell of their hearts / To eat dusty bread" (19).

12. Mary Daly records her conversations with animals in *Gyn/Ecology* as well (466 n. 47); eco-feminism is a central value for the type of lesbian feminism that both Daly's and Gearhart's work exemplifies.

13. For a reading of *Woman and Nature* as an epic poem, see Ostriker, *Stealing*

the Language, 228–32; for a critique of organic sisterhood, see Haraway, "Manifesto for Cyborgs," 216. Griffin's art metaphors here are, of course, similar to the novelization of CR that I discuss in Chapter Two.

14. This is King's reading of the "lesbian continuum" in Adrienne Rich's "Compulsory Heterosexuality and Lesbian Existence," which, by asserting that all women are lesbians, attempts magically to do away with homophobia. See *Theory in Its Feminist Travels*, 135.

15. Both *The Wanderground* and *Woman on the Edge of Time*, for example, devote considerable attention to showing how "process" works in their imagined futures; Gearhart depicts telepathic meetings among the Hill Women, and Piercy the "shaping controversy" over what kinds of interventions in nature her utopian society will make.

16. We can see this understanding in a number of feminist-critical essays of the decade, as the later version of Ellen Morgan's "Humanbecoming: Form and Focus in the Neo-Feminist Novel" evidences. Morgan suggests of novels like *The Female Man* that "The fantasy is still the only forum for the depiction of women successfully breaching all the barriers of sexual caste, and it serves the important function of taking the reader where neither the realistic novel nor the real woman has yet been able to go. It expands our store of images of what is possible" (Brown and Olson 277).

17. Margaret Atwood's *The Handmaid's Tale* (1986) is a later example of this category of feminist SF; twenty years after *Walk to the End of the World*, Charnas finished the trilogy with *The Furies* (1994). There is an interesting essay to be written on the varieties of feminisms and the debates between them that Charnas's trilogy encompasses, which is unfortunately beyond my scope here.

18. I discuss the role of protagonists' submission to psychiatry in Chapter Two, comparing *Woman on the Edge of Time* to *Ella Price's Journal*.

19. In "Manifesto for Cyborgs," Haraway argues that *The Female Man* is not a utopian novel, a reading of the novel in a context of more recent SF and other "cyborg" works by women, and especially by women writers of color (220). In that context, Haraway's argument seems right to me; just as compelling, though, are a number of analyses that treat the novel as utopian. Rather than performing an extended analysis of Whileaway to "decide" its utopianness, let me suggest here that critical readings of the novel, including my own, that have identified it as utopian have done so because it fits so nicely with the more clearly utopian and dystopian novels of the 1970s, and because Russ uses recognizably utopian strategies.

20. To see the difference a feminist critique of these issues makes, compare *Benefits* with John Shirley's *A Song Called Youth* trilogy (*Eclipse, Eclipse Penumbra*, and *Eclipse Corona*) in which the primary way that the neo-fascist right carries out its genocidal policies is by killing people of color; only in one minor instance in the entire trilogy does Shirley posit reproductive control as part of the right's program. While Shirley does identify fundamentalist Christianity as a significant avenue to power for the right, he minimizes the importance of its ideas about gender, the family, and reproductive rights. Billed as "the ultimate cyberpunk saga," Shirley's work demonstrates the political limitations of cyberpunk itself as an overwhelmingly male-dominated literary movement. For a different political critique of cyberpunk's sexism, see Nicola Nixon, "Cyberpunk: Preparing the Ground for Revolution or Keeping the Boys Satisfied?"; and Andrew Ross, "Cyberpunk in Boystown."

21. On the historical alliance of anti-porn feminists with the Right, see, among

others, Gayle Rubin, "Thinking Sex: Notes for a Radical Theory of the Politics of Sexuality" (1984). For a poststructuralist reading that sees such an alliance as "discursive," see Judith Butler, "The Force of Fantasy: Feminism, Mapplethorpe, and Discursive Excess"; and Teresa de Lauretis's critique in *The Practice of Love: Lesbian Sexuality and Perverse Desire* 143–48.

22. Clearly, Praxis's murdering Mary's baby in Fay Weldon's *Praxis* also engages this argument about women, feminism, and reproduction.

23. For a reading of *A Weave of Women* in relation to issues of Jewish feminism in the decade, see Leslie Brody.

Chapter Six
The Sex/Race Analogy

"What Chou Mean *WE*, White Girl?"
—Lorraine Bethel[1]

The first wave of feminism in the United States was shaped by the analogy feminists drew between the situation of women and the situation of slaves, as exemplifed by the title of Elizabeth Cady Stanton's 1860 address to the New York State Legislature, "A Slave's Appeal." Historians such as Blanche Glassman Hersh have recognized the centrality of the woman/slave analogy (Hersh's book is called *The Slavery of Sex*) and of feminists' experiences in the abolitionist movement to their politics and rhetoric. Second-wave feminism was shaped just as profoundly by the sex/race analogy, and by the Movement's grounding in the Civil Rights Movement. Though the sex/race analogy in second wave feminism has been attacked, and some would argue discarded, it was a foundational rhetorical strategy for the emergent Women's Liberation Movement, and it continues to be used in feminist theory.

Jane Gallop provides a shorthand version and a typical account of the importance of the sex/race analogy to literary feminism in *Around 1981: Academic Feminist Literary Theory*. She takes particular note of the section subtitled "Invisible Women" in Susan Koppelman Cornillon's 1972 anthology, *Images of Women in Fiction: Feminist Perspectives*. Arguing that "In 1972, white feminist critics blithely propose to join black men, offering 'the invisible woman' as counterpart to 'the invisible man'" (93), Gallop suggests that "the analogy fulfills a wish" (91): the wish to analogize into being a feminist movement like the Civil Rights movement, the wish to analogize into being a feminist writing that is like Ellison's in, what Cheri Register called in 1975, *Invisible Man*'s appeal "to common multi-racial feelings of insignificance and alienation" (23). Gallop notes as well that, "thanks to the impact of black feminist writing, we now know to ask what place that gesture leaves for the black woman," citing such important black feminist works as bell hooks's *Ain't I a Woman?* and the anthology titled *All the Women Are White, All the Blacks Are Men, But Some of Us Are Brave: Black Women's Studies*, both published in 1982 (93). This shorthand version typifies white feminists' dismissals of the analogy: it marks the "bad old days" before black women taught "us" better. Such a dismissal cannot, however, account for the power of that analogy, nor for its historical origins and importance.[2]

The sex/race analogy of the Women's Liberation Movement of the 1970s cannot be dismissed so simply as white women's racism; that is only one of its meanings. However flawed as an analysis of sex, race, and the relations between them, not least because of its erasure of women of color, the sex/race analogy was nonetheless a founding rhetoric of second-wave feminism: it permeated every kind of Movement writing and analysis, from outlines for consciousness raising, to theoretical works, to literary criticism, to poetry and fiction—permeating tactics, analyses, scholarship, and literature.[3] It was, as Florynce Kennedy argued in her essay in *Sisterhood Is Powerful*, "too perfect to ignore," even for some black women (493).[4] To dismiss the analogy is to oversimplify the tasks, of both internal and external legitimation in particular, that feminists understood themselves to be undertaking in the late 1960s and 1970s, and to refuse to see the ways the analogy continues to function in contemporary feminist theory.

Lisa M. Walker's 1993 essay, "How to Recognize a Lesbian: The Cultural Politics of Looking Like What You Are," focuses on the femme lesbian as the blind spot in contemporary feminist theories, raising crucial questions about the privileging of the visible, and of "how discourses about race and gender/sexuality coalesce and what they reveal/conceal about each other" (878). Walker works with what she names "the visibility/invisibility trope," which she discusses in a lengthy footnote addressing problems with it suggested to her by readers. Walker's analysis of "privileging the visible" in works by white feminist theorists demonstrates the continuing importance, indeed, the inescapability, of the sex/race analogy for feminist theory. In this chapter, I trace out a particular history of that analogy, focusing on its emergence as a crucial legitimating rhetorical strategy for feminists in the 1970s, and tracing as well a literary critical/historical aspect of its use in feminist fictional re-visionings of Ralph Ellison's *Invisible Man*. I conclude by returning to a speculative account of how the analogy continues to function in feminist theory.

One way of understanding the historical force of the analogy in the 1970s is to see it as a crucial way that feminists familiarized the radical newness of their task. Susan Koppelman Cornillon's introduction to *Images of Women in Fiction*, to take up Gallop's example again, refers to "new courses," "new perspectives," "new forms of analysis growing out of new consciousness," "new directions for women in reading and understanding fiction," "new directions and depths for women in their personal paths," the "newest insistence" by women on equality, and a "new scholarship fund for women" established with the proceeds from the volume—all these usages of "new" appear in four-and-a-half pages (ix–xiii). The substitution of "the invisible woman" for "invisible man" in this volume that Gallop notes crosscuts the introduction's catalogs of newness and of beginnings (six usages), anchors readers in a more familiar mode of political thinking, a comfortable and respectable metaphor for oppression. The Women's Liberation Movement of the 1970s—in its academic and literary forms as well as in its political forms—was fundamentally shaped by precisely this tension between the radically new and the respectably analogized, or, to shift the terms somewhat, between the speculative, utopian, or fantastic and the historical.

Another important way to understand the analogy is to locate its emergence in Women's Liberation's declaration of independence as a political movement. The sex/race analogy appears as early as 1964, in Casey Hayden and Mary King's "SNCC Position Paper (Women in the Movement)," and became increasingly prevalent as Women's Liberation developed into its own political movement.[5] Alice Echols lays out the political context from which Women's Liberation emerged in the late sixties: both the Civil Rights Movement and the New Left shifted their focuses to emphasize "organizing on behalf of one's own group" (37). This strategy would become the core principle of Women's Liberation; in the late 1960s, however, it worked to marginalize white women in both these movements. In the Civil Rights Movement, as black power superseded an earlier emphasis on integration, white activists left the movement, were purged from it, and/or felt themselves increasingly peripheral to it. At the same time, Students for a Democratic Society (SDS) began to focus on draft resistance and campus organizing. The rise of the Black Panthers and of Weathermen, with their rejections of non-violence and abandonment of the ideals of "beloved community," alienated many black and white women who had been active workers for Civil Rights and against the war in Vietnam. The SDS's move toward draft resistance in particular marginalized women activists by allowing them only a supporting role on behalf of men (Echols 36–38).

When Left women began to organize on their own behalf within Left organizations, they encountered real hostility toward their liberation. At one demonstration in 1969, for example, men in the audience began shouting "Take it off!" and "Take her off the stage and fuck her!" at the women speakers (Echols 117; D'Emilio and Freedman 311). At the June 1969 SDS convention, factional infighting erupted over a resolution about women's liberation. One speaker referred to "pussy power," another to Stokely Carmichael's famous pronouncement about women's position in the movement ("prone"). While it became clear from the audience's heckling that "this sort of undisguised and public contempt for women's liberation was no longer acceptable in SDS circles," the resolution affirming women's liberation as a revolutionary task was nonetheless defeated, and feminist activists "discerned that the SDS's interest in women's liberation was primarily opportunistic" (Echols 124). While Marge Piercy argued in "The Grand Coolie Damn" (1969) that "Any attempts to persuade men that we are serious are a waste of precious time and energy" since "they are not our constituency" (R. Morgan 492), feminists continued through the early part of the 1970s to try to do precisely that. The sex/race analogy was the most important strategy for convincing men—and Leftist men in particular—of the importance of the Women's Liberation Movement.[6] Given the hostility toward Women's Liberation on the Left, feminists' practice of enlisting black liberation movements to legitimize their own was a crucial rhetorical strategy.

The analogy operated inside the emergent Movement as well—it was at least as important to address that analogy to white women as to men. Piercy's essay, for instance, appeared in *Sisterhood is Powerful,* a book clearly directed to a female readership. In it, she refers to herself repeatedly as a "house nigger" in the Left, an oppressed person with just enough privileges to prevent her from seeing the depth of her oppression. In "The Grand Coolie Damn," the sex/race analogy functions specifically to bridge the theoretical and political divide between "politicos" and "feminists"—between "politicos" coming out of the New Left, who argued that women's oppression was based in capitalism, and "feminists" coming out of the Civil Rights Movement, who argued that women's oppression was based in male supremacy, as Echols identifies the distinction (51–53). Piercy's painstaking analysis of how the Left operates in precisely the same way as capitalism claims for women the status of exploited worker, and demonstrates to "politicos" the importance of Women's Liberation.[7] Cross-cutting this analysis, the sex/race analogy claims for sexism (male supremacy, male chauvinism, and male liberalism, in Piercy's three-part formulation) the ideological power of racism, and opens her primarily politico-style analysis to "feminists." In bridging the disjunction between "politico" and "feminist" analyses of women's oppression, the sex/race analogy plays an important role in Piercy's appeal to sisterhood—a two-fold appeal based first in the pain of the absence of sisterhood ("how separated from my sisters I have been") and second in the future vision of a Movement of sisters ("for the next few years it would be healthiest for us to work as if we were essentially all the Movement there is") (R. Morgan 490, 492). Piercy's move to bridge the different analyses thus stands as a gesture to bring together both groups of women, in a utopian vision of sisterhood that would be the Movement.

The sex/race analogy has its limits, however, in Piercy's rhetorical strategies of futurity for the Movement. On one hand, the analogy solidifies the need for a movement, as Piercy argues that "We are oppressed, and we will achieve our liberation by fighting for it the same way as any other oppressed group" (R. Morgan 482). On the other hand, as Piercy argues, "Nowhere on earth are women free now, although in some places things are marginally better. What we want we will have to invent ourselves," suggesting that no movements for social change, including movements for black liberation, can provide an adequate model for a post-patriarchal world (R. Morgan 491). In Piercy's essay, then, the analogy exists in tension with its failure, its familiarity crosscut by the radical newness of Women's Liberation, just as it does in Susan Koppelman Cornillon's introduction to *Images of Women in Fiction.*

Redstockings Manifesto, also included in *Sisterhood is Powerful,* is another useful example of how the sex/race analogy functions in feminist theory in the 1970s, and how that theory is, at base, fantastic and utopian. The Manifesto argues: "We identify with all women. We define our best interest as that of the poorest, most brutally exploited woman" (R. Morgan 600). At the heart of this argument is a fantasy of that woman built out of the belief that "our" experience of sexism enables "us" to understand "her" experience of racism. Redstockings' analysis, like much radical feminist analysis in the 1970s, uses the analogy and then back-constructs it: "Male supremacy is the oldest, most basic form of domination. All other forms of exploitation and oppression (racism, capitalism, imperialism, etc.) are extensions of male supremacy: men dominate women, a few men dominate the rest"; sex is like race because sexism created racism (R. Morgan 599). Logically, this political analysis leads them to assert: "We repudiate all economic, racial, educational or status privileges that divide us from other women" (R. Morgan 600). Echols sees this position as suggesting "that a multi-class and multi-racial movement could be achieved if white, middle-class women would simply renounce their privileges and altruistically identify with women who were less privileged than they." Echols adds, "It was a nice fantasy, but . . . it did not materialize" (145).[8]

Shulamith Firestone's *The Dialectic of Sex* (1970) is perhaps the clearest example of combining the sex/race analogy with the speculative utopian/fantastic elements of feminist theory. Her chapter on race, "Racism: The Sexism of the Family of Man," argues that "*racism is a sexual phenomenon*" and "*racism is sexism extended*" (122; emphasis original). Firestone asserts that race relations in America are "a macrocosm of the hierarchical relations within the nuclear family," with the white man as father, white woman as mother, and black man and woman as son and daughter, which enables her to apply the revised Oedipal narrative from her chapter on "Freudianism" to construct relational psychodramas of envy, identification, and hatred (122). The problems with this analysis are obvious. Because of the white woman's position in what Firestone names the "sex/race system," her racism can only be "inauthentic" and "hysterical" because it is based in an "illusion of power" that she does not possess (132, 124).[9] While Firestone criticizes Eldridge Cleaver's *Soul on Ice* for having "no conception of the black woman as a human being in her own right" (138), black women fare little better in her analysis; the very few black women she quotes are cited to exemplify black women's mystified acceptance of the machismo of Black Power politics. Racism in *The Dialectic of Sex* becomes wholly subsumed to Firestone's argument that the family is the primary site of oppression—of racial as well as of sexual oppression. Her proposal in the chapter, "Conclusion: The Ultimate Revolution," calls for "cybernetic socialism," which would free "women from their reproductive biology by every means available," thus abolishing the nuclear family altogether, and by implication abolishing the Oedipal psychodrama of racism that grows out of it (269, 233).

The sex/race analogy works in Firestone's analysis, as it does in others', insofar as it collapses oppressive structures into each other on the basis of *cause, origin, source*: it is a top-down model of oppression based on the primary agent of that oppression (white men),[10] and organizes individual instances of oppression into a linear history (sexism, then racism, colonialism, capitalism, etc.). This top-down model and linear history of oppression posited in the sex/race analogy was very much in keeping with the theoretical drive of some kinds of radical feminism in the 1970s: since "radical" equalled "root," radical feminist analyses like Firestone's located the root cause of all oppression, and proposed to eliminate it. Logically, then, all other oppressive structures would fall like dominoes, or collapse like a house of cards with the base yanked out. More than the "place" of black women, in Gallop's phrase, is missing from such an analysis; such top-down models of both oppression and liberation sidestep theorizing the process of change itself.

Todd M. Lieber, in a 1972 essay on *Invisible Man*, provides a useful and concise sense of the meanings of the visibility /invisibility trope in the 1970s:

. . . "invisibility" suggests the situation of a group stripped of its native culture and forced to adhere to alien standards and values while its own cultural qualities were ignored; socially it reflects the conditions of a group whose basic plight was long overlooked or pushed into obscure shadows; perhaps most significantly it embodies the complex psychological dilemmas of men [sic] without a sense of vital group identity, whose sense of individual human identity is often denied by the dominant society. (86)

The visibility/invisibility trope is, of course, ironic in the sense that it turns *hyper*visibility into *in*visibility. That is, the Other named as invisible is unseen as an individual, while simultaneously hypervisible as a stereotype, or, in Invisible Man's own metaphor, a "walking nightmare" (Ellison 4–5).[11] Lieber's explanation captures nicely the dynamic of individual and group identity, and, despite his generic *men* here, hints at the trope's usefulness for feminists trying to create a politicized gender consciousness that would be as effective in organizing women as a politicized race consciousness had been for African Americans.

In emergent feminist literary criticism, the sex/race analogy coalesced with the visibility/invisibility trope; it played out specifically in a number of comparisons between feminist fiction and *Invisible Man*. Ellen Morgan, for example, defended feminist fiction from the charge of "propaganda" by citing *Invisible Man* as an example of the way that "passionate consciousness of oppression not only does not preclude, but can well call forth the creation of art" (Brown and Olson 276).[12] Cheri Register located Ellison's novel as a "precedent" for the kind of "personalized polemic" she advocated as consciousness-raising fiction, arguing that *Invisible Man* "was successful not because it exposed conditions that were completely foreign to whites in America, but because it appealed to common, multiracial feelings of insignificance and alienation, showing how much more intense they are when institutionalized" (23). Early feminist critics frequently cited *Invisible Man* either prescriptively or descriptively as a model for feminist fiction; a large number of women fiction writers with varying degrees of allegiance to the Movement used Ellison's novel as a model. Among the realist novels of the decade with important references to invisibility and to *Invisible Man* are these: Dorothy Bryant's *Ella Price's Journal* (1972), which links invisibility with both aging and with freedom; Joyce Carol Oates's *Do with Me What You Will* (1973), which associates marriage with women's becoming visible; Margaret Atwood's *Lady Oracle* (1976), which is similar to Bryant in linking invisibility to freedom; and Marilyn French's *The Women's Room* (1977), especially its opening scenes. What these examples are meant to suggest is that the sex/race analogy had an important literary history, in addition to or alongside of its theoretical history in the Women's Liberation Movement.

While images of invisibility abound in feminist realist fiction in the 1970s, the two most explicit re-visionings of Ellison's novel in the decade are works of science fiction: James Tiptree, Jr.'s (Alice Sheldon's) story, "The Women Men Don't See" (1973), and Joanna Russ's novel, *The Female Man* (1975). What Sarah Lefanu describes as "the plasticity of science fiction and its openness to other literary genres" is clearly at issue here, as is the long tradition in science fiction of representing some notion of otherness in its use of aliens, extraterrestrials, and nonhumans (9).[13] In these two works, the generic tendency toward exploring otherness comes together with feminism's focus on women as other, as a part of what Lefanu calls "the extraordinary relationship between feminism and science fiction that developed in the 1970s and continues to the present day" (7). That "extraordinary relationship," as Lefanu suggests, developed from a similarity in questions; she writes, "Feminism questions a given order in political terms, while science fiction questions it in imaginative terms" (100); both science fiction and feminism ask "what if" questions, as I discuss in Chapter Five. Both feminist science fiction and feminist theory in the decade were utopian, and both used the sex/race analogy to further their speculations. Intertextually, the widespread use of the sex/race analogy in feminist theory helped make Ellison's novel particularly available for re-visioning within emergent feminist science fiction, as readings of "The Women Men Don't See" and *The Female Man* will demonstrate.

"The Women Men Don't See" may be the most elegant "invisible woman" story of the decade, meticulous in its re-visioning of Ellison, and important in its own right as an instance of Tiptree's (relatively) successful male impersonation.[14] I want to discuss this story at some length, for it encompasses a number of important themes for feminist readers of *Invisible Man*. After a plane crash in a remote area of Mexico, the male narrator, Don Fenton, and one of the two nondescript women passengers, Ruth Parsons, make an overnight trip through the swamp to bring back fresh water. Don, clearly puzzled by Ruth, tries repeatedly to understand her by setting her into sexist stereotypes. He imagines Ruth as a rape victim; her "obtrusive recessiveness" seems to him an invitation to rape (191). Ruth's competence leads him to imagine her as "Such a decent ordinary little woman, a good girl scout" (199). He suggests she ought to be married, and then concludes, "What was wrong with her? Well, what's wrong with any furtively unconventional middle-aged woman with an empty bed" (204). None of these attempts to categorize her lead Don to any real understanding; Ruth is no more visible to him than she was at the beginning of the story, when he saw her and her daughter Althea as a "double female blur" (176–77).

When Don tries to talk to Ruth about feminism, however, he begins to realize the depth of his non-understanding, the radical alterity of her experience. Ruth tells him that women's liberation is "doomed" because

> Women have no rights, Don, except what men allow us. Men are more aggressive and powerful, and they run the world. When the next real crisis upsets them, our so-called rights will vanish like—like that smoke. We'll be back where we always were: property. And whatever has gone wrong will be blamed on our freedom, like the fall of Rome was. You'll see. (204–5)

What women do, Ruth argues, is survive: "We live by ones and twos in the chinks of your world-machine." Rather than a "guerrilla operation," as Don suggests her language implies, Ruth says the better metaphor for women in a male-dominated world is the opossum: "Think of us as opossums, Don. Did you know that there are opossums living all over? Even in New York City." Ruth tells Don that she dreams "sometimes of— of going away" (205–6).

"Going away" is precisely what she does. When a pair of extraterrestrials find Ruth and Don in the swamp, Ruth arranges to go with them to their planet, taking Althea as well. "We don't mind what your planet is like; we'll learn—we'll do anything!" she pleads; "We don't want to come back!" (214, 215). Don tries to protect Ruth from the aliens, accidentally shooting her instead, in a neat figuration of the uselessness of men's protection. At the end of the story, after Ruth and Althea have left, Don understands that their disappearance will not cause "any bother, any trouble at all"; he has learned from Ruth that the disappearance of two opossums is nothing significant. But Don can only marvel at what he perceives as the weirdness, the insanity of going "sight unseen to an alien world." He still cannot understand the depth of Ruth's alienation, the reason she leaves: he wonders, "How could a woman choose to live among unknown monsters, to say good-bye to her home, her world?" and cannot see that *he* is the unknown monster, and that Earth was never *her* home, *her* world. Ruth and Don are aliens to each other still at the end of the story; Don concludes, "Two of our opossums are missing" (217).

"The Women Men Don't See" re-visions *Invisible Man* in important ways.[15] When Ruth argues that women "live by ones and twos in the chinks of your world machine," readers must be reminded of Invisible Man's hibernation in his "warm hole"—his basement "in a building rented strictly to whites," carrying on his "battle with Monopolated Light and Power" (5–7).[16] Moreover, Tiptree's central metaphor in "The Women Men Don't See"—the metaphor of the opossum—plays on Invisible Man's "hibernation." For hibernation, after all, can be seen as an extended period of "playing possum," of holding still long enough to shake off predators. This is how Invisible Man came to be underground in the first place, falling through the street hole while running away. "So I would stay here until I was chased out," he determines (558). At the end of the novel, Invisible Man decides that hibernation is not enough, because there is a "possibility that even an invisible man has a socially responsible role to play" (568). "Please, a definition," Ellison writes in the Prologue: "A hibernation is a covert preparation for a more overt action" (13). Ruth has given up entirely on the possibility of playing a socially responsible role; when she comes out of hiding, when she emerges from Don's stereotypes, it is only to make another kind of escape—to go off with aliens somewhere else. The difference in duration becomes a difference in kind: where Ellison depicts Invisible Man's hibernation as a temporary respite, Tiptree's story suggests that playing possum—constantly, always, inevitably—is women's natural state in a male-dominated society.

The Female Man also draws on *Invisible Man* in its use of the metaphor of invisibility in two important instances. One reason Joanna changes into a man, she says, is that she rarely sees women: "I think it's a legend that half the population of the world is female; where on earth are they keeping them all?" She gives us this list of visible men:

My doctor is male.
My lawyer is male.
My tax-accountant is male.
The grocery-store-owner (on the corner) is male.
The janitor in my apartment building is male.
The president of my bank is male.
The manager of the neighborhood supermarket is male.
My landlord is male.
Most taxi-drivers are male.
All cops are male.
All firemen are male.
The designers of my car are male.
The factory workers who made the car are male.
The dealer I bought it from is male.
Almost all my colleagues are male.
My employer is male.
The Army is male.
The Navy is male.
The government is (mostly) male.
I think most people in the world are male. (203–4)

Like Tiptree's opossums and Ellison's Invisible Man, Russ's women are out there somewhere, hidden or hiding from Joanna. Joanna says that she doubts that "most of the women are put into female-banks when they grow up and that's why you don't see them" (204), but she offers no alternative explanation. This discussion of women's invisibility is clearly a consciousness-raising device: what would the world look like, Russ asks us to consider, if we actually saw all of the women who allegedly inhabit it?

Jael the assassin's experience of invisibility in *The Female Man* is less comic than Joanna's. Russ specifically links Jael's invisibility to violence —as Ellison similarly links invisibility and violence. When Jael goes to do business with one of the Manlanders, the Manlander engages her in a long conversation about reuniting the sexes. As the conversation becomes more and more cliched, Jael feels herself "Sliding down the slippery gulf into invisibility." As the Manlander begins to set his arguments about the advantages of a sex-integrated society into generic masculine pronouns, Jael feels "drained of personality" (178). The conversation ends with the Manlander's insisting that Jael have sex with him: "It doesn't matter what you say. You're a woman, aren't you? This is the crown of your life. This is what God made you for" (181). Because the Manlander has a "gadget" in his ear "that screens out female voices," he cannot hear Jael's refusal, and can't see her anger (180). Jael summons up her "hysterical strength" (192)—an adrenaline surge—and kills him. The other Js (Joanna, Jeannine, and Janet) ask her whether killing the Manlander was necessary; Jael replies that, necessary or not, she liked it (184).

Jael kills the Manlander because he can neither see nor hear her, because he makes her invisible. Russ links Jael's feeling invisible to a dream she has afterward, sleeping off the effects of hysterical strength. Jael dreams about guilt, "not human guilt, but the helpless, hopeless despair that would be felt by a small wooden box or geometric cube if such objects had consciousness; it was the guilt of sheer existence." Russ insists, though, that this guilt of sheer existence is specifically *women's*: the guilt of the survivor of rape, the guilt of demanding attention from men, the guilt of original sin, the guilt of refraining from making scenes, the guilt of women's "radical inferiority" that comes with possessing female genitalia (194). Jael refuses to believe this guilt comes from murder. On the contrary, she argues, the guilt is the motive for her murders. Only murder allows her to exist; only on the verge of death can her victims acknowledge her existence.

For every drop of blood shed there is restitution made; with every truthful reflection in the eyes of a dying man I get back a little of my soul; with every gasp of horrified comprehension, I come a little more into the light. See? It's *me*!

I am the force that is ripping out your guts; I, I, I, the hatred twisting your arm; I, I, I, the fury who has just put a bullet in your side. It is I who cause this pain, not you. It is I who am doing it to you, not you. It is I who will be alive tomorrow, not you. Do you know? Can you guess? Are you catching on? It is I, who you will not admit exits.

Look! Do you *see me*? (195; emphasis original)

In Russ's formulation, women's invisibility is dangerous. It is dangerous to women's possibility for happiness, as Joanna's transformation suggests, and it is especially dangerous to men, who can only be convinced of women's existence through violence.

Like Jael, Ellison's Invisible Man experiences people's refusal to see him as a temptation to violence: "It's when you feel like this that, out of resentment, you begin to bump people back." When Invisible Man bumps back, he nearly kills the white man on the street, but refrains when he realizes that, as far as the white man is concerned, he "was in the midst of a walking nightmare": "Something in this man's thick head had sprung out and beaten him within an inch of his life" (4–5). Russ's Jael, in a re-visioning of this scene, *must* kill a man who cannot see her. "Would he have awakened at the point of death?" Invisible Man asks; Jael answers in the affirmative, insisting that the Manlander die with his eyes open, insisting she receive that "truthful reflection" in his eyes (Ellison 5; Russ 195). Invisible Man also asks whether death could free the white man "for wakeful living," a question Jael answers implicitly in the negative. No such "wakeful living" is possible for men in *The Female Man*, just as the utopian future of Whileaway becomes possible only after the plague or an army of Jaels rids the planet of the male sex.

In Tiptree's story, men *don't* see women—don't see them, at least, except under the most extraordinary of circumstances, when beings even more alien than women make women visible. In Russ's novel, men *can't* see women—can't see them, it seems, under penalty of death. Women's invisibility may be—and the contingency of the alternate-universe plot poses this as a possibility rather than a certainty—dangerous to men, if women organize, and if the Js cooperate with Jael. Even women don't see each other, Russ points out in Joanna's discussion of invisibility, but that can change. After Jeannine agrees to help Jael, she suddenly sees that the "streets are full of women" (209). Once she chooses sides in Jael's literal battle of the sexes, she can then, and only then, begin to see the previously hidden population of women. In Ellison's novel, people *don't* see Invisible Man: his invisibility results from "a peculiar disposition of the eyes of those with whom I come into contact. A matter of construction of their *inner* eyes, those eyes with which they look through their physical eyes upon reality" (3). The burden of *Invisible Man* is its attempt to "tell you what was really happening when your eyes were looking through" (568), a claim that insists on our ability to change the disposition of those inner eyes—a claim that rests, ultimately, on the novel's ability to raise the consciousnesses of its readers.

The visibility/invisibility trope is especially well-suited to the consciousness-raising novel because it so clearly links changes in individual perceptions to changes in social reality. Ellison's final line—"Who knows but that, on the lower frequencies, I speak for you?" (568)—suggests the burden of representativeness that the CR novel carries. The novel's claim to "speak for" readers invites us to end the novel by affirming our similarity to and shared feelings with Invisible Man, to affirm our identification with his feelings of alienation and his oppression. Such affirmations are structurally similar to the practice of CR, in which participants built their knowledge of male domination out of the commonalities in their personal narratives, shifting the interpretive terrain of these narratives from the personal to the political, from the individual to the systemic—indeed, from the invisible to the visible. For white women readers grounded in the sex/race analogy of the late 1960s and 1970s, the affirmation at the end of *Invisible Man* that he does "speak for [them]" could be read as affirming the analogy itself.

Invisibility is not a "natural" or inevitable metaphor for women's oppression; Tiptree's and Russ's uses of it in their texts construct specific and detailed readings—re-visionings, even rewritings—of Ellison's novel. The coalescing of the discourses of sex and race encapsulated in the sex/race analogy and played out in the visibility/invisibility trope have influenced readings of *Invisible Man* as well as these rewritings. Carolyn Sylvander's 1975 essay, "Ralph Ellison's *Invisible Man* and Female Stereotypes," borrows a technique from Alice Walker's "In Search of Our Mother's Gardens" (1974); Sylvander takes Ellison's discussions of racial stereotypes from *Shadow and Act* and inserts "appropriate substitutes" (language about gender) as a way to critique Ellison's women characters, just as Walker used bracketed insertions to rewrite Virginia Woolf's story of Judith Shakespeare as a story of Phillis Wheatley. Both Sylvander and Walker bring the discourses of sex and race together, enlisting their perceived structural and rhetorical similarities to illuminate each other.

Mary Rohrberger's reading of the sexual politics of *Invisible Man* focuses on the analogy. "A reader today," she argues, "must be aware of the invisibility and impotence of women in society." Despite what she sees as the novel's depiction of women as "one-dimensional figures playing roles in a drama written by men," Rohrberger argues that "there is some hidden knowledge concerning women that hovers just below the surface of the invisible man's consciousness" (130). It is, I suggest, precisely the history of the sex/race analogy in second-wave feminism and the literary history of feminist rewritings of *Invisible Man* that make this hovering knowledge apparent.[17] That is, one kind of consciousness raising can be seen in this historical context to contain another, whether "consciously" experienced by the character or not.

These rewritings and readings illuminate *Invisible Man*'s importance to feminism in the 1970s, and help us understand why all those images of invisible women populate feminist fiction, theory and Movement writing, literary criticism, and poetry. Feminist readers and rewriters of *Invisible Man* affirm that the visibility/invisibility trope speaks for them—culturally, socially, and psychologically, to return to the terms Lieber uses to address the trope—even while the "details" of race must be rewritten or bracketed. In "Theories of Feminist Criticism: A Dialogue" (1975), Carolyn Heilbrun and Catharine Stimpson make a case for the usefulness to feminist readers of a wide range of non-feminist texts: "Skepticism of authority is like a contagious disease," they write, "Since most structures of authority are masculine, to question them *per se* may lead us to question masculine authority *per se*" (72). Reading *Invisible Man* as a text that challenges race-based authority enabled feminist readers and rewriters to (re)frame precisely the challenge to "masculine authority *per se*" that Stimpson and Heilbrun advocate—by slipping along the sex/race analogy.

As early as 1975, Jo Freeman qualified the importance of the sex/race analogy, granting that it was all-pervasive, but then going on to argue that "What was most potent to the most people, however, was not this analogy, but the idea of equality, and equality *now*, that accompanied it" (*Politics* 28). Over the course of the decade, the urgency to legitimate feminism both to men in the movements from which Women's Liberation emerged and to women who could be "converted" gave way to the urgency of the critique of racism in the movement, and to the development of a feminism that was both accountable and specific to women of color. Importantly, much of the work to move race, ethnicity, and color to the top of feminist agendas was done by lesbians. Where Piercy had used the sex/race analogy to call into being a feminist sisterhood in "The Grand Coolie Damn," these later works refuted—sometimes even while using—the sex/race analogy as a way of pointing out the pain of racism in the feminist movements and lesbian communities that had developed since the late 1960s.

Yet neither the visibility/invisibility trope nor the sex/race analogy disappeared, not even from the tremendously influential anthologies by women of color from the late 1970s and early 1980s.[18] Perhaps the most striking evidence for the inescapability of the sex/race analogy comes in its use in the anthology whose title was most designed to refute it: *All the Women Are White, All the Blacks Are Men, But Some of Us Are Brave: Black Women's Studies* (1982). The analogy appears only in the essay, "Racism—A White Issue," where Ellen Pence describes her experience as a white woman coming to understand the significance of racism in the women's movement:

> I started seeing the similarities with how men have excluded the participa-
> tion of women in their work through Roberts Rules of Order, encouraging us to
> set up subcommittees to discuss *our* problems but never seeing sexism as their
> problem. It became clear that in many ways I act the same way toward women
> of color, supporting them in dealing with *their* issues. As with liberal men's rec-
> ognition of the oppression of women, I recognized the oppression of Third
> World people but never understood that I personally had anything to gain by
> the elimination of racism. While I fully understood how sexism dehumanizes
> men, it never crossed my mind that my racism must somehow dehumanize me.
> (Hull, Scott, and Smith 46)

Pence's strategy here is to use the experience of white feminists dealing
with men as a structural device to understand the experience of women
of color dealing with white women; the analogy has shifted to put white
women in the position occupied by white men in the earlier uses. "The
oppression of men toward women is in so many ways parallel to the oppression of white women toward women of color," she explains. Pence
uses the sex/race analogy not to convince white women that they are
oppressed, but rather that they are oppressors, and to make intelligible
to white women readers the feelings of women of color: "The lessons
we've learned so well as women must be the basis for our understanding of ourselves as oppressive to the Third World women we work with"
(Hull, Scott, and Smith 46–7).

Pence's essay occupies an uneasy place in *But Some of Us Are Brave*: it
both contradicts the book title's refutation of the sex/race analogy and
addresses a "we" of white women where the title addresses an "us" of
black women. Its contradictory position in the book may serve to ironize
the analogy, by inviting readers to see the sex/race analogy as a strategy
specific to white feminists (as a "white issue" like racism itself); alternatively, white women readers may find Pence's use of the analogy familiar, and read its address as a bridge to the anthology's dominant "us."
If Pence's use of the sex/race analogy was included as a consciousness-
raising device for white readers, though, it is a strategy absent from the
volume's outline for consciousness raising about racism—"Face-to-Face,
Day-to-Day—Racism CR"—which frames more complex and nuanced
questions about the interrelations of gender, sexuality, and race.

This Bridge Called My Back (1981, 1983), to take another of these important anthologies, uses the visibility/invisibility trope repeatedly. In
the anthology's introduction, the editors use the trope to explain the
subject of the first section of the anthology, "Children Passing in the
Streets: The Roots of Our Radicalism." The texts in this section address
both the *hyper*visibility of race in children's lives and the *in*visibility of
race to light-skinned or assimilated children of color raised with, as

Chrystos writes, "all the whitest advantages" (Moraga and Anzaldúa 18); the editors describe the section as addressing the question of "how visibility/invisibility as women of color forms our radicalism" (Moraga and Anzaldúa xxiv). In her essay in the collection, "Invisibility is an Unnatural Disaster: Reflections of an Asian American Woman," Mitsuye Yamada not only uses the trope but also refers specifically to Ellison's novel in so doing; both the trope and the reference are part of Yamada's strategy to claim for Asian-American women the politically liminal status of "the visible minority that is invisible" (Moraga and Anzaldúa 36).

Another essay in *This Bridge*, Cheryl Clarke's "Lesbianism: An Act of Resistance," demonstrates that the sex/race analogy was not specific to white women in the late 1970s and early 1980s—just as it was not a decade earlier. Clarke, a black lesbian feminist writer, locates the "historic connection between the oppression of African peoples in North America and the universal oppression of women" in the fact that "racism and sexism have been produced by the same animal"; she argues that "the white man learned, within the structure of heterosexual monogamy and under the system of patriarchy, to relate to black people—slave or free—as man *relates* to a woman, viz. as property, as a sexual commodity, as a servant, as a source of free or cheap labor, and as an innately inferior being" (Moraga and Anzaldúa 130–31).[19]

Especially interesting in Clarke's essay is the combination of the radical feminist use of the sex/race analogy, as these passages demonstrate, together with a different version of the analogy. In making her case for the forcefulness of lesbian resistance, Clarke draws a series of parallels between ways of living as a lesbian and ways of living as an African American, a series that deploys the visibility/invisibility trope in its reference to passing.

Many women are only lesbians to a particular community and *pass* as heterosexuals as they traffic among enemies. (This is analogous to being black and passing for white with only one's immediate family knowing one's true origins.) . . . . Many women are politically active as lesbians, but may fear holding hands with their lovers as they traverse heterosexual turf. (This response to heterosexual predominance can be likened to the reaction of the black student who integrates a predominately white dormitory and who fears leaving the door of her room open when she plays gospel music.) There is the woman who engages in sexual-emotional relationships with women and labels herself *bisexual*. (This is comparable to the Afro-American whose skin-color indicates her mixed ancestry yet who calls herself "mulatto" rather than black.) . . . And then there is the lesbian who is a lesbian anywhere and everywhere and who is in direct and constant confrontation with heterosexual presumption, privilege, and oppression. (Her struggle can be compared to that of the Civil Rights activist of the 1960's who was out there on the streets for freedom, while so many of us viewed the action on the television.) (Moraga and Anzaldúa 129–30)

Here, as in Lisa Walker's essay on the femme lesbian that I cited earlier, the sex/race analogy has shifted along the dual meanings of *sex* as biological sex and as sexuality to make *lesbian* rather than *woman* the term of comparison. This shift has given the analogy not only a new meaning but also another arena in lesbian/gay/queer theory.

The stable term, as it is throughout the history of the analogy I trace, is *race*, and *race* rendered specifically as black. While the visibility/invisibility trope has been used to name a variety of racial, ethnic, gendered, and sexual identities, the sex/race analogy always works to attribute to the sex term the presumed stability and unity of the race term, and always uses some version of the visibility/invisibility trope. Ed Cohen makes this argument in discussing the use of "race" as a model for gay identity in "Who Are 'We'? Gay 'Identity' as Political (E)motion" (1991); the essay he critiques (Steven Epstein's "Gay Politics, Ethnic Identity: The Limits of Social Constructionism" [1987]) evidences the analogy's move into lesbian/gay/queer theory.

Here the explicit parallel drawn between "race" and "sexuality," familiar to so many polemical affirmations of (non-racial) identity politics, is meant to evoke an underlying and apparently indisputable common sense that naturalizes this particular choice of political strategy almost as if the "naturalness" of racial "identity" could confer a corollary stability upon the less "visible" dynamics of sexuality. (74)

Cohen reminds us that the analogy naturalizes and makes self-evident both its terms, and "elides the complex processes of social differentiation that assign, legitimate, and enforce qualitative distinctions between 'types' of individuals" (74).

Even in its more contemporary versions—the essay Cohen critiques is from 1987, and Lisa Walker reads essays in feminist theory from 1985, 1987, and 1990—the sex/race analogy works by fantasy, just as it did in it earlier versions. First, in its use of *race*, it represents a fantastic vision of African-American identity, community, and politics—uncontested, uncontradictory, unproblematic—that is shaped by a simultaneous nostalgia for and forgetting of the Civil Rights Movement, as if identity, community, and politics had never been the subjects of struggle. Second, the analogy attempts to forge out of that nostalgia and forgetting an equally fantastic vision of a self-evident identity, community, and politics of *sex*, whether construed as gender or as sexuality. Third, implicit in the setting together of the two is a fantasy of coalition, whether joined by the structural similarity of the systems of domination or by the parallel strategies of resistance. And, just as the radical feminist "domino theory" of the early 1970s (in which dismantling patriarchy would cause all systems of domination to fall) works to side-step the process of change itself, the fantasy of coalition implicit in the sex/race analogy sidesteps the processes and practices that would make such coalition possible. Small wonder that it was in science fiction versions of CR narratives that the sex/race analogy found its most perfect literary form in the 1970s.

In its original form, the sex/race analogy was part of the Women's Liberation Movement's declaration of independence from other social movements in the late 1960s and the crisis of legitimating that movement in the face of real hostility; it facilitated white feminists' identifying with Invisible Man, and functioned to make Ellison's novel especially available for feminist re-vision, as Tiptree's and Russ's works exemplify. Even as the urgency of legitimating feminism gave way to the urgency of the critique of racism in the women's movement, though, the sex/race analogy did not disappear; it continued to operate even in the same texts that worked to discredit it. To dismiss the analogy as simply outdated or as bad feminism is to ignore its continuing appeal—to fantastic visions of gender, sexual identity, and coalition—and its continuing rhetorical power to raise consciousness. To dismiss the analogy is also to dismiss the crucial importance of *Invisible Man* to the development of feminist fiction, for just as feminists claim earlier figures like Woolf and de Beauvoir as literary-theoretical "mothers" and models for the Women's Liberation Movement, so too ought we to claim our literary- theoretical "fathers."

Notes

1. This is the title of Bethel's poem from *Conditions Five: The Black Women's Issue.*
2. I want to make it clear here that I am expanding and refining Gallop's argument; her three chapters on feminist literary criticism and theory in the 1970s in *Around 1981* are the very best readings of this material I have encountered. For an important critique of Gallop's reading of *Conjuring* in *Around 1981*, see Ann duCille, "The Occult of True Black Womanhood: Critical Demeanor and Black Feminist Studies"; duCille specifically critiques the gesture of the I-used-to-be-a-racist version of a "critical apologia" that I am invoking here (612–17); see below for a discussion of the sex/race analogy in *But Some of Us Are Brave.*
3. A sampling of the metaphors of politicized invisibility includes these: "Consciousness-Raising," which asks, "Do you ever feel invisible?" under the topic of sex and sex-roles (Koedt, Levine, and Rapone, 280–81); Dale Spender, *Invisible Women: The Schooling Scandal*; Robin Morgan, *Sisterhood Is Powerful*, which has a section subtitled "Invisible Women: Psychological and Sexual Repression"; and Alicia Suskin Ostriker, *Stealing the Language: The Emergence of Women's Poetry in America*, which cites Joyce Carol Oates's collection, *Invisible Woman*, and Robin Morgan's poem, "The Invisible Woman," as specific examples of women poets' using "the figure of invisibility as a feminine attribute" (65).
4. Kennedy argues that she was refused admission to law school "not because I was black, but because I was a woman," and suggests that black women may have the leverage of race to redress discrimination by sex: "I leaned on the

ethnic angle, saying that some of my more cynical friends thought I was being discriminated against because I was a Negro. . . . Law-school admissions opened the door just wide enough for *me*, but not for my friend Pat Jones, who was a Barnard graduate, with a slightly higher law aptitude level and slightly lower undergraduate average, but white" (R. Morgan 500–501).

5. For a discussion of the Hayden-King paper, see Evans, 85–88. It is perhaps useful to note that de Beauvoir also used the analogy in *The Second Sex*.

6. Naomi Weisstein's "'Kinde, Kuche, Kirche' as Scientific Law: Psychology Constructs the Female" exemplifed the importance of the analogy to a general audience in its 1969 publication in *Psychology Today* under the title, "Woman as Nigger." Weisstein's essay attacked the sex-based assumptions of clinical psychology, but only briefly drew the analogy at the end, when she compared the list of appropriate female traits to "a typical minority group stereotype of inferiority" (R. Morgan, 244); the *Psychology Today* version of the essay inserted the phrase "woman as nigger" at this point. *Sisterhood is Powerful* attributes the phrase, "Woman is the nigger of the world," to Yoko Ono in its collection, "Verbal Karate (Statistical and Aphoristic Ammunition)" (R. Morgan, 634).

7. See Firestone, *The Dialectic of Sex*, for a different strategy; where Piercy invites politicos into sisterhood, Firestone attacks and tries to shame them into sisterhood (37–42).

8. Echols rightly points out the limitations of Redstockings' "pro-woman line" and of consciousness raising: both rest on assumptions of the universality of women's experience, thus ignoring differences of race and class, among others (153).

9. For a later and quite differently nuanced version of "whiteness = maleness," see Marilyn Frye, "On Being White: Thinking Toward a Feminist Understanding of Race and Race Supremacy," wherein Frye suggests that white women's "radical feminism is treacherous to the white race as presently constructed and instituted in this country"; note as well her reference to *Invisible Man* as "a book of considerable value to feminists" in this essay (125, 119).

10. In "Lesbianism: An Act of Resistance," Cheryl Clarke makes this point; see below.

11. I want to thank one of the anonymous reviewers for *Women's History Review* for a provocative suggestion that the cruelty of scopophilia, of women's hypervisibility as feminist film scholars theorized it in the 1970s (see, e.g., Laura Mulvey, "Visual Pleasure and Narrative Cinema"), cross-cuts my examples of invisibility.

12. That feminist fiction required defending against the charge of "propaganda" is amply demonstrated by the book reviews of the period, as I discussed in Chapter Four.

13. See Ursula L. Le Guin, "American SF and the Other"; Le Guin qualifies this assumption that aliens represent "the sexual Alien, and the social Alien, and the cultural Alien, and finally the racial Alien," suggesting that it is more potentially than actually true; most SF has been, from a political perspective, "brainless regressivism" (97–99). See also Joanna Russ, "Images of Women in Science Fiction," for a similar argument about gender, which concludes, "There are plenty of images of women in science fiction. There are hardly any women" (Koppelman Cornillon, 91).

14. For a discussion of the effect of the Tiptree pseudonym, see Ursula K. Le Guin, "Introduction to *Star Songs of an Old Primate* by James Tiptree, Jr.": Tiptree withdrew "The Women Men Don't See" from Nebula Award consideration

in 1974 because of the "false pretenses" involved in "the evidence it gave that a man could write with full sympathy about women" (182). In *Feminism and Science Fiction*, Lefanu argues that the story raises "questions about the nature of feminine and feminist writing," in large part because of its macho narrator, but also because of the Tiptree signature (122).

15. Marleen S. Barr argues in *Feminist Fabulation: Space/Postmodern Fiction* that readers ought to see a relationship between "The Women Men Don't See" and Zora Neale Hurston's short fiction (40–41); while Barr's is a provocative recasting of literary history (and itself a fabulation of that history, given that Hurston's stories remained uncollected and largely out of print until Alice Walker published the Hurston Reader in 1979, and *Spunk: The Selected Stories* appeared in 1985), her argument that "Ruth and Althea use women's invisibility to demand women's visibility" can also serve to underline the importance of reading Tiptree's text in relation to Ellison's. See also her *Lost in Space: Probing Feminist Science Fiction and Beyond*, for the essay "Science Fiction's Invisible Female Men: Joanna Russ's 'When It Changed' and James Tiptree's 'The Women Men Don't See,' " which takes its epigraph from *Invisible Man*, but does not develop the comparison.

16. The "everyday rebellions" of feminism (in Gloria Steinem's phrase) are quite similar to Invisible Man's battle, and this similarity is part of the attractiveness of the sex/race analogy.

17. See also Yvonne Fonteneau, "Ralph Ellison's *Invisible Man*: A Critical Reevaluation" (1990), for her discussion of women in *Invisible Man* and in critical accounts of the novel.

18. Two of these important anthologies were *Conditions: Five: The Black Women's Issue* (1979), a journal issue that "immediately set a record in feminist publishing by selling three thousand copies in the first three weeks that it was available," eventually sold ten thousand copies in two printings, and became the basis for *Home Girls: A Black Feminist Anthology* (1983), as editor Barbara Smith explained in the introduction to the later work (xlviii); and *This Bridge Called My Back: Writings by Radical Women of Color* (1981, 1983), which sold twenty thousand copies in its first edition. Both *Home Girls* and the second edition of *This Bridge* were published by Kitchen Table: Women of Color Press, which was founded in 1980 specifically to publish work by women writers of color.

19. Clarke also cites Firestone's analysis of racism from *The Dialectic of Sex* in an approving, if qualified, way (135–36).

Conclusion

> "Somethin's, like, crossed over in me. I can't go back—I just couldn't live."
>
> — *Thelma & Louise*

The moment in *Thelma & Louise*, when Thelma indicates that she has somehow "crossed over," signals the film's use of CR narrative strategies. Unlike Fay Weldon's *Praxis*, with its imperative to "Watch Praxis. Watch her carefully. Look, listen, learn. Then safely, as they say to children, cross over" (109), Thelma's "crossing over" is anything but safe. How CR narrative strategies migrated from fiction to film, and how CR itself became deadly in the process, is the focus of this Conclusion. I begin by discussing two crucial reasons the CR novel form has largely disappeared from fiction: the ubiquity of the form as a factor in constraining its ability to do political work, and changes in feminist political thinking, most notably a shift toward a model of coalition politics. Next, I turn to *Thelma & Louise* itself, both as an example of the migration of the CR form into film, and as a text that occasioned a lively public debate over the nature and meaning of feminism itself, just as CR novels such as *The Women's Room* and *The Color Purple* had during the 1970s and early 1980s. Finally, I describe briefly some of the venues other than fiction currently available for both "soft" and "hard" CR, as fiction has ceased to be a privileged venue even for reading-based versions of CR.

The CR novel lost a great deal of its ability to do political work when it became too successful a form, when its conventions became so widely available to non- or even anti-feminist writers that feminism itself could become something the protagonist must have her consciousness raised "above." Alison Lurie's novel, *The Truth About Lorin Jones* (1979), exemplifies the way that the CR novel form became available to anti-feminist arguments by the end of the 1970s. Lurie uses the historical mothers device that I discussed in both realist and science fiction CR novels in

Chapter Five; her protagonist, Polly, begins research for a biography of Lorin Jones, a painter. Initially, Polly sees Lorin Jones in ways very similar to the ways that feminists in the early seventies see Sylvia Plath: "an unrecognized genius destroyed by the male establishment" (31). How Polly comes to see Lorin Jones differently is the novel's plot.

Polly discovers over the course of her research that there are two ways of telling Lorin's story. One of the possible narratives is to portray Lorin as "an innocent victim" of patriarchy, a narrative Lurie identifies repeatedly in the novel not only as feminist, but as feminism itself. Polly also discovers that it is possible to portray Lorin as "a neurotic, ungrateful genius" (324), based on what she learns from the men who were Lorin's lovers. Choosing which story to tell necessarily entails certain life choices for Polly: if she writes the "feminist" book, Polly will become "an angry, depressed lesbian feminist," and if she tells the story from the perspective of the men in Lorin's life, Polly will become "a selfish, successful career woman" (324). Polly chooses neither of these options; she decides to write a biography that includes all the versions of Lorin Jones that she has collected, "the real story . . . the whole truth with all the contradictions left in" (327). And she decides to write the book in Key West with Lorin's last lover; she believes this will prevent her from becoming, as he tells her Lorin was, "a damaging, rejecting woman" (327).

The Truth About Lorin Jones is an anti-feminist feminist CR novel—or perhaps a "postfeminist" CR novel, if we understand "postfeminism" to be a critique of feminism as no longer adequate for women. Lurie uses the historical mother device and other conventions of the CR novel to make an argument about the limits of feminism's explanatory power—uses, in other words, some of the conventions of the feminist CR novel to reject feminism itself.[1] By 1979, after these conventions had been circulating for a decade, inside and outside of the women's movement, in best-sellers as well as in more obscure novels, in works by feminist and non-feminist writers, the CR novel form had been so firmly established that it became available not only to non-feminist writers, but also to anti- (or "post-") feminist writers as well. It had become "authoritative discourse" in Bakhtin's sense: having the authority, in Bakhtin's examples, "of religious dogma, or of an acknowledged scientific truth, or of a currently fashionable book," as he argues in "Discourse in the Novel" (343). What Polly learns in *The Truth About Lorin Jones* is what protagonists in the CR novel nearly always learn from their historical mothers: the courage to lead an unconventional life. The difference here, though, is that Lurie perceives feminism itself to be conventional. Lurie tells us that Lorin Jones's story is too complex for a feminism that Polly understands as being unable to encompass contradictions; Polly thus comes to reject feminism, politics, lesbianism, and participating in a women's community as limited and conventional. Instead of feminism, Lurie poses an individual solution at the end of the novel—writing a different book and having a relationship with Lorin Jones's lover—in a stunning transvaluation of the politics of the CR novel, even in its "soft" versions. Where other writers pose feminism as an alternative to the individual solution, a way of writing (and living) beyond the marriage-or-death conventions of women's (literary) lives, Lurie poses feminism as itself one of those conventions.

When feminism itself becomes a convention within a novel form that emerged from the Women's Liberation Movement, we can begin to see why it lost its usefulness. Jean E. Kennard explores the conventions of feminist fiction in the 1970s to explain the reading strategies these conventions create for feminist readers of *The Yellow Wallpaper*. Kennard suggests these conventions change very quickly. By 1977, she points out, Marilyn French could already argue that the plot by which "leaving her husband and taking a lover can indicate that a woman is searching for self-fulfillment," a plot that developed only in the early 1970s, is already "a convention of the women's novel" (71–72). "By what process," Kennard asks, "does the convention become too conventional?" (72). Part of that process is simply success: when the conventions of the CR novel came to so permeate fiction by women, especially popular and best-selling fiction, they lost their connection to the political movement from which they emerged. These conventions became—as Rosalind Coward argued in the early 1980s that they always already were—more closely aligned with "the popular" than with feminism, especially the conventions of depicting sexuality, as I discuss in Chapter Three. This success, coupled with the political changes that feminism underwent, made the CR novel form no longer sufficient for feminist fiction. The success of the CR form turned it into an authoritative discourse—a discourse that still had enough internal persuasion to be struggled with and against, as Lurie's use of its conventions and devices suggest, but against which writers measured other internally persuasive discourses. Moreover, the ubiquity of the CR narrative form had spread to film in the late 1970s and early 1980s, so that a number of popular Hollywood films in this period contained elements of the CR narrative—usually deploying those elements in storylines that were not specifically feminist, as I argued in Chapter Four.

Another factor in the decline of the CR form in fiction is that both political and reading strategies changed significantly in the 1980s. While some of the strategies and devices of the CR novel remained useful, frequently these devices served a different kind of narrative. Sherley Anne Williams's historical novel *Dessa Rose* (1986), for example, uses elements of the CR novel, perhaps most notably the multiple characters device, tracing the lives of Dessa, an escaped slave, and Ruth, a white woman abandoned by her gambler husband. Williams's novel, though, uses the multiple character device as part of a very different kind of feminist political narrative. Dessa discovers her common bond with Ruth in their vulnerability to sexual assault by white men: "The white woman was subject to the same ravishment as me; this the thought that kept me awake. I hadn't knowed white mens could use a white woman like that, just take her by force same as they could with us" (220). This scene is an elegant rendering of the CR "click" moment, and such a bond between black and white women is, of course, a long-standing theme in works by both black women and white women arguing for black freedom.[2] What is different in *Dessa Rose* is that this discovery of a common bond does not take on a life of its own—it strengthens Dessa's and Ruth's ability to work together and creates the possibility for friendship between them, but it does not become itself a distinct or separate struggle. Indeed, one of the most striking differences from the CR novel of the 1970s is that Dessa and Ruth go their separate ways by the end of the novel; their alliance, while clearly important to both of them in teaching them freedom, is not permanent. Dessa wonders about Ruth at the end of the book, but then closes the novel on a different note: "We have paid for our children's place in the world again and again . . ." (260).

Ruth's whiteness had been, and does not entirely cease to be, something that makes it very difficult for Dessa to trust her. The bond between Dessa and Ruth over their shared vulnerability to sexual assault helps Dessa learn that Ruth too is at risk in their work. But the work itself—selling and re-selling the escaped slaves to raise money so they can settle in the West, and so Ruth too can start over—does not change. In Williams's novel, then, feminism, figured as that bond between Dessa and Ruth, strengthens their coalition without changing the nature of the work to be done. Feminism in this novel enables work for other kinds of freedom, and enables women in particular to understand freedom, but the novel's vision of sisterhood is limited.

Dessa Rose emerges from a different model for feminist politics from the one that is central to *The Color Purple* and the CR novels of the 1970s. That model is coalition politics, most famously articulated by Bernice Johnson Reagon in her essay, "Coalition Politics: Turning the Century." Reagon's essay is based on a speech given at the West Coast Women's Music Festival in 1981, a "women-only" festival celebrating women's culture and feminist politics. Reagon takes feminists to task for believing that the label "women-only" would make the Festival into a safe, nurturing, homogeneous event. Women are not a homogeneous group, she argues, and "women-only" designations cannot be limited to white women or to lesbians; feminism is a space of difference, coalition, and challenge, not of nurturing or of "home." Racism and homophobia will appear in "women-only" spaces, and must be confronted. Moreover, Reagon argues, coalition must and does happen because no group, even the tiniest, can be both politically active and homogeneous, and political work is not by definition nurturing. The "little barred rooms" created when activists mistake "home" for political work are not only illusory in their homogeneity, but also liable to be disrupted by others who believe they should be included (358–59).

The model of coalition politics has been enormously influential in feminist theory, as it has also been in feminist fiction. Few works of fiction capture this model as clearly as Octavia Butler's science fiction trilogy, *Xenogenesis* (*Dawn* [1987], *Adulthood Rites* [1988], and *Imago* [1989]). Where much feminist science fiction in the 1970s was, as I argued in my discussion of Le Guin's *The Left Hand of Darkness* in Chapter Five, concerned with the elimination of gender, Butler's novels focus both on its interrelations with race (coded here as species) and on its proliferation. In the *Xenogenesis* novels, Butler depicts a third sex, neither male nor female, called *ooloi*, which human characters refer to using the pronoun "it." Butler's gender system differs from Le Guin's in that it adds rather than subtracts sex-gender identities; where Le Guin populates Gethen with individuals who combine both human sexes, Butler gives us males, females, and neuters. Where Le Guin's novel worked toward androgyny, Butler's trilogy works toward a radical multiplicity. More importantly, Butler's gender system becomes further complicated by human-alien interbreeding in five-parent sets (one each human male, human female, alien male, alien female, and alien ooloi), so that species identity and gender identity become interdependent in their "construct" offspring. If we see extra-terrestrials as metaphoric racial "others"—a conventional interpretation of works involving human-alien relations— then we can see Butler's work, with its focus on the interrelations between species and gender, race and gender, in relation to later feminist theories that establish gender as one among several oppositions, structures, or social categories that (over) determine individual identity.[3]

Moreover, the plot that sets the trilogy in motion dramatizes the argument Reagon makes in her essay about coalition as a means of survival. Donna Haraway summarizes the issues nicely in her description of Butler's *Dawn*:

Butler tells the story of Lilith Iyapo, whose personal name recalls Adam's first and repudiated wife and whose family name marks her status as the widow of the son of Nigerian immigrants to the United States. A black woman and a mother whose child is dead, Lilith mediates the transformation of humanity through genetic exchange with extraterrestrial lovers/rescuers/destroyers/genetic engineers, who reform earth's habitats after the nuclear holocaust and coerce surviving humans into intimate fusion with them. It is a novel that interrogates reproductive, linguistic, and nuclear politics in a mythic field structured by late twentieth-century race and gender. (221)

Butler's *Xenogenesis* trilogy, read against both earlier feminist science fiction and late CR novels like *The Color Purple*, exemplifies the shift in theoretical models underlying feminist fiction. Where the CR novels depended on using readers' identification with their protagonists to transact CR, Butler's novels ask readers to read for differences. The theoretical differences in the feminisms out of which the novels develop thus require different reading strategies. The CR narrative form does not and cannot work with these reading strategies, which is one of the important reasons for the form's disappearance in fiction.

Another, perhaps more minor, factor in the disappearance of the CR form from fiction may be the disappearance of housewife protagonists from fiction in the 1980s. It may be the case that the CR narrative form migrated into other media because feminist fiction moved away from depicting women who don't work for wages, while housewives still figure in film, for instance, or other media. As Resa L. Dudovitz points out in her study of women's best-sellers, "Fewer stories of housewives . . . are appearing on the bestseller lists" in the 1980s (165). Was the CR narrative form simply unable to survive the movement of white, middle-class, married women into the paid work force of the past twenty years? Was the CR novel shaped at its core by the generational experiences of the young women in the Women's Liberation Movement who read in these novels some visions of the lives they were most afraid of leading—their mothers'?[4] The audience for contemporary fiction is primarily composed of white, middle-class, educated women; it is not surprising that novels directed toward such readers would change to reflect their experience—or their fantasies.

What followed the CR novel on the bestseller list was the "sex and success" novel, also called the "shopping and fucking" novel.[5] Dudovitz characterizes the bestsellers of the 1980s this way:

Many of the current American or British female characters create financial empires, achieve international success as writers or actresses, or climb to lofty executive positions. Whereas at one time the heroine's work situation functioned in the text as a kind of window dressing, the bestsellers of the 1980s focus on her active participation in a particular industry such as clothing or perfume, or even the stock market and Wall Street, and provide a certain amount of insight into the workings of areas in which women have traditionally and non-traditionally worked. . . . The boardroom has replaced the kitchen as the prime narrative site in the contemporary bestsellers published in the United States. (165)

What Dudovitz calls the "superwoman novel" of the 1980s itself began to wane by the end of the 1980s, a phenomenon that Dudovitz attributes to its being "over-exploited" (189), in much the same way that I have argued the CR novel became too conventional by the end of the previous decade. The "superwoman novel" of the 1980s reflects the emergence of a particular kind of postfeminism: a postfeminism that erases the history of political struggle which enabled women to break into some of the industries and positions represented. Under this erasure, neither sex nor success, neither shopping nor fucking, takes on the political resonances these issues had in the CR novels of the 1970s.[6]

It is not my intention simply to argue that the CR novel disappeared from fiction because housewives did. Rather, taken together with the substantial differences between the feminisms of the 1970s and the 1990s, the move away from housewife-protagonists might be seen as a shift in who counts as an "ordinary" or "average" woman. With the much greater and more complex attention to racial issues and racism in post-1970s feminism—and the corresponding degree of critical, scholarly, and popular attention to works by feminist writers of color—the assumption that the "ordinary" or "average" woman is white and middle-class has been eroded, at least to some extent. The CR novel was by no means solely about housewives, but the sheer number of examples of housewife protagonists does underline the extent to which it was a form both by and about white women (with Piercy's Connie in *Woman on the Edge of Time* and Walker's Celie in *The Color Purple* as counter-examples). The early-seventies argument that white women better proved feminist analyses because their status was uncomplicated by racial issues— that white women were "more women" than women of color—has by now almost entirely disappeared from feminism, though racism itself, of course, has not. Similarly, traces remain in contemporary feminism of the radical feminist domino theory of oppressions—holding that sexism as the original division of labor created racism, capitalism, etc.— but those who still subscribe to that theory insist nonetheless that race and class intersect with gender in ways that substantially affect the impact of gender oppression on women who occupy different positions.

Fiction by women writers of color will not, despite Gayle Greene's hope at the end of *Changing the Story*, take up where white women's fiction has left off. The CR novel is not especially useful to the feminism of the 1990s, for its insistence (most of the time) on gender as primary and other issues as secondary no longer fits contemporary feminist analysis. The theoretical and practical political concerns of feminism change when women of color are no longer marginalized and silenced. Gender means something different when we look carefully at its construction by race, ethnicity, and class, and the sex/race analogy always oversimplified both gender and race. Even CR itself has changed, as it has been taken up in "unlearning racism" workshops.[7] Thus feminist critics of contemporary fiction must see past the hegemony of the CR novel in order to see what has come after the feminist high renaissance of the 1970s.

The CR narrative form did not disappear, however conventional it had become, however far the women's movement had moved from the political theory on which it was based, however substantially reading strategies for feminist fiction had changed. Instead, in the early 1990s, it resurfaced in a film that catalyzed a new round of public and mass-media debates over the meaning of feminism. The media furor over *Thelma & Louise* was hardly a new phenomenon, and much of the discourse surrounding the film is strikingly similar to debates about the CR novels of the 1970s, and about *The Color Purple* in the early 1980s. The repetitions seem almost eerie, with (some) critics and feminist movement writers arguing vehemently that *Thelma & Louise* was *not* a feminist film, just as *The Women's Room* had vehemently been disclaimed in the late 1970s, and just as (some) black feminists had disclaimed *The Color Purple* in the early 1980s. Critic Margaret Carlson argued in *Time* that the film's version of liberation could not be feminist because the title characters were "free to behave like—well, men," rather than in some presumably authentic women's way; columnist Ellen Goodman dismissed the film as "a PMS movie, plain and simple" (in Schickel 54); Elayne Rapping argued that, despite the film's grounding in the issues of second-wave feminism, "I certainly don't think it's a feminist movie" ("Feminism Gets the Hollywood Treatment" 30). Popular texts, both fiction and film, have been and continue to be used to draw lines and set limits about what feminism is and what it means.

Thelma & Louise is a particularly rich example of the political problems posed by popular texts, meticulous in its use of CR strategies, even as it combines CR with the conventions of other genres, such as the road or buddy movie and the Western. "Somethin's, like, crossed over in me," Thelma tells Louise in one of the most important scenes in the film, "I can't go back—I just couldn't live." In a later scene, Thelma says, "I feel awake—wide awake. I don't remember ever feeling this awake. Know what I mean? Everything looks different. You feel like that too? Like you got something to look forward to?" The film offers several possible explanations for Thelma's crossing over or awakening, including her first orgasm ("You finally got laid properly," Louise says), her discovery of competence ("I just feel like I got a knack for this shit," she tells Louise), and her coming to a kind of self-expression through outlaw behavior ("You've always been crazy," Louise says, "this is just the first chance you've ever had to really express yourself"). Thelma's "crossing over" marks the film's engagement with feminist narrative strategies of CR.

Understanding *Thelma & Louise* as a CR narrative clarifies a number of important issues within the film itself, enabling a better reading of the film's peculiar status and use as a cultural artifact. That link to CR helps explain the film's appeal, especially to women who had some exposure to CR narratives in their earlier forms, in 1970s fiction and/or in the Women's Liberation Movement. That link to CR also helps account for the film's political deployment by feminists: the large number of women who attended a speech by Anita Hill wearing "Graduate of Thelma & Louise Finishing School" buttons; the t-shirt that sold widely at the 1992 abortion rights march on Washington showing Thelma and Louise sitting in the convertible aiming their guns, captioned "George Bush, Meet Thelma & Louise"; the bumpersticker that proclaimed "Thelma & Louise in '92."[8]

The use of images from the film in feminist politics marks as well the way the film, like the CR novel, makes consciousness-raising not only the subject but the objective of its narrative—the way it transacts CR as well as demonstrates it. I argue in Chapter Two that the CR novel has designs on its readers' consciousnesses as well as its characters', and enacts consciousness-raising as a transaction between author, character, and reader. Similarly, the responses of feminist viewers who use the images of the film in political work or to make political arguments about women's anger demonstrate two levels of the film's transaction of CR: first, viewers recognize that transaction having taken place in their own viewing, and second, they attempt to re-deploy it, to transact it again in another arena by juxtaposing the film with a current political issue.

Perhaps most important in examining *Thelma & Louise* as a CR narrative is the film's use of what I call (citing Alice Echols) in Chapter Three the stereographic view of sexuality. Like most post-1970s CR narratives, the film splits apart that view, using Thelma's rape or near-rape (as well as the hints of Louise's) as evidencing sexual oppression, and awkwardly but insistently providing a view of heterosexual awakening and freedom in Thelma's one-night stand with J.D. The rape scene in the film evidences an increasing attentiveness to some feminist concerns and analysis in mainstream Hollywood film; like *The Accused* (1988), *Thelma & Louise* presents an acquaintance rape, and does so in a way that clearly marks its violence.[9] Moreover, and this is clearly one of the sources of controversy about the film and its greatest source of pleasure for feminist viewers, *Thelma & Louise* insistently contextualizes the acquaintance rape, establishing it as the worst instance among many of men's contempt for women.

Many viewers of the film argue that Thelma's sexual pleasure with J.D., coming so soon after the attempted rape, is the least "realistic" part of the film. As Sarah Schulman puts it, "In real life, of course, very few battered and assaulted women would leap into a light-hearted, passionate, and sexually awakening one-night stand with a man they do not know" (34). This scene has been difficult for reviewers and critics to explain; most have read it as a move to contain the threat of lesbianism developing out of the theme of female bonding, or as an imitative generic move playing out the buddy-movie formula.[10] Without denying either of these readings, I would argue as well that the film's invocation of heterosexual pleasure is a necessary and essential feature of its CR narrative. The links the film makes between sexual violence and finding strength through fighting back, and between sexual pleasure and self-expression, follow the conventions of the CR novel's treatment of heterosexuality. The duality of heterosexual violence and pleasure— the location of heterosexuality as the simultaneous site of women's victimage and of women's freedom—completes the film's link to the CR narratives of the 1970s. Importantly, when Thelma finds heterosexual pleasure, she finds it as an active participant: "Wait, wait," she tells J.D., and takes control of the sexual activity. Only after Thelma has asserted control can she find pleasure: the power relations at the heart of CR narratives of heterosexuality construct women's power to express sexuality over and against men's power to make women into objects, and the film's depiction of heterosexuality makes that same turn.[11]

Moreover, *Thelma & Louise* presents Thelma's consciousness raising as taking shape in imitating or impersonating other people's language, an important formal feature of CR that I discussed in Chapter Two. When Thelma learns to defy her husband, she quotes Louise's words, "You're not my father, you're my husband," then adds, "Go fuck yourself." When she robs the liquor store, she imitates not only J.D.'s actions, but more specifically his spiel as he recited it to her.[12] When she pulls her gun on the police officer, virtually all of her conversation with him is a parody of his discourse, culminating in her polite command, "will you step into the trunk, please?" Even the officer's plea for mercy because he has a wife and kids becomes a parody in Thelma's mouth. "Better be sweet to them," she says, "especially your wife. My husband wasn't sweet to me and look how I turned out." The appropriation of others' language, especially through parody, is a central feature of the practice of CR, a heteroglossic re-figuring of events and affects. This passage from *The Female Man* exemplifies it nicely:

"I am the gateway to another world," (said I, looking in the mirror) "I am the earth-mother; I am the eternal siren; I am purity," (Jeeze, new pimples) "I am carnality; I have intuition; I am the life-force; I am selfless love." (Somehow it sounds different in the first person, doesn't it?)

Honey (said the mirror, scandalized) Are you out of your fuckin' *mind*? (205; emphasis original)

The CR novel most frequently parodies the discourses of patriarchal pronouncement either by showing us the protagonist's repetition of something believed earlier in the novel in parodic form later on, or, more simply, by putting these discourses into the mouths of fools. Like Thelma, protagonists learn by repetition, imitation, and parody.

Even the silence at the heart of the film—about what happened to Louise in Texas—can be linked to the film's use of CR narrative form. "I know what's making you run," the detective tells her, "I know what happened to you in Texas." "It happened to you, didn't it," Thelma asks, "in Texas, I mean—that's what happened to you—you was raped," but Louise refuses to discuss it, indeed, stops the car to make clear the vehemence of her refusal. Even unnarrated, the events in Texas are constantly referred to in Louise's refusal to go through Texas, her saying that that's where she learned how to shoot, and so forth. This kind of reference—what happened to Louise in Texas—can be linked directly to the CR novel's drive to name the unnameable, to its political burden of speaking the realities of women's lives that had not yet appeared in fiction. The tension between speech and silence, memory and repression, that this kind of reference enacts can be seen in Joan Didion's *Play It As It Lays*, in Maria's continual reference to her illegal abortion as "something that happened to her in Encino," a phrase used repeatedly in the novel, even though the story of the abortion is told to us. "What happened in Texas," like Didion's "something that happened in Encino," works as what folklorist Susan Kalčik calls a "kernel story" in her analysis of narrative structure of women's rap groups in the 1970s (7). Kalčik's essay title gives examples from her research: ". . . like Anne's gynecologist or the time I was almost raped." The film's kernel story enables us to see Louise's process of CR in the film as well as Thelma's: the recurrence of "Texas" as a figuration for unnamed violence against women (probably, we believe, sexual violence) links the two women's experience, establishing them as a (very small but nonetheless fully functioning) CR group. Thelma's CR is, of course, the more obvious, particularly in the moment of insight where she says, "I'm not sorry that son of a bitch is dead. I'm just sorry it was you that did it and not me." Nonetheless, Louise's realization that "Jimmy's not an option" and that both she and he had gotten "what we settled for" surely counts.

The film also contains a small redeployment of the sex/race analogy, a convention of the CR novel and of 1970s feminism that I discuss in Chapter Six. Manohla Dargis summarizes the scene:

a key scene in *Thelma & Louise* has a black Rastafarian cycle incongruously into the picture. . . . The stormtrooper-turned-crybaby wiggles a small, white, very wormy finger through an airhole after the women leave, only to have the Rasta blow back the exhaust of his spliff in reply. The American landscape has ceased to be the exclusive province of white masculinity. (88)

This scene is gratuitous, serving only as a brief moment of comic relief as the tension of the police pursuit of Thelma and Louise escalates. It is also the sole appearance of a black person in the film. The only logical reading of this scene in the film is that Thelma and Louise's liberation from conventional femininity and from the law opens up the landscape to other freedoms, in a repetition of the radical feminist domino theory of oppressions. In this scene, the film suggests that women's liberation is indeed everybody's liberation.[13]

Extratextually, the link to the CR novel helps account for the controversy that surrounded the film, and particularly for the arguments that its depictions of men characters were appalling, as so many of the CR novels of the 1970s received similar critical responses. "Men can't be that bad," argued the critics, especially but not exclusively men, in response to the CR novel, as I argue in Chapter Four. John Leo's widely quoted review of *Thelma & Louise*, "Toxic Feminism on the Big Screen," argued that "All males in this movie exist only to betray, ignore, sideswipe, penetrate, or arrest our heroines"; Fred Bruning described the men as "crooks, studs, tyrants, or ninnies"; and *Playboy*'s Asa Baber (not surprisingly, given the venue) argued that "The most primitive message behind *Thelma & Louise* is that a lot of men need killing these days." Richard Grenier in *Commentary* uses a particularly interesting rhetorical strategy to make his case: "When they are not actual rapists, they are violent (to women), insulting (to women), surly (to women), charming but treacherous (to women), and in all possible other ways obnoxious (to women)" (52). Grenier's insistent repetition of "(to women)" clearly is supposed to make us doubt the "fairness" of the portrayals, and the parentheses emphasize the marginality of women's perceptions. *Thelma & Louise*, like *The Women's Room*, is held to be just too "one-sided" by these critics.

Particular readings and misreadings of the ending also become clearer in relation to the film's use of CR narrative. We see the car in midair; we see it begin to arc downward into the Grand Canyon and lose a hubcap; we know that Thelma and Louise must necessarily die in the crash at the bottom. But we do not see them crash and we do not see them die—the screen fades to white and we see instead earlier scenes from the film. Viewers of *Thelma & Louise* similarly insist on finding some kind of openness in the film's ending: "they drive off into the sky," or "they get to the other side," some viewers explain, or, as my button insists, "Thelma and Louise Live!" or, as one version of the t-shirt goes further, "Thelma and Louise Live Forever."[14] Critics make a range of metaphors out of the film's open ending: "escaping the frame that confines them" (L. Braudy 29); "escaping closure" (Glancy); "a triumphant apotheosis" (Murphy 29); "an apotheosis, a flight into forever" (Chumo 24); "[pushing] over the edge of the world" (Rafferty 86). Cathy Griggers produces a camp reading that takes the kiss at the end as central:

Kiss and die. Thelma and Louise are floating afterwards—below them death awaits, expansive, a canyon of empty air, a finite moment of infinite possibility. *They could care less.* The kiss is the final dare, perhaps, or better, a letting go until there's nothing left but the momentary clasping of hands, limbs, *for however long it lasts.* But don't be mistaken; these women are already falling when they kiss. They don't die because they kiss, rather they kiss because they're going to die. (132–33; emphasis original)

Such insistences are more than simply idiosyncratic bad readings or willful misreadings. Griggers argues that "aberrant" readings like hers are especially fetishized in camp readings, but are in fact "generally 'normative' for any readership" (134). The readership of *Thelma & Louise* that insists on the open ending of the film—whether as the opening of a lesbian narrative or as the suspension of the laws of physics (as Laws of the Father, perhaps?)—is shaped by the open ending of the CR novel.

As I argue in Chapter Two, CR novels almost always employ open endings, ending, for instance, half-way through a sentence, on the verge of action, or with a decision made but not yet executed; this is the type of ending Rachel Blau DuPlessis calls "writing beyond the ending," identifying it as an essential narrative strategy of twentieth-century women's fiction. The CR novel employs that strategy in sometimes extravagantly self-conscious ways—with Jong's Isadora Wing in the bathtub waiting for her husband, with Russ's promise of freedom in the final line of *The Female Man* ("On that day we will all be free"), with Dorothy Bryant's Ella Price just beginning to inhale the anaesthetic before her abortion (the novel ends with "I feel . . ."). Thelma and Louise do live if we read the ending of the film as if it were a consciousness-raising novel—as if their driving off into the sky were a beginning rather than an ending.

At the same time, of course, we do know that they die. The formal ambiguity of the film—the driving off into the sky and running the film backward through every shot of Thelma and Louise together and smiling[15]—enables viewers to have it both ways. On one hand, feminist viewers can see Thelma's and Louise's death as telling the truth about patriarchy: that women's freedom is not possible within a system of patriarchy, that feminism (here figured simply as breaking patriarchal rules) has costs and consequences for women. *Patriarchy kills women* is how we might read this ending—or, alternatively, and more in keeping with the anti-feminist backlash of the 1980s and early 1990s, *feminism kills women.* On the other hand, viewers can see the open ending of the film as mimicking the practice of CR: the earlier scenes from the film are gathered up and handed over to viewers as the summing up at the end of the CR meeting.

And yet, I want to suggest that *Thelma & Louise*'s political weight is ultimately limited by its use of the conventions of popular film. The film's generic gestures toward buddy-movies, road movies, and Westerns, which may be transgressive to some extent simply in populating those genres with women outlaws, in the end contain the film's feminism.[16] Importantly, Thelma and Louise are alone even when they are together, unable to connect with any other women—and, indeed, there are almost no other women characters in the film. While Pat Dowell lauds the film for its vision of "sisterhood" (30), that sisterhood includes only Thelma and Louise. The waitress at the bar where Louise shoots Harlan, virtually the only other woman character with any lines,[17] tells Hal Slocum that "neither of those two was the murderin' type," thus refusing the film's central truth: that any woman can become "the murderin' type" if pushed far enough, that respectable housewives and waitresses can be motivated by a specifically female and indeed feminist rage. Like the CR novel, and, indeed, like CR itself in its slippage from "hard" to "soft" versions over the course of the 1970s, aspects of the film seem to point in more radical directions, but fail in the end to get there. The glory that is Thelma and Louise's road trip is a profoundly Western-generic glory in the end: the lone rangers of the highways set against the backdrop of red rock monuments, consciousness raising that can never become transformative political change or do any work, but remains only a fleeting, individual experience of freedom and power.

Even so, the film's feminism cannot ultimately be decided on the basis of a close reading, cannot ultimately be contained textually. *Thelma & Louise* has done work as a feminist text: the film has been used by feminists to mark the legitimacy of feminist anger, the disruptive possibilities of that anger's transformation into power, and this has been its greatest pleasure for feminist viewers.[18] But such pleasure, as affirming as it may be of our own sense of feminism's radicality, as confirming of the righteousness and moral high ground of feminist anger, may also mark a sense of radical failure. Linda Brodkey and Michelle Fine have suggested that "outrageous acts" and "extraordinary methods" are the recourse of women who "despair over adamant institutional refusal to listen and act" in the face of women's oppression (93). The deployment of images from *Thelma & Louise* by mainstream feminists marks, I suggest, a specific historical moment of a very real sense of impotence, of powerlessness, that feminists felt in the early 1990s. What answer could feminists provide to the Clarence Thomas confirmation, the William Kennedy Smith rape trial — "spectacles," as Kirsten Marthe Lentz points out, "which have shown us in tortured detail that the justice system does not serve women of all racial and sexual categories" (398)? [19] What could we do with George Bush but fantasize shooting him, given that he — like Harlan, the rapist, or like Earl, the harassing trucker — was utterly unafraid of us, utterly disrespectful toward us, despite whatever weapons we held to his head? What kind of dialogue is possible when even modest feminist reforms become demonized in Pat Buchanan's vision of "feminazis"? Louise's too-late, "You watch your mouth, buddy," after she's killed Harlan is precisely how many feminists felt after women voters in particular turned Bush and Quayle out of office. In this political context, it is not surprising that *Thelma & Louise* became a sort of cult film for feminists, just as Susan Faludi's *Backlash* became a best-seller that same year. It is also not surprising that the film generated the controversy that it did, for in the 1990s as in the 1970s, no vision of feminism is or could be uncontested.

Those contestations no longer play out in fiction as a, or the, privileged arena. To some extent, we can see the move of CR narrative strategies into film (and Hollywood film in particular) as marking the movement's success in influencing discourses about violence against women, and about women's anger. If one of the primary goals of CR was, as Redstockings argued in their manifesto, to create and further women's class consciousness as women, that class consciousness, or gender consciousness as we might more accurately name it, is now ubiquitous in United States culture. As Bonnie J. Dow points out in her analysis of the *Lifetime* "network for women," this gender consciousness can be used to deliver a market segment for advertisers; Susan Douglas argues in her "Narcissism as Liberation" chapter in *Where the Girls Are* that the fitness and cosmetics industries likewise appropriated feminist discourses for their advertising purposes during the 1980s; Naomi Wolf goes so far as to argue in *Fire with Fire* that advertising itself provides a better feminism than the movement currently does, citing the Nike "Just Do It" campaign.[20] Certain kinds of basic feminist ideas no longer require either consciousness raising or fiction, particularly the kinds of analysis generated by self-help-oriented, "soft" CR.

Indeed, arguably one of the primary arenas in United States culture for the self-help versions of "soft" CR is the television talk show. Talk shows frequently focus on women and girls, often working- and lower-middle-class women and girls. That talk shows relentlessly personalize and pathologize problems which cry out for feminist political analysis does not contradict the point, nor does the presence of "experts" conceal the ways the talk show format resembles some versions of the CR group. The non-expert guests share personal narratives, and answer questions from both host and audience members; the talk-show format in fact resembles nothing so much as the stage-managed, performed CR I describe in Chapter Two at a Women Against Pornography conference in 1979. At this conference, the WAP organizers began with speeches, then a slide show, and these were followed by a "speakout" in which, as Brooke Williams described it, a series of "excerpts from letters from women around the country were read, describing harrowing incidents with porn" ("porn again" 24). The comparison here lies in the ways that talk shows, like the performed CR of WAP, maintain tight control over both the topic and the analysis; just as Williams perceived after the speakout that "the only admissible experiences with porn were real horror stories" ("porn again" 25), the only admissible analyses in talk shows are analyses of individual pathology. Even racism, which receives more attention on talk shows than in almost any other arena of contemporary culture, is treated as prejudice, as attitudes and beliefs that are best solved by educating individuals; systemic or institutional racism is rarely addressed.[21] Television talk shows may help forward a kind of feminist literacy when the shows address women's issues, but the shows' overwhelming emphasis on analyzing these issues as individual problems with individual solutions does not allow for CR as such, and indeed may preclude political or systemic analyses on the part of viewers.[22]

Another important venue for something like the CR group in contemporary United States feminism by the middle 1990s has been created by information technologies, including the Internet, the World Wide Web, and topical bulletin boards and chat rooms. While some electronic list-serves are specifically academic and professionally-oriented (WMST-L, for example[23]), others engage a broader range of issues and topics, and depend on exchanges of personal narratives, political diatribes, and everything in between. Such venues depend on access to computer technology and to the Internet, which makes them a particular province of college women—tending toward the young and the middle-class, the professional and the academic. Carla Sinclair's *Net Chick: A Smart-Girl Guide to the Wired Web* (1996), which bills itself as "the only guide to stylish, post-feminist, modern grrrl culture" (4), provides a directory of women's web sites, including a handful of explicitly feminist ones. Most of these are campy, cultural, musical, fashionable—too hip to be serious, and indeed, postfeminist in any number of senses of the term.[24] At the same time, even the most postfeminist of web sites has the potential to be a useful place for the exchange of information, and for the encouraging of a kind of attitude which begins in gender consciousness but need not end there. Some kinds of postfeminism, I suggest, may be proto-feminist in their effects.

A critical and related venue for the feminism of young women in particular is the Riot Grrrl movement in alternative music.[25] Norah Salmon explains the movement's varieties of separatism:

Riot grrl bands separate from corporate rock assimilation by establishing their own independent record labels, from radio assimilation by making their music unplayable on FCC policed airwaves, from mainstream record store exploitation by being independently distributed or by selling directly to alternative record stores, and from pop music's vapid appeal to mainstream audiences by making music that is socio-politically charged. (10)

Much of the music, as Salmon points out, using examples from lyrics by Bikini Kill, both eroticizes the figure of the "rebel girl" and establishes sexuality as "a mode of agency in resistance to oppression" (15). Perhaps a signal connection between Riot Grrls and second-wave feminism is a shared attitude of defiance; the lyrics of groups like Bikini Kill and the rhetoric of some web sites echo—sometimes eerily—the style of second-wave manifestos, the hyperbole of SCUM or the theatricality of WITCH, reminding us, as Brodkey and Fine note, that "the outrageous is . . . of untold pedagogical value" (93).

Accompanying the music and the web sites are the self-published, self-consciously "amateur" 'zines.[26] Deeply influenced by the DIY (do it yourself), anti-professional, and anti-slick ethos and aesthetics of punk and post-punk music, 'zines are often remarkably similar to the some of the early writings of the Women's Liberation Movement, in their mimeographed, sold-on-the-streetcorner quality in particular. At the same time, however, 'zines tend to be produced by individuals rather than by groups, and thus to rely heavily on the single personal narrative rather than on a collection of them. Thus, like the CR novel itself, 'zines may often function as testimony of the absent member.

In this respect, 'zines operate like more established publications of the feminist press—*off our backs, Ms., On the Issues, Sojourner, Hurricane Alice*, just to name a few—which also provide individual narratives to serve as testimonies. By contrast, though, 'zines tend to appeal to younger and much narrower audiences, and to emphasize a specifically "grrrl"-oriented politics and aesthetics. When, for instance, feminist-political alternative rock begins to find its way into "mainstream" feminism, it does so with some ambivalence. *Ms.* published an article on Tribe 8's controversial appearance at the Michigan Womyn's Music Festival, and *On the Issues* on the groups that are "where the pulse of young feminism beats" (Saraco 26). The particular issue of *OTI* in which Saraco's article appeared catches nicely this ambivalence. The cover story by Sheila Jeffreys, "How Orgasm Politics Has Hijacked the Women's Movement," disparages body piercings and tattoos as what she calls the "sexuality of self-mutilation and slavery" (21); seven pages later, the full-page photo collage accompanying Margaret R. Saraco's article on rock visually celebrates the multiply-pierced and tattooed Lunachicks, Tribe 8, and Ani DiFranco. Some of the ambivalence demonstrated in *OTI* about the political valences of personal style is simply generational difference, while some has deeper roots in substantive political disagreements.[27]

In any case, the various sites of grrrl culture—web sites, music, 'zines—offer to young women much the same kind of potential CR as did the CR novel of the 1970s. Julie E. Cooper, reviewing a recent book on rock and roll for the *Nation*, makes an argument about Grrrl music that bears a remarkable similarity to my arguments about fiction in the 1970s:

> . . . the first record by Bikini Kill, a feminist Riot Grrrl band, begins when singer Kathleen Hanna announces, "We're Bikini Kill, and we want a revolution girl-style now!" While a girl can become a feminist by listening to records in isolation, she can only start a revolution by participating in collective political action. (33)

Cooper quite accurately catches the importance of Riot Grrrl music to women's individual feminist self-fashioning, to the perceptual shift that "becoming feminist" might entail, as well as the limitations of such self-fashioning if it does not lead to political action.

No study of consciousness raising can ignore what is the most significant arena for feminist discourse outside the Movement: Women's Studies. The curriculum of Women's Studies provides what Cheri Register identified as the crucial supplement to feminist fiction: "factual information about the status of women from other sources" (23). "Introduction to Women's Studies" classes often serve as sites for CR, whether deliberately or not, places in which feminist literacy becomes politicized as students begin to see their experience in relation to broader, national and international systems. The importance of CR to Women's Studies courses is simultaneously one of the great joys and great burdens of teaching such courses: on one hand, the CR processes of individual students can be enormously powerful resources for the class, while, on the other, "soft" CR can pull on a classroom like a kind of quicksand into which the material at hand sinks out of sight.

Many recent critiques of Women's Studies have seized upon this latter tendency as evidence of the intellectual bankruptcy of the discipline. Such critiques of Women's Studies in most respects simply replay the critiques of CR itself (as bourgeois, as therapeutic, or as self-indulgent) among late 1960s radicals, as eerily as the controversy about *Thelma &*

Louise in the early 1990s replayed the "men can't be that bad" debates.[28] At the same time, however, many of these critiques are underwritten by right-wing think tanks in conjunction with other attacks on higher education, which does differentiate them from New Leftist sniping at Women's Liberation.[29] Given the resources of some of these critics of Women's Studies, it seems clear that disavowing or abandoning the CR component of the Intro course will not appease them. We—faculty and other defenders of the field—might more usefully turn our energies toward defending CR as a critical learning strategy, and link it to similar learning strategies in disciplines other than Women's Studies. To do so successfully requires that we address the difference between "soft" and "hard" CR, and shift our emphasis toward the latter.

In "Small Group Pedagogy: Consciousness Raising in Conservative Times," Estelle B. Freedman proposes a concrete solution to the difficulty of both covering the material in the Intro course and making space for students' necessary personal applications of it. Her "Introduction to Feminist Studies" course assigns students to meet biweekly in small groups, in which they are asked to address CR-style questions and keep a notebook of their meetings. Students then write up an (ungraded but required) account of their groups at the end of the term.[30] Freedman's students' accounts of their small-group experiences demonstrate the continuing value and importance of CR, particularly as a way of processing "factual information about the status of women from other sources" in relation to students' own experience. Building the CR process formally into the course design requires that students take it seriously; asking students to evaluate the process makes room for students' dissent, critique, and theorizing. The structure Freedman lays out here enables "hard" CR: not only do students narrate and assemble their experiences, but they also interrogate and connect those experiences and narratives to the course materials.[31]

Consciousness raising will happen in the Intro course, as it will in other Women's Studies courses; many (if not most) students do reflect on their own experiences in relation to new knowledge about women, gender, and feminism. What Freedman's account of her course and course design suggests is that we can structure our courses to incorporate a better (more intellectually sound, more politically and theoretically sophisticated) version of it. At the same time, we can avoid the quicksand of "soft" CR in the classroom, better enabling the intellectual work and rigor of the discipline.

To use CR effectively in the 1990s, in and out of our classrooms, our academic work, and our political work, we must retrieve it from its use as metaphor. CR is not simply feminist literacy; it is not simply awareness of women's issues; it is not simply a reading strategy for fiction; it is not simply a practice of raising women's self-esteem. These metaphorical uses of the term work in much the same way that the sex/race analogy did: via a simultaneous nostalgia for and forgetting of the struggles of the Women's Liberation Movement, CR as metaphor for anything vaguely feminist invokes a fantastic vision of a self-evident identity, community, and politics. Too, CR as a metaphor implicitly or explicitly creates a self-evident narrative of political progress, which distracts us from the more difficult work of tracing out what feminism has and has not accomplished. In these ways, the use of CR as a metaphor leaps over the real work and the real contestations, the difficult arguments and dissenting visions, the fractures and fault-lines which make contemporary feminism anything but self-evident.

This book has traced a specific recent history of consciousness raising and its relationship to the fiction that emerged from the Women's Liberation Movement. By exploring questions about the meanings and contests for meaning around issues of sexuality, men, the future, the relationships between sex and race, and CR itself, I hope to clear some ground for what has come since the feminist high renaissance of the 1970s, in fiction, in movement practice, and in feminist theory. We can neither forget the 1970s nor simply invoke that decade nostalgically, if we are to continue working for women's freedom.

Notes

1. For another reading of *The Truth About Lorin Jones* as "postfeminist," see Greene, 199.
2. The most famous nineteenth-century example is Harriet Jacobs's *Incidents in the Life of a Slave Girl*, which not only presents a crucial alliance between Linda Brent and Mrs. Bruce as a means to Linda's gaining her freedom, but also meticulously details the harmful effects on white women of masters' sexual abuse of women slaves.
3. For an elegant summation of this perspective in feminist theory, see de Lauretis, "Feminist Studies/Critical Studies: Issues, Terms, and Contexts."
4. See Ruth Rosen, "The Female Generation Gap," for a view of second-wave feminism as motivated by young women's attempts to forge different lives from their mothers'.
5. See Rita Felski, "Money, Sex, and Power."
6. This disappearance of the housewife-protagonist was never total, of course, and she remains a staple of detective fiction in particular, as part of the convention of the amateur sleuth (Jill Churchill's comic mysteries about widowed housewife Jane Jeffry are good examples), and of romance (including romances written by men, as *The Bridges of Madison County* exemplifies). Examples in the 1990s include Olivia Goldsmith's housewife-turned-writer in *The First Wives Club* (1992), a revenge narrative played for broad comedy in the film version, and Marge Piercy's housewife-turned-homeless-housecleaner in *The Longings of*

Women (1994), a much more overtly political novel about women's impoverishment after divorce.

7. For a discussion of such workshops in relation to Women's Studies teaching, see Estelle Freedman, "Small Group Pedagogy."

8. In "Anita Hill and Revitalizing Feminism," Deborah Sontag notes the *Thelma & Louise* buttons in Hill's audience; the various buttons and bumperstickers were sold widely in feminist bookstores; the "Meet George Bush" t-shirt was a popular souvenir among my students who attended the 1992 march.

9. Whatever else reviewers and critics of *Thelma & Louise* have debated, this depiction of rape is the sole unquestioned, perhaps unquestionable, feminist element of the film. Elayne Rapping's "Feminism Gets the Hollywood Treatment" is especially smart on this point. To see this depiction of rape as the stunning progress it is, one need only compare it to the rape scene in Paul Mazursky's *Blume in Love* (1973). When Blume rapes his ex-wife as part of his campaign to win her back, the scene is played for comedy, as evidence of his pathetic desperation. More disturbing than the scene itself was the feminist critical (non) response: Molly Haskell, as late as 1978, specifically pointed to the rape scene as exemplifying Mazursky's risk-taking and freedom from ideology, of which she heartily approved ("A Woman's Movement" 72); Gail Rock, reviewing the film in *Ms.*, simply overlooked the scene.

10. See, e.g., Pat Dowell, 29.

11. Two critics—Sharon Willis and Manohla Dargis—point specifically to the film's eroticizing J.D. as instances of its use of gender reversal, which we might see as the film's technical underlining of Thelma's agency in the sex scene.

12. Roy Grundmann argues that Thelma's imitative behavior in the robbery makes her a "stand-in for her ex-lover" (36); Peter N. Chumo II argues, by contrast, that Thelma, "makes the role her own and adjusts the robbery to suit her own tastes" (24).

13. Perhaps one might argue that even the "stormtrooper-turned-crybaby," as Dargis calls him, is liberated in his transformation, particularly if we read his tears in relation to the "sensitive man" of the 1970s, liberated from the constraints of conventional masculinity by tears.

14. I am indebted to my students who took me to see *Thelma & Louise* several times and collected their own and their friends' impressions of the ending; thanks to Curtis Bowman, Michelle Holley, and Fran Slater in particular.

15. This backwards running of the film contains an unusual choice of shots: the moment when they are stopped by the police officer. In the context of the body of the film, it is clear that their smiles here are forced and artificial, the surface (women's) obedience to (a man's) power required in the situation ("Oh my God, he's a Nazi," Louise says when the officer gets out of his car). In the context of the other shots in this collage, however, their smiles seem to refer instead to their later pleasure at having outwitted the officer.

16. Virtually every reviewer compares the film to *Butch Cassidy and the Sundance Kid*, for instance, and several compare it to *Easy Rider*.

17. There are two other women characters who speak: the waitress at the Oklahoma City motel coffee shop who teases Louise about her passionate good-bye kiss with Jimmy, and a woman police officer or sheriff who appears very briefly, speaking into her radio, at the beginning of the first chase scene. We also hear women speaking in the backgrounds in most of the coffee shops in the film.

18. For a version of this argument, see Kirsten Marthe Lentz, "The Popular

Pleasures of Female Revenge (Or Rage Bursting in a Blaze of Gunfire)," which discusses *Thelma & Louise* together with other films depicting women with guns.

19. The network television version of *Thelma & Louise,* because it necessarily eliminated the profanity and explicit sexual references (so that Harlan's "suck my cock" became "clean my clock," for example), replayed a very interesting dynamic from the Thomas-Hill hearings. In the hearings, we heard only Hill (and her interrogators) use the language of harassment; it is in the nature of such proceedings that the accused need never demonstrate his capacity to use such language. Similarly, in the televised version of the film, absent the men characters' profanity and verbal harassment, the women's violent responses must necessarily seem excessive, far removed from self-defense or legitimate anger. In the midst of arguments that "men can't be that bad," questions of women's credibility thus become central.

20. See Dow's critique of Wolf's position in the Afterword to *Prime-Time Feminism* 211–13.

21. Oprah Winfrey has, for example, done several shows devoted to racism in the past few years; all of them without exception have forwarded the individualist analysis.

22. Of course, oppositional readings of talk shows are possible; viewers may choose to supplement the shows' emphasis on individual solutions with their own systemic analyses, and thus to use the shows as CR-style testimony. But these analyses do not come from the shows themselves. It is clear, I think, that I am not generally sympathetic to arguments that talk-show culture is feminist as such, though I am somewhat more sympathetic to an analysis of talk shows as forwarding gay and lesbian visibility—but here, too, I would set this under the rubric of literacy rather than CR. That is, the issue of visibility is a question of literacy, of basic awareness of the existence and ubiquity of gay men and lesbians, rather than a political analysis of heterosexism or homophobia.

23. WMST-L is a list moderated by Joan Korenman, designed for the exchange of information about Women's Studies, including job postings, calls for papers, and topical discussions about Women's Studies teaching and research.

24. Sinclair's own web site celebrates Camille Paglia, for instance, whose appeal to "webgrrls" Michelle Wodtke Franks' analysis describes this way: "The message . . . (to suck it up, quit whining and don't let the current conspiratorial feminist discourse make you a victim) holds appeal for a generation that has greatly benefitted from the activism of the second wave combined with a generational cynicism that embraces conspiracy theories" (3). Franks looks specifically at the *Nrrdgrrl!* and *geekgirl* sites (http://www.winternet.com/~ameliaw/nrrdfaq. html and http://www.youth.nsw.gov.au/rob.upload/friendly/fintro.html, respectively), arguing that these sites represent not postfeminism but a version of Donna Haraway's metaphor of the cyborg.

25. The term Riot Grrrl or Grrl refers loosely to a wide range of music, 'zines, and web sites (among other kinds of cultural production) made by young women, sometimes working with young men. Salmon argues that Riot Grrls constitute a kind of youth separatist movement with strongly pro-feminist and anti-corporate politics.

26. The term *'zine* derives from *fanzine,* a newsletter-style, amateur production surrounding bands or other mass-/pop-culture phenomena such as science fiction.

27. For a smart exploration of the meaning of style in lesbian communities in

particular, one aspect of what's at stake in the *OTI* issue, see Arlene Stein, "Style Wars and the New Lesbianism."

28. Perhaps the most influential of these critiques of Women's Studies is Daphne Patai and Noretta Koertge, *Professing Feminism: Cautionary Tales from the Strange World of Women's Studies* (1994); Alice Kessler-Harris's review in *Academe* is useful in contextualizing this volume. See Ruth Conniff, "Warning: Feminism Is Hazardous to Your Health," for an account of the Independent Women's Forum attempt to link Women's Studies to "an all-out assault on medical science" (34), which includes an account of Koertge's presentation at the IWF conference Coniff describes.

29. Sommers's *Who Stole Feminism?* is the best example. For an account of these attacks that follows the money, see Ellen Messer-Davidow, "Manufacturing the Attack on Liberalized Higher Education"; Annette Kolodny makes an important link between attacks on tenure and attacks on Women's Studies in "Why Feminists Need Tenure," as does Messer-Davidow in "Doing the Right Thing."

30. Full disclosure: I was one of the Teaching Assistants for this course in 1988; to Freedman's conclusions, I would add that the small group structure enabled the larger discussion sections to focus primarily on the course material. Since Freedman's article appeared in *NWSA Journal* in 1990, others have duplicated this structure, often with great success.

31. The sheer number of Freedman's students who incorporate language and concepts from course materials into their accounts of the small group process evidences this point.

Works Cited

Abbott, Sidney and Barbara Love. "Is Women's Liberation a Lesbian Plot?" In Gornick and Moran, 436–51.

Acker, Kathy. *Blood and Guts in High School.* 1978. Rpt. New York: Grove, 1989.

———. *Kathy Goes to Haiti.* 1978. Rpt. in *Literal Madness.* New York: Grove, 1988, 1–170.

Alberts, Mimi. Rev. of *Play It As It Lays* by Joan Didion. *off our backs,* November 1971, 20.

———. Rev. of *Small Changes* by Marge Piercy. *off our backs,* October 1973, 12.

Alcoff, Linda. "Cultural Feminism Versus Post-Structuralism: The Identity Crisis in Feminist Theory." *Signs* 13, 3 (Spring 1988) 405–36.

Alice Doesn't Live Here Anymore. Dir. Martin Scorsese. 1974.

Alper, Rika, Pris Hoffnung, and Barbara Solomon. "i eat your flesh plus i drink your blood (the double features of the abortion business)." *off our backs,* October 1972, 10–11.

Alther, Lisa. *Kinflicks.* 1975. Rpt. New York: Knopf, 1976.

Althusser, Louis. "Ideology and Ideological State Apparatuses (Notes Toward an Investigation)." *Lenin and Philosophy.* New York: Monthly Review Press, 1971, 121–73.

"Altitude Sickness" Rev. of *Fear of Flying* by Erica Jong, *Times Literary Supplement,* 26 July 1974, 813.

Andersen, Margaret. "Feminism as a Criterion of the Literary Critic." 1975. Rpt. in Brown and Olson, 1–10.

Ann. "NOW: a new perspective?" *off our backs,* July 1974, 9.

Atkinson, Ti-Grace. "Lesbianism and Feminism: Justice for Women As 'Unnatural.'" 1970. Rpt. in *Amazon Odyssey.* New York: Links, 1974, 131–34.

———. "The Institution of Sexual Intercourse." 1968. Rpt. in *Amazon Odyssey.* New York: Links, 1974, 13–23.

Atwood, Margaret. *The Handmaid's Tale.* New York: Fawcett, 1986.

———. *Lady Oracle.* 1976. Rpt. New York: Ballantine, 1987.

———. *Surfacing.* 1972. Rpt. New York: Warner Books, 1984.

Baber, Asa. "Guerilla Feminism." *Playboy,* October 1991, 45.

Bakhtin, Mikhail M. "Discourse in the Novel." *The Dialogic Imagination.* Trans. Caryl Emerson and Michael Holquist, ed. Michael Holquist. Austin: University of Texas Press, 1981, 259–422.

Barker-Plummer, Bernadette. "News as a Political Resource: Media Strategies and Political Identity in the U.S. Women's Movement, 1966–1975." *Critical Studies in Mass Communication* 12 (1986): 306–24.

Barr, Marleen S. *Feminist Fabulation: Space/Postmodern Fiction.* Iowa City: University of Iowa Press, 1992.

———. *Lost in Space: Probing Feminist Science Fiction and Beyond.* Chapel Hill: University of North Carolina Press, 1993.

Barry, Kathleen. "Deconstructing Deconstruction (or, Whatever Happened to Feminist Studies?)." *Ms.,* January/February 1991, 83–85.

Bartky, Sandra Lee. "Toward a Phenomenology of Feminist Consciousness." In *Feminism and Philosophy,* ed. Mary Vetterlin-Braggin, Frederick A. Elliston, and Jane English. Totowa, N.J.: Littlefield, Adams, 1977, 22–37.

Baumgardner, Jennifer. "*Who* Shot Andy Warhol?" Rev. of *I Shot Andy Warhol,* dir. Mary Harron. *Ms.,* May/June 1996, 73–74.

Baym, Nina. *Woman's Fiction: A Guide to Novels by and about Women in America 1820–1870.* Ithaca, N.Y.: Cornell University Press, 1978.

Beck, Evelyn Torton, ed. *Nice Jewish Girls: A Lesbian Anthology.* Trumansburg, N.Y.: Crossing Press, 1982.

Berlant, Lauren. "Race, Gender, and Nation in *The Color Purple.*" *Critical Inquiry* 14 (Summer 1988): 831–59.

bernice. "keeping an eye on iwy in the midwest." *off our backs,* July 1975, 23.

Bird, Caroline. *Born Female.* Rev. ed. New York: Pocket, 1971.

Bloch, Alice. "In Praise of Criticism." Letter, *Chrysalis* 4 (1977): 9.

Blum, Linda M. "Feminism and the Mass Media: A Case Study of *The Women's Room* as Novel and Television Film." *Berkeley Journal of Sociology* 27 (1982): 1–26.

Bobo, Jacqueline. "Sifting Through the Controvery: Reading *The Color Purple.*" *Callaloo* 12 (Spring 1989): 332–42.

Bogan, Louise. "Women." *The Blue Estuaries.* New York: Ecco, 1977, 19.

Boyle, Kay. *The Underground Woman.* New York: Holt, 1975.

Braudy, Leo. "Satire into Myth." *Film Quarterly* 45 (Winter 1991–92): 28–29.

Braudy, Susan. "A Day in the Life of Joan Didion." *Ms.,* February 1977, 65–68, 108–9.

———. "She Only Laughs When It Hurts." Rev. of *Making Ends Meet* by Barbara Howar. *Ms.,* June 1976, 95–96.

Brodkey, Linda and Michelle Fine. "Presence of Mind in the Absence of Body." In *Disruptive Voices: The Possibilities of Feminist Research,* ed. Michelle Fine. Ann Arbor: University of Michigan Press, 1992. 77–95.

Brody, Leslie. "From Where We Came and to Whom We Speak: American Religious and Secular Jewish Feminist Contributions, 1970–1986." Unpublished M.A. paper, Women's Studies, University of Cincinnati, Winter 1997.

Broner, E. M. *Her Mothers.* 1975. Rpt. Bloomington: Indiana University Press, 1985.

———. *A Weave of Women.* 1978. Rpt. Bloomington: Indiana University Press, 1985.

Brown, Cheryl L. and Karen Olson, eds. *Feminist Criticism: Essays on Theory, Poetry and Prose.* Metuchen, N.J.: Scarecrow, 1978.

Brown, Helen Gurley. *Sex and the Single Girl.* 1962. Rpt. New York, Pocket, 1963.

Brown, Rita Mae. "Reflections of a Lavender Menace: Remembering When Lesbians Challenged the Women's Movement." *Ms.,* July/August 1995, 40–47.

———. *Rubyfruit Jungle.* 1973. Rpt. New York: Bantam, 1977.

Broyard, Anatole. "Two Heroines." Rev. of *Rachel, the Rabbi's Wife* by Silvia Tennenbaum and *The High Cost of Living* by Marge Piercy. *New York Times Book Review,* 22 January 1978, 14.

Bruning, Fred. "A Lousy Deal for Women—and Men." *MacLean's*, August 12, 1991, 9.

Brunsdon, Charlotte. "A Subject for the Seventies." *Screen* 23, 3–4 (1982): 20–29.

Bryant, Dorothy. *Ella Price's Journal.* Philadelphia: Lippincott, 1972.

———. *The Kin of Ata Are Waiting for You.* Originally published as *The Comforter* in 1971. Berkeley, Calif.: Moon Books, 1976.

Bryant, Sylvia. "The Incredible Shrinking Movement? Some Thoughts on Star Trek, Feminist Anonymity, and Hillary's Cookies." Paper given at "Feminist Generations," Bowling Green State University, February 1996.

Burris, Barbara. "The Fourth World Manifesto." In Koedt, Levine, and Rapone, 322–57.

Butler, Cheryl B. "The Color Purple Controversy: Black Woman Spectatorship." *Wide Angle* 13, 3 & 4 (1991): 62–69.

Butler, Judith. "The Force of Fantasy: Feminism, Mapplethorpe, and Discursive Excess." *differences* (1990): 20–28.

Butler, Octavia. *Xenogenesis* trilogy: *Dawn.* New York: Warner, 1987. *Adulthood Rites.* New York: Warner, 1988. *Imago.* New York: Warner, 1989.

Cabrillo, Toni. "N.O.W.'s Rush to Judgment: The *American Psycho* Connection." *On the Issues,* Summer 1996, 20.

Campbell, Karlyn Kohrs. "The Rhetoric of Women's Liberation: An Oxymoron." *Quarterly Journal of Speech* 59 (February 1973): 74–86.

"Can We Talk? An *OTI* Dialogue with Tammy Bruce and Julianne Malveaux." *On the Issues,* Summer 1996, 16–21, 56–58.

Castro, Ginette. *American Feminism: A Contemporary History,* trans. Elizabeth Loverde-Bagwell. New York: New York University Press, 1990.

Chapman, Frances. Reply to Laura Chester, "erica's poems." *off our backs,* April 1972, 30.

———. "The Wrong Side of the Dream." Rev. of *Fruits and Vegetables* by Erica Jong. *off our backs,* December 1971, 10.

Charnas, Suzy McKee. *The Furies.* New York: TOR, 1994.

———. *Motherlines.* 1978. Rpt. New York: Berkley, 1979.

———. *Walk to the End of the World.* 1974. Rpt. New York: Berkley, 1978.

Chesler, Phyllis. *Women and Madness.* New York: Avon, 1973.

Chester, Laura. "erica's poems." *off our backs,* April 1972, 30.

Cheung, King-Kok. " 'Don't Tell': Imposed Silences in *The Color Purple* and *The Woman Warrior*." *PMLA* (1988): 162–74.

Chrystos. "He Saw." In Moraga and Anzaldua, 18–19.

Cixous, Hélène. "The Laugh of the Medusa." 1975. Rpt. in *New French Feminisms: An Anthology,* ed. Elaine Marks and Isabelle de Courtivron. Amherst: University of Massachusetts Press, 1980, 245–64.

———. "Sorties." 1975. Rpt. in Marks and de Courtivron, 90–98.

Clarke, Cheryl. "Lesbianism: An Act of Resistance." In Moraga and Anzaldua, 128–37.

Cleaver, Eldridge. *Soul on Ice.* New York: McGraw-Hill, 1968.

Clemons, Walter. "Beware of the Man." Rev. of *Fear of Flying* by Erica Jong, *Newsweek,* 12 November 1973, 111.

Coal Miner's Daughter. Dir. Michael Apted. 1980.

Cohen, Ed. "Who Are 'We'? Gay 'Identity' as Political (E)Motion (A Theoretical Rumination)." In *Inside/Out: Lesbian Theories, Gay Theories,* ed. Diana Fuss. New York: Routledge, 1991, 71–92.

Cohen, Marcia. *The Sisterhood: The True Story of the Women Who Changed the World.* New York: Simon, 1988.

Coming Home. Dir. Hal Ashby. 1978.

Conniff, Ruth. "Warning: Feminism Is Hazardous to Your Health." *Progressive,* April 1997, 33–36.

"Consciousness-Raising." In Koedt, Levine, and Rapone, 280–81.

Cooper, Julie E. "Ideologizing Rock." Rev. of *Rhythm and Noise* by Theodore Gracyk. *The Nation,* 23 December 1996, 32–33.

Cosell, Howard. "Why I Support the ERA." *Ms.* (Special Issue on Men), October 1975, 78.

Coward, Rosalind. "Are Women's Novels Feminist Novels?" In Showalter, *New Feminist Criticism,* 225–39.

Cowie, Elizabeth, Claire Johnston, Cora Kaplan, Mary Kelly, Jacqueline Rose, and Marie Yates. "Representation vs. Communication." In *No Turning Back: Writings From the Women's Liberation Movement 1975–1980,* ed. Feminist Anthology Collective. London: Women's Press, 1981, 238–45.

Cragin, 'Becca. "Post- (Lesbian) -Feminism: Academic Construction of the 70s." Paper given at "Feminist Generations," Bowling Green State University, February 1996.

Crawford, Mary and Roger Chaffin. "The Reader's Construction of Meaning: Cognitive Research on Gender and Comprehension." In *Gender and Reading: Essays on Readers, Texts, and Contexts,* ed. Elizabeth A. Flynn and Patrocinio P. Schweikart. Baltimore: Johns Hopkins University Press, 1986, 3–30.

Crew, Margie. Rev. of *Riverfinger Woman* by Elana Nachman. *off our backs,* December 1974, 22.

Cross, Tia, Freada Klein, Barbara Smith, and Beverly Smith. "Face-to-Face, Day-to-Day—Racism CR." In Hull, Scott, and Smith, 52–56.

Daly, Mary. *Gyn/Ecology: The Metaethics of Radical Feminism.* Boston: Beacon, 1978.

Damon, Gene [Barbara Grier]. "The Least of These: The Minority Whose Screams Haven't Yet Been Heard." In R. Morgan, 333–43.

Dargis, Manohla. "'Thelma & Louise' and the Tradition of the Male Road Movie." In *Women and Film,* ed. Pam Cook et al. Philadelphia: Temple University Press, 1993, 86–92.

Davis, Angela Y. "Rape, Racism and the Myth of the Black Rapist." *Women, Race and Class.* New York: Random House, 1983, 172–201.

Davis, Flora. *Moving the Mountain: The Women's Movement in America Since 1960.* New York: Simon & Schuster, 1991.

de Beauvoir, Simone. *The Second Sex.* 1949. Rpt. trans. H. M. Parshley. New York: Vintage, 1974.

"Defining the fight." *off our backs,* April 1970, 14.

de Lauretis, Teresa. "Feminist Studies/Critical Studies: Issues, Terms, and Contexts." In *Feminist Studies/Critical Studies,* ed. Teresa de Lauretis. Bloomington: Indiana University Press, 1986, 1–19.

———. *The Practice of Love: Lesbian Sexuality and Perverse Desire.* Bloomington: Indiana University Press, 1994.

D'Emilio, John and Estelle B. Freedman. *Intimate Matters: A History of Sexuality in America.* New York: Harper, 1988.

Densmore, Dana. "Independence from the Sexual Revolution." In Koedt, Levine, and Rapone, 107–18.

Didion, Joan. *Play It As it Lays.* 1970. Rpt. New York: Pocket, 1978.

———. "The Women's Movement." *New York Times Book Review*, 30 July 1972, 1–2, 14.

Dillon, Millicent. "Literature and the New Bawd." *The Nation*, 22 February 1975, 219–221.

Dinnersteen, Dorothy. *The Mermaid and the Minotaur: Sexual Arrangements and Human Malaise*. Reprint New York: Harper and Row, 1976.

Donovan, Josephine, ed. *Feminist Literary Criticism: Explorations in Theory*. Lexington: University of Kentucky Press, 1975.

———. *Feminist Theory: The Intellectual Traditions of American Feminism*. 1986 2nd ed. New York: Ungar, 1993.

Douglas, Carol Anne. Rev. of *Small Changes* by Marge Piercy. *off our backs*, October 1973, 12.

Douglas, Carol Anne, evgenia b., and Tacie Dejanikus. "how feminist is therapy?" *off our backs*, September 1976, 2–3, 22–3.

Douglas, Susan J. *Where the Girls Are: Growing Up Female with the Mass Media*. New York: Times, 1994.

Dow, Bonnie J. *Prime-Time Feminism: Television, Media Culture, and the Women's Movement Since 1970*. Philadelphia: University of Pennsylvania Press, 1996.

Dow, Bonnie J. and Lisa Maria Hogeland. "When Feminism Meets the Press, Our Real Politics Get Lost." *On the Issues*, Winter 1997, 12–13.

Dowell, Pat. "The Impotence of Women." *Cineaste* 18, 4 (1991): 28–30.

Dreifus, Claudia. "Sterilizing the Poor." *Feminist Frameworks*. 2nd ed., ed. Alison M. Jaggar and Paula S. Rothenberg. New York: McGraw-Hill, 1984, 58–66.

———. *Woman's Fate: Raps from a Feminist Consciousness-Raising Group*. New York: Bantam, 1973.

duCille, Ann. "The Occult of True Black Womanhood: Critical Demeanor and Black Feminist Studies." *Signs* 19,3 (Spring 1994): 591–629.

Dudovitz, Resa L. *The Myth of Superwoman: Women's Bestsellers in France and the United States*. London and New York: Routledge, 1990.

Duffy, Martha. "Stiff Upper Lib." Rev. of *Small Changes* by Marge Piercy. *Time*, 20 August 1973, 81–82.

Duncan, Erika. "Showing Our Wounds." Letter *Chrysalis* 4 (1977): 8–9.

DuPlessis, Rachel Blau. *Writing Beyond the Ending: Narrative Strategies of Twentieth-Century Women Writers*. Bloomington: Indiana University Press, 1985.

Durbin, Karen. "The Walking Wounded." Rev. of *Female Friends* by Fay Weldon. *Ms.*, December 1974, 30, 34.

Dworkin, Andrea. "Antifeminism." *Trivia* 2 (Spring 1983): 6–35.

Dworkin, Susan. "The Strange and Wonderful Story of the Making of 'The Color Purple.'" *Ms.*, December 1985, 66–70, 94–95.

———. "Sex and Excess." Rev. of *Some Do* by Jane DeLynn. *Ms.*, December 1978, 38, 41.

Ebert, Roger. "A Man and a Woman." Rev. of *An Unmarried Woman*, dir. Paul Mazursky. *Film Comment*, March 1978, 26–32.

Echols, Alice. *Daring to be BAD: Radical Feminism in America 1967–1975*. Minneapolis: University of Minnesota Press, 1989.

Edelson, Carol. "supreme court ruling." *off our backs*, February/March 1973, 4.

"Editorial: Notes from the Third Year." In Koedt, Levine, and Rapone, 300–301.

Ehrenreich, Barbara, Elizabeth Hess, and Gloria Jacobs. *Re-Making Love: The Feminization of Sex*. Garden City, N.Y.: Doubleday, 1986.

Ehrenstein, David. "Melodrama and the New Woman." Rev. of *An Unmarried Woman*, dir. Paul Mazursky. *Film Comment*, September 1978, 59–62.

Ellison, Ralph. *Invisible Man.* 1947. Rpt. New York: Vintage, 1972.

Evans, Nancy Burr. "The Value and Peril for Women of Reading Women Writers." In Koppelman Cornillon, 308–14.

Evans, Sara. *Personal Politics: The Roots of Women's Liberation in the Civil Rights Movement and the New Left.* New York: Vintage, 1980.

Fairbairns, Zoe. *Benefits.* London: Virago, 1979.

Faludi, Susan. *Backlash: The Undeclared War Against American Women.* New York: Crown, 1991.

Felman, Shoshana. "Women and Madness: The Critical Phallacy." *Diacritics* (Winter 1975): 2–10.

Felski, Rita. *Beyond Feminist Aesthetics: Feminist Literature and Social Change.* Cambridge, Mass: Harvard University Press, 1989.

———. "Money, Sex, and Power." Paper given at the Modern Language Association, December 1994.

"The Feminists: A Political Organization to Annihilate Sex Roles." In Koedt, Levine, and Rapone, 368–78.

Findlen, Barbara, ed. *Listen Up: Voices from the Next Feminist Generation.* Seattle: Seal Press, 1995.

Fetterley, Judith. *The Resisting Reader: A Feminist Approach to American Literature.* Bloomington: Indiana University Press, 1978.

Firestone, Shulamith. *The Dialectic of Sex.* New York: Morrow, 1970.

Fisher, Bev, Anne Hatfield, and Marie Khouri. "a house divided." *off our backs,* Oct 1971, 11.

Flynn, Elizabeth A. and Patrocinio P. Schweikart, eds. *Gender and Reading: Essays on Readers, Texts, and Contexts.* Baltimore: Johns Hopkins University Press, 1986.

Fonteneau, Yvonne. "Ralph Ellison's *Invisible Man*: A Critical Reevaluation." *World Literature Today* 64, 3 (Summer 1990): 408–12.

Franks, Michelle Wodtke. "Reinterpreting the Manifesto: grrls, geeks, and surfing the 3rd wave." Unpublished paper for "Feminist Theory," Women's Studies 731, University of Cincinnati, December 1996.

Freccero, Carla. "Notes of a Post-Sex-Wars Theorizer." In *Conflicts in Feminism,* ed. Marianne Hirsch and Evelyn Fox Keller. New York: Routledge, 1990. 305–325.

Freedman, Estelle B. "Separatism as Strategy: Female Institution Building and American Feminism, 1870–1930." *Feminist Studies* 5, 3 (Fall 1979): 512–29.

———. "Small Group Pedagogy: Consciousness Raising in Conservative Times." *NWSA Journal* 2, 4 (Autumn 1990): 602–23.

Freeman, Jo. *The Politics of Women's Liberation.* New York: Longman, 1975.

Freeman, Susan Kathleen. "From the Lesbian Nation to the Cincinnati Lesbian Community: Lesbian Feminists' Construction of a Local Discourse in the 1970s." Unpublished M.A. paper, Women's Studies, University of Cincinnati, May 1995.

French, Marilyn. *The Women's Room.* 1977. Rpt. New York: Jove, 1978.

Friedan, Betty. *The Feminine Mystique.* 1963. Rpt. New York: Dell, 1974.

Friedman, Susan Stanford. "Beyond White and Other: Relationality and Narratives of Race in Feminist Discourse." *Signs* 21, 1 (Autumn 1995): 1–49.

Fritz, Leah. *Dreamers and Dealers: An Intimate Portrait of the Women's Movement.* Boston: Beacon, 1979.

Frye, Joanne S. *Living Stories, Telling Lives: Women and the Novel in Contemporary Experience.* Ann Arbor: University of Michigan Press, 1986.

Frye, Marilyn. "On Being White: Thinking Toward a Feminist Understanding of Race and Race Supremacy." *The Politics of Reality: Essays in Feminist Theory.* Freedom, Calif.: Crossing Press, 1983, 110–27.

Fuss, Diana. "Reading Like a Feminist." *differences* 1, 2 (Summer 1989): 77–92.

Gallop, Jane. *Around 1981: Academic Feminist Literary Theory.* New York: Routledge, 1992.

Gearhart, Sally Miller. *The Wanderground: Stories of the Hill Women.* Watertown, Mass.: Persephone, 1979.

Gerrity, Diane Rowan. "Two women, lost on the freeways." Rev. of *Play It As It Plays* by Joan Didion and *Such Good Friends* by Lois Gould. *Christian Science Monitor,* 4 September 1970, 11.

Gilman, Charlotte Perkins. *Herland.* 1915. Rpt. New York: Pantheon, 1979.

Girlfriends. Dir. Claudia Weill. 1978.

Gitlin, Todd, and Carol S. Wolman. Rev. of *An Unmarried Woman,* dir. Paul Mazursky. *Film Quarterly* 32, 1 (Fall 1978): 55–58.

Glancy, Diane. "Columbus Meets Thelma and Louise / And the Ocean Is Still Bigger Than Any of Us Thought." *Women's Review of Books,* July 1992, 13.

Goldman, Robert, Deborah Heath, and Sharon L. Smith. "Commodity Feminism." *Critical Studies in Mass Communication* 8 (1991): 333–51.

Goldsmith, Olivia, *The First Wives Club.* New York: Poseidon Press, 1992.

Gordon, Mary. *Final Payments.* New York: Random, 1978.

Gornick, Vivian and Barbara K. Moran, eds. *Woman in Sexist Society: Studies in Power and Powerlessness.* New York: Basic, 1971.

Gosier, Diane, L. N. Gardel, and Alice Aldrich. "now or never." *off our backs,* Dec. 1974, 23.

Gould, Lois. *Final Analysis.* 1974. Rpt. New York: Farrar, 1988.

———. *Such Good Friends.* 1970. Rpt. New York: Farrar, 1988.

Gray, Paul. "Blue Genes." Rev. of *Kinflicks* by Lisa Alther. *Time,* 22 March 1976, 80.

Greene, Gayle. *Changing the Story: Feminist Fiction and the Tradition.* Bloomington: Indiana University Press, 1991.

Grenier, Richard. "Killer Bimbos." *Commentary,* September 1991, 50–52.

Griffin, Susan. *Woman and Nature: The Roaring Inside Her.* New York: Harper, 1978.

Griggers, Cathy. "*Thelma and Louise* and the Cultural Generation of the New Butch-Femme." In *Film Theory Goes to the Movies,* ed. Jim Collins, Hilary Radner, and Ava Preacher Collins. New York: Routledge, 1993, 129–41.

Grundmann, Roy. "Hollywood Sets the Terms of the Debate." *Cineaste* 18, 4 (1991): 35–36.

Hacker, Marilyn. "Science Fiction and Feminism: The Work of Joanna Russ." *Chrysalis* 4 (1977): 67–79.

Haraway, Donna. "A Manifesto for Cyborgs: Science, Technology, and Socialist Feminism in the 1980s." 1985. Rpt. in *Feminism/ Postmodernism,* ed. Linda J. Nicholson. New York: Routledge, 1990, 190–233.

Harris, Trudier. "On *The Color Purple,* Stereotypes, and Silence." *Black American Literature Forum* 18, 4 (1984): 155–61.

Haskell, Molly. Rev. of *Fear of Flying* by Erica Jong. *Village Voice,* 22 November 1973, 27.

———. "A Woman's Movement." Rev. of *An Unmarried Woman,* dir. Paul Mazursky. *New York,* 6 March 1978, 72–73.

Heart like a Wheel. Dir. Jonathan Kaplan. 1983.

Heilbrun, Carolyn and Catharine Stimpson. "Theories of Feminist Criticism: A Dialogue." In Donovan, 61–73.

Henderson, Mae G. "*The Color Purple*: Revisions and Redefinitions." *Sage* 2 (Spring 1985), 14–26.

Hersh, Blanche Glassman. *The Slavery of Sex: Feminist-Abolitionists in America.* Urbana: University of Illinois Press, 1978.

Heywood, Leslie and Jennifer Drake. "We Learn America like a Script: Activism in the Third Wave, or, Enough Phantoms of Nothing." Multi-media presentation given at "Feminist Generations," Bowling Green State University, February 1996.

Hite, Molly. "Romance, Marginality, Matrilineage: Alice Walker's *The Color Purple* and Zora Neale Hurston's *Their Eyes Were Watching God.*" *Novel* (Spring 1989): 257–73.

Hochman, Sandra. *Walking Papers.* New York: Viking Press, 1971.

Hogeland, Lisa Maria. "Fear of Feminism." *Ms.,* November/December 1994, 18–21.

———. "Learning from the 70s: Unresolved Issues from the Second Wave." Paper given at "Feminist Generations," Bowling Green State University, February 1996.

Hollibaugh, Amber and Cherrie Moraga. "What We're Rollin Around in Bed With: Sexual Silences in Feminism." 1981. Rpt. in Snitow, Stansell, and Thompson, 394–405.

Holly, Marcia. "Consciousness and Authenticity: Toward a Feminist Aesthetic." In Donovan, 38–47.

hooks, bell. *Ain't I a Woman? Black Women and Feminism.* Boston: South End Press, 1982.

———. "Dissident Heat." *Outlaw Culture: Resisting Representations.* New York: Routledge, 1994.

———. "Writing the Subject, Reading *The Color Purple.*" In *Reading Black, Reading Feminist: A Critical Anthology,* ed. Henry Louis Gates, Jr. New York: Meridian, 1990, 454–70.

Hotaling, Debra, and Mary Munsil. "Professing and Policing: Personal and Critical Receptions of *Fear of Flying.*" Paper presented at the Modern Language Association, December 1994.

Howe, Florence. "Feminism and Literature." In Koppelman Cornillon, 253–77.

Huff, Linda. *A Portrait of the Artist as a Young Woman: The Writer as Heroine in American Literature.* New York: Ungar, 1983.

Hull, Gloria T., Patricia Bell Scott, and Barbara Smith, eds. *All the Women Are White, All the Blacks Are Men, But Some of Us Are Brave: Black Women's Studies.* Old Westbury, N.Y.: Feminist Press, 1982.

"Isadora & Adrian, John & Mimi." Rev. of *Fear of Flying* by Erica Jong and *John & Mimi: A Free Marriage* by John and Mimi Lobell. *Atlantic,* December 1974, 125–26.

Jeffreys, Sheila. "How Orgasm Politics Has Hijacked the Women's Movement." *On the Issues,* Spring 1996, 18–21, 58–59.

Jelinek, Estelle. "anais reconsidered." *off our backs,* December 1974, 18–19.

JGS. "money doesn't talk, it swears: abortion industry in new york." *off our backs,* 14 December 1970, 4–5.

Johnson, Joyce. *Minor Characters.* Boston: Houghton, 1983.

Jones, Beverly. "The Dynamics of Marriage and Motherhood." 1970. Rpt. in R. Morgan, 49–66.

Jong, Erica. "The Artist as Housewife." In Klagsbrun, 111–22.

———. "Comments on Joan Reardon's '*Fear of Flying*: Developing the Feminist

Novel': A Letter to the Author." *International Journal of Women's Studies* 1, 6 (November/ December 1978): 625–26.

———. *Fanny: Being the True History of the Adventures of Fanny Hackabout-Jones: A Novel.* New York: New American Library, 1981.

———. *Fear of Flying.* New York: Holt, 1973.

———. *How to Save Your Own Life.* 1977. Rpt. New York: Signet, 1978.

Joreen [Jo Freeman]. "The BITCH Manifesto." 1970. Rpt. in Koedt, Levine, and Rapone, 50–59.

———. "The Tyranny of Structurelessness." In Koedt, Levine, and Rapone, 285–99.

Juhasz, Suzanne. " 'The Blood Jet': The Poetry of Sylvia Plath." In Brown and Olson, 111–30.

Julia. Dir. Fred Zinnemann. 1977.

Kalčik, Susan. " '. . . like Anne's gynecologist or the time I was almost raped': Personal Narratives in Women's Rap Groups." *Journal of American Folklore* 88 (Jan-March 1975): 3–11.

Katz-Stoker, Fraya. "The Other Criticism: Feminism vs. Formalism." In Koppelman Cornillon, 315–27.

Kearon, Pamela. "Man-Hating." In Koedt, Levine, and Rapone, 78–80.

Kempton, Sally. "Cutting Loose." *Esquire,* July 1970, 53–57.

Kennard, Jean E. "Convention Coverage or How to Read Your Own Life." *New Literary History* (1981): 69–88.

———. "Personally Speaking: Feminist Critics and the Community of Readers." *College English* 43, 2 (1981): 140–45.

Kennedy, Florynce. "Institutionalized Oppression vs. The Female." In R. Morgan, 492–501.

Keohane, Nannerl O., Michelle Z. Rosaldo, and Barbara C. Gelpi, eds., *Feminist Theory: A Critique of Ideology.* Chicago: University of Chicago Press, 1982.

Kessler-Harris, Alice. Rev. of *Professing Feminism: Cautionary Tales from the Strange World of Women's Studies* by Daphne Patai and Noretta Koertge, and *The Feminist Classroom* by Frances A. Maher and Mary Kay Thompson Tetreault. *Academe,* November-December 1995, 65–67.

King, Katie. *Theory in Its Feminist Travels: Conversations in U.S. Women's Movements.* Bloomington: Indiana University Press, 1994.

Klagsbrun, Francine, ed. *The First Ms. Reader.* New York: Warner, 1973.

Koedt, Anne. "Lesbianism and Feminism." In Koedt, Levine, and Rapone, 246–58.

———. "The Myth of the Vaginal Orgasm." In Koedt, Levine, and Rapone, 198–207.

Koedt, Anne, Ellen Levine, and Anita Rapone, eds. *Radical Feminism.* New York: Quadrangle, 1973.

Kolodny, Annette. "Dancing Through the Minefield: Some Observations on the Theory, Practice, and Politics of a Feminist Literary Criticism." 1981. Rpt. in Showalter, 144–67.

———. "Some Notes on Defining a 'Feminist Literary Criticism.' " 1975. Rpt. in Brown and Olson, 37–58.

———. "Why Feminists Need Tenure." *Women's Review of Books,* February 1996, 23–24.

Koppelman Cornillon, Susan, ed. *Images of Women in Fiction: Feminist Perspectives.* Bowling Green, Oh.: Bowling Green University Popular Press, 1972.

Krouse, Agate Nesaule. "Toward a Definition of Literary Feminism." In Brown and Olson, 279–90.

laGuardia, Dolores and Hans P. Guth, eds. *American Voices: Multicultural Literacy and Critical Thinking.* 2nd ed., Mountain View, Calif.: Mayfield, 1996.

Laurence, Margaret. *The Diviners.* New York: Knopf, 1974.

Lefanu, Sarah. *Feminism and Science Fiction.* 1988. Rpt. Bloomington: Indiana University Press, 1989.

Le Guin, Ursula K. "American SF and the Other." 1973. Rpt. *The Language of the Night: Essays on Fantasy and Science Fiction,* ed. Susan Wood. New York: Putnam, 1979, 97–100.

———. *The Dispossessed.* 1974. Rpt. New York: Avon, 1975.

———. "Introduction to *Star Songs of an Old Primate.*" 1978. Rpt. *The Language of the Night,* ed. Susan Wood. New York: Putnam, 1979, 179–84.

———. "Is Gender Necessary?" In *The Language of the Night,* ed. Susan Wood. New York: Putnam, 1979, 161–70.

———. *The Left Hand of Darkness.* 1969. Rpt. London: Granada, 1975.

Lehmann-Haupt, Christopher. "Novels with Anxious Moments." Rev. of *The Autograph Hound* by John Lahr and *Surfacing* by Margaret Atwood. *New York Times,* 7 March 1973, 41.

———. "Nuances of Women's Liberation." Rev. of *Fear of Flying* by Erica Jong and *A Different Woman* by Jane Howard. *New York Times,* 6 November 1973, 35.

———. "The Old Point of View Problem." Rev. of *Final Analysis* by Lois Gould and *The Wonder Worker* by Dan Jacobson. *New York Times,* 2 April 1974, 37.

———. Rev. of *The High Cost of Living* by Marge Piercy. *New York Times,* 19 January 1978, C18.

———. Rev. of *The Women's Room* by Marilyn French. *New York Times,* 27 October 1977, C20.

Lentz, Kirsten Marthe. "The Popular Pleasures of Female Revenge (Or Rage Bursting in a Blaze of Gunfire)." *Cultural Studies* 7, 3 (October 1993): 374–405.

Leo, John. "Toxic Feminism on the Big Screen." *U.S. News & World Report,* 10 June 1991, 20.

Leonard, John. "Ugliness and Expertise." Rev. of *Such Good Friends* by Lois Gould and *The Production* by Daniel Brown. *New York Times,* 19 May 1970, 37.

Leonard, Vickie. "c-r: it ain't what it used to be." *off our backs,* February 1980, 17.

———. Rev. of *Braided Lives* by Marge Piercy. *off our backs,* April 1982, 23.

———. "She Was a Big, Strong Woman." Rev. of *Vida* by Marge Piercy. *off our backs,* June 1980, 19.

Lessing, Doris. *The Four-Gated City.* 1969. Rpt. New York: Bantam, 1970.

———. *The Golden Notebook.* 1962. Rpt. New York: Bantam, 1973.

Lieber, Todd M. "Ralph Ellison and the Metaphor of Invisibility in Black Literary Tradition." *American Quarterly* 24 (1972): 86–100.

Light, Alison. "Fear of the Happy Ending: *The Color Purple,* Reading, and Racism." In *Plotting Change: Contemporary Women's Fiction,* ed. Linda Anderson. London: Edward Arnold, 1990, 103–17.

Lippard, Lucy. "Sweeping Exchanges: The Contribution of Feminism to the Art of the 1970s." *Art Journal* 40 (1980): 362–65.

Lorde, Audre. "An Open Letter to Mary Daly." In Moraga and Anzaldua, 94–97.

"Loving Another Woman." Interview. In Koedt, Levine, and Rapone, 85–93.

Lurie, Alison. *Real People.* 1969. Rpt. New York: Avon, 1970.

———. *The Truth About Lorin Jones.* 1989. Rpt. New York: Avon, 1990.

Lydon, Susan. "The Politics of Orgasm." In R. Morgan, 219–28.

MacKinnon, Catharine A. "Desire and Power: A Feminist Perspective." *Marxism and the Interpretation of Culture*, eds. Cary Nelson and Lawrence Grossberg. Urbana: University of Illinois Press, 1988, 105–16.

———. "Feminism, Marxism, Method, and the State: An Agenda for Theory." *Feminist Theory: A Critique of Ideology*, ed. Nannerl O. Keohane et al. Chicago: University of Chicago Press, 1982, 1–30.

Maio, Kathi. Rev. of *I Shot Andy Warhol*, dir. Mary Harron. *Sojourner*, May 1996, 29–30.

Martin, Biddy. "Lesbian Identity and Autobiographical Difference(s)." In *The Lesbian and Gay Studies Reader*, ed. Henry Abelove, Michele Aina Barale, and David M. Halperin. New York: Routledge, 1993, 77–103.

McDermott, Patrice. "On Cultural Authority: Women's Studies, Feminist Politics, and the Popular Press." *Signs* 20, 3 (Spring 1995): 668–84.

McDowell, Deborah E. "New Directions for Black Feminist Criticism." In Showalter, 186–99.

McMullen, Wayne J., and Martha Solomon. "The Politics of Adaptation: Steven Spielberg's Appropriation of *The Color Purple*." *Text and Performance Quarterly* 14 (1994): 158–74.

Messer-Davidow, Ellen. "Doing the Right Thing." *Women's Review of Books*, February 1992, 19–20.

———. "Manufacturing the Attack on Liberalized Higher Education." *Social Text* 36 (Fall 1993): 40–80.

Meyerowitz, Joanne. "Beyond the Feminine Mystique: A Reassessment of Post-War Mass Culture, 1946–1958." In *Not June Cleaver: Women and Gender in Post-War America, 1945–1960*, ed. Joanne Meyerowitz. Philadelphia: Temple University Press, 1994. 229–62.

Millett, Kate. *Sexual Politics*. New York: Ballantine, 1970.

Mitchell, Juliet. *Woman's Estate*. 1971. Rpt. New York: Vintage, 1973.

Modleski, Tania. "Feminism and the Power of Interpretation: Some Critical Readings." *Feminist Studies/Critical Studies*. ed. Teresa de Lauretis. Bloomington: Indiana University Press, 1986, 121–38.

———. "Why Do We Still Fear Flying?" *The University of Michigan Papers in Women's Studies* 1, 4 (June 1975): 107–12.

Moers, Ellen. *Literary Women*. Garden City: Anchor, 1977.

Moraga, Cherríe and Gloria Anzaldúa, eds. *This Bridge Called My Back: Writings By Radical Women of Color*. 2nd ed. New York: Kitchen Table: Women of Color Press, 1983.

Morgan, Ellen. "Humanbecoming: Form and Focus in the Neo-Feminist Novel." In Koppelman Cornillon, 183–205.

———. "Humanbecoming: Form and Focus in the Neo-Feminist Novel," revised version. In Brown and Olson, 272–78.

Morgan, Robin. "Goodbye to All That." 1970. Rpt. *Masculine / Feminine*, ed. Betty Roszak and Theodore Roszak. New York: Harper, 1970, 241–50.

———. "Portrait of the Artist as Two Young Women." *Lady of the Beasts*. New York: Random House, 1976, 31–33.

———, ed. *Sisterhood Is Powerful: An Anthology of Writings From the Women's Liberation Movement*. New York: Vintage, 1970.

Morris, Meaghan. *The Pirate's Fiancee: Feminism, Reading, Postmodernism*. London and New York: Verso, 1979.

Moylan, Tom. *Demand the Impossible: Science Fiction and the Utopian Imagination*. New York: Methuen, 1986.

Mulvey, Laura. "Visual Pleasure and Narrative Cinema." 1975. Rpt. in *Feminisms: An Anthology of Literary Theory and Criticism*, ed. Robyn R. Warhol and Diane Price Herndl. New Brunswick: Rutgers University Press, 1991, 432–42.

Murphy, Kathleen. "Only Angels Have Wings." *Film Comment* 27 (July 1991): 26–29.

Nachman/Dykewomon, Elena. *Riverfinger Women.* Tallahassee, Fl.: Naiad Press, 1992.

Nelson, Cary, and Lawrence Grossberg, eds. *Marxism and the Interpretation of Culture.* Urbana: University of Illinois Press, 1988.

New York Radical Women. "Principles." In R. Morgan, 583–84.

Nin, Anais. Letter. *Everywoman.* 5 March 1971, 3.

Nine to Five. Dir. Colin Higgins. 1980.

Nixon, Nicola. "Cyberpunk: Preparing the Ground for Revolution or Keeping the Boys Satisfied?" *Science Fiction Studies* 19 (1992): 219–35.

Norma Rae. Dir. Martin Ritt. 1979.

Oates, Joyce Carol. *Do with Me What You Will.* New York: Vanguard, 1973.

Ohmann, Richard. "The Shaping of a Canon: U.S. Fiction, 1960–1975." *The Politics of Letters.* Middletown, Conn.: Wesleyan University Press, 1987, 68–91.

O'Reilly, Jane. "The Housewife's Moment of Truth." In Klagsbrun, 11–22.

Orenstein, Gloria Feman. "Is There Feminist Fiction Before Consciousness Raising?" Letter, *Chrysalis* 4 (1977): 7–8.

Ostriker, Alicia Suskin. *Stealing the Language: The Emergence of Women's Poetry in America.* Boston: Beacon, 1986.

Payne, Carol Williams. "Consciousness Raising: A Dead End?" In Koedt, Levine, and Rapone, 282–84.

Pence, Ellen. "Racism—A White Issue." In Hull, Scott, and Smith, 45–51.

Peslikis, Irene. "Resistances to Consciousness." In R. Morgan, 379–81.

Piercy, Marge. *Braided Lives.* New York: Fawcett, 1982.

———. "The Grand Coolie Damn." 1969. Rpt. in R. Morgan, 473–92.

———. *The Longings of Women: A Novel.* New York: Fawcett Colombine, 1994.

———. *Small Changes.* Greenwich, Conn.: Fawcett, 1974.

———. *Woman on the Edge of Time.* New York: Fawcett, 1976.

Pipino, Mary Frances. " 'I Have Found My Voice': The Italian-American Woman Writer." Diss., Univ. of Cincinnati, 1996.

Plath, Sylvia. "The Jailor." Rpt. in R. Morgan, 572–74.

Poppe, Terri. Rev. of *In Her Day* by Rita Mae Brown. *off our backs*, November 1976, 15.

Pratt, Annis. "The New Feminist Criticism." 1971. Rpt. in Brown and Olson, 11–20.

Prescott, Peter S. "Pipe Dreams." Rev. of *Lady Oracle* by Margaret Atwood. *Newsweek*, 4 October 1976, 62, 64.

Rabinowitz, Peter J. *Before Reading: Narrative Conventions and the Politics of Interpretation.* Ithaca, N.Y.: Cornell University Press, 1987.

Radicalesbians. "The Woman-Identified Woman." In Koedt, Levine, and Rapone, 240–45.

Radway, Janice A. *Reading the Romance: Women, Patriarchy, and Popular Literature.* Chapel Hill: University of North Carolina Press, 1984.

Rafferty, Terrence. "Outlaw Princesses." *New Yorker*, 3 June 1991, 86–88.

Raphael, Jody. Rev. of *Walking Papers* by Sandra Hochman. *off our backs*, March 1972, 26.

Rapone, Anita. "The Body is the Role: Sylvia Plath." In Koedt, Levine, and Rapone, 407–12.

Rapping, Elayne. *The Culture of Recovery: Making Sense of the Self-Help Movement in Women's Lives.* Boston: Beacon, 1996.

———. "Feminism Gets the Hollywood Treatment." *Cineaste* 18, 4 (1991): 30–32.

———. "The Ladies Who Lynch." *On the Issues,* Spring 1996, 7–9, 56.

———. *The Movie of the Week: Private Stories, Public Events.* Minneapolis, University of Minnesota Press, 1992.

Reagon, Bernice Johnson. "Coalition Politics: Turning the Century." In *Home Girls: A Black Feminist Anthlogy,* ed. Barbara Smith. New York: Kitchen Table: Women of Color Press, 1983, 356–68.

Redstockings, ed. *Feminist Revolution.* New Paltz: Redstockings, 1975.

———. "*Ms.*" *off our backs,* July 1975, 28–33.

———. "Redstockings Manifesto." In R. Morgan, 598–601.

Reed, Evelyn. "Women: Caste, Class, or Oppressed Sex?" 1970. Rpt. in *Feminist Frameworks,* 2nd ed., ed. Alison M. Jagger and Paula S. Rothenberg. New York: McGraw-Hill, 1984.

Register, Cheri. "American Feminist Literary Criticism: A Bibliographical Introduction." In Donovan, 1–28.

Ribera, Doris. "Women in Women's Eyes." *Everywoman,* 12 January 1971, 9.

Rich, Adrienne. "The Burning of Paper Instead of Children." 1968. Rpt. in *The Fact of a Doorframe.* New York: Norton, 1984. 116–19.

———. "Compulsory Heterosexuality and Lesbian Existence." 1980. Rpt. in Snitow, Stansell, and Thompson, 177–205.

———. "The Images." *A Wild Patience Has Taken Me This Far.* New York: Norton, 1981, 3–5.

———. "It is the Lesbian in Us . . ." *On Lies, Secrets, and Silence.* New York: Norton, 1979, 199–202.

———. "When We Dead Awaken: Writing as Re Vision." 1971. Rpt. in *On Lies, Secrets, and Silence.* New York: Norton, 1979, 33–49.

Rich, B. Ruby. "Review Essay: Feminism and Sexuality in the 1980s." *Feminist Studies* 12, 3 (Fall 1986): 525–61.

Rigney, Barbara Hill. *Madness and Sexual Politics in the Feminist Novel: Studies in Bronte, Woolf, Lessing, and Atwood.* Madison: University of Wisconsin Press, 1978.

Robinson, Lillian S. "Dwelling in Decencies: Radical Criticism and the Feminist Perspective." 1971. Rpt. in Brown and Olson, 21–36.

Rohrberger, Mary, " 'Ball the Jack': Surreality, Sexuality, and the Role of Women in *Invisible Man.*" In *Approaches to Teaching Ralph Ellison's* Invisible Man, ed. Susan Resneck Parr and Pancho Savery. New York: Modern Language Association, 1989: 124–32.

Rose, Ellen Cronan. "Review Essay: American Feminist Criticism of Contemporary Women's Fiction." *Signs* 18, 2 (1993): 346–75.

Rosen, Ruth. "The Female Generation Gap: Daughters of the Fifties and the Origins of Contemporary American Feminism." In *U.S. History as Women's History: New Feminist Essays,* ed. Linda K. Kerber, Alice Kessler-Harris, and Kathryn Kish Sklar. Chapel Hill: University of North Carolina Press, 1995, 313–34.

Rosenstein, Harriet. "Reconsidering Sylvia Plath." In Klagsbrun, 213–40.

Rosenthal, Lucy. "Ideology and Fiction: A Delicate Balance." Rev. of *Small Changes* by Marge Piercy. *Ms.,* September 1973, 29–31.

Ross, Andrew. "Cyberpunk in Boystown." In *Strange Weather: Culture, Science, and Technology in the Age of Limits*. London: Verso, 1991, 137–67.

Roszak, Betty and Theodore Roszak, eds. *Masculine/Feminine*. New York: Harper, 1969.

Rowbotham, Sheila. *Woman's Consciousness, Man's World*. Hammondsworth, UK: Penguin, 1973.

———. *Women, Resistance and Revolution*. 1972. Rpt. New York: Vintage, 1974.

Rowbotham, Sheila, Lynn Segal, and Hilary Wainwright, eds. *Beyond the Fragments: Feminism and the Making of Socialism*. 1979. Rpt. Boston: Alysoun, 1981.

Rubin, Gayle. "Thinking Sex: Notes for a Radical Theory of the Politics of Sexuality." 1984. Rpt. in *American Feminist Thought at Century's End: A Reader*, ed. Linda S. Kauffman. Cambridge: Blackwell, 1993, 3–64.

———. "The Traffic in Women: Notes on the 'Political Economy' of Sex," 1975. Rpt. in *Feminist Frameworks*, 2nd ed., eds. Alison M. Jagger and Paula S. Rothenberg. New York: McGraw-Hill, 1984, 155–71.

Ruby, Jennie. "*Off Our Backs*." In *Women and Media: Content, Careers, and Criticism*, ed. Cynthia M. Lont. New York: Wadsworth, 1995, 41–53.

Rukeyser, Muriel. "Kaethe Kollwitz." 1968. Rpt. *The Norton Anthology of Literature by Women: The Tradition in English*, ed. Sandra M. Gilbert and Susan Gubar. New York: Norton, 1983, 1783–87.

Russ, Joanna. *The Female Man*. New York: Bantam, 1975.

———. "Images of Women in Science Fiction." In Koppelman Cornillon, 79–94.

———. "What Can a Heroine Do? Or Why Women Can't Write." In Koppelman Cornillon, 3–20.

Ryan, Barbara. *Feminism and the Women's Movement: Dynamics of Change in Social Movement Ideology and Activism*. New York: Routledge, 1992.

Salmon, Norah. "Systemic Oppression, Youths, and Political Agency." Unpublished paper for "Feminist Theory," Women's Studies 731, University of Cincinnati, December 1996.

Sanborn, Sara. "A Feminist Jacqueline Susann?" Rev. of *The Women's Room* by Marilyn French. *Ms.*, January 1978, 30, 34.

Saraco, Margaret R. "Where Feminism Rocks." *On the Issues*. Spring 1996, 26–8, 57.

Sayers, Sohnya, Anders Stephason, Stanley Aronowitz, and Frederic Jameson, eds. *The 60s Without Apology*. Minneapolis: University of Minnesota Press, 1984.

Schickel, Richard. "Gender Bender." *Time*, 24 June 1991, 52–56.

Schrager, Cynthia D. "Self-Help or Self-Harm?" Rev. of *I'm Dysfunctional, You're Dysfunctional: The Recovery Movement and Other Self-Help Fashions*, by Wendy Kaminer, and *Women and Self-Help Culture: Reading Between the Lines*, by Wendy Simonds. *The Women's Review of Books*, October 1992, 1, 3–4.

Schulman, Sarah. "The Movie Management of Rape." *Cineaste* 18, 4 (1991): 34–35.

Schwartz, Lynne Sharon. " 'How Foolish I Was: How Mellow I've Become.' " Rev. of *Burning Questions* by Alix Kates Shulman. *Ms.*, March 1978, 40–41.

Schwartz, Tony. "Woman as Pinball." Rev. of *Praxis* by Fay Weldon. *Newsweek*, 4 December 1978, 102.

Sedgwick, Eve Kosofsky. "Queer and Now," *Tendencies*. Durham: Duke University Press, 1993, 1–22.

Segal, Lore. Rev. of *Play It As It Lays* by Joan Didion. *New York Times Book Review*, 9 August 1970, 6, 18.

Segerberg, Marsha. "re/de/e/volving: feminist theories of science." *off our backs*, March 1979, 12–3, 29.

Shelley, Martha. "Notes of a Radical Lesbian." In R. Morgan, 343–48.

Sherfey, Mary Jane. "A Theory of Female Sexuality." In R. Morgan, 245–56.

Shirley, John. *A Song Called Youth* trilogy. *Eclipse.* New York: Warner, 1988. *Eclipse Penumbra.* New York: Warner, 1989. *Eclipse Corona.* New York: Warner, 1990.

Showalter, Elaine. "Critical Cross-Dressing: Male Feminists and the Woman of the Year." In *Men in Feminism*, eds. Alice Jardine and Paul Smith. New York: Methuen, 1987, 116–32.

———, ed. *The New Feminist Criticism: Essays on Women, Literature, and Theory.* New York: Pantheon, 1985.

———. "Toward a Feminist Poetics." 1979. Rpt. in Showalter, 125–43.

———. "Women Writers and the Female Experience." 1971. Rpt. in Koedt, Levine, and Rapone, 391–406.

Shreve, Anita. *Women Together, Women Alone: The Legacy of the Consciousness-Raising Movement.* New York: Viking, 1989.

Shulman, Alix Kates. *Burning Questions.* 1978. Rpt. Seattle: Thunder's Mouth Press, 1990.

———. *Memoirs of an Ex-Prom Queen.* 1972. Rpt. Chicago: Academy Chicago, 1985.

———. "Organs and Orgasms." In Gornick and Moran, 198–206.

———. "Sex and Power: Sexual Bases of Radical Feminism." *Signs* 5, 4 (1980): 590–604.

Silkwood. Dir. Mike Nichols. 1983.

Simons, Margaret A. "Racism and Feminism: A Schism in the Sisterhood." *Feminist Studies* 5, 2 (Summer 1979): 384–401.

Sinclair, Carla. *Net Chick: A Smart-Girl Guide to the Wired World.* New York: Holt, 1996.

Slonczewski, Joan. *Door into Ocean.* 1985. Rpt. New York: Arbor House, 1986.

Smith, Barbara. "Introduction." In *Home Girls: A Black Feminist Anthology*, ed. Barbara Smith. New York: Kitchen Table: Women of Color Press, 1983, xix–lvi.

———. "Toward a Black Feminist Criticism." 1977. Rpt. in Showalter, 168–85.

Snitow, Ann. "Feminism and Motherhood: An American Reading." *Feminist Review* 40 (Spring 1992): 32–51.

———. "Women's Private Writings: Anais Nin." In Koedt, Levine, and Rapone, 413–18.

Snitow, Ann, Christine Stansell, and Sharon Thomson, eds., *Powers of Desire: The Politics of Sexuality.* New York: Monthly Review Press, 1983.

Solanis, Valerie. "Excerpts from the SCUM Manifesto." In R. Morgan, 577–83.

Sommers, Christina Hoff. *Who Stole Feminism? How Women Have Betrayed Women.* New York: Simon & Schuster, 1994.

Sontag, Deborah. "Anita Hill and Revitalizing Feminism." *New York Times*, 26 April 1992, L+ 31.

Spender, Dale. *Invisible Women: The Schooling Scandal.* London: Writers and Readers, 1982.

Stanton, Elizabeth Cady. "A Slave's Appeal: Speech to the Judiciary Committee, New York State Legislature." In *Man Cannot Speak for Her*, Vol. II, *Key Texts of the Early Feminists*, ed. Karlyn Kohrs Campbell. Westport, Conn.: Greenwood, 1989, 167–86.

Stein, Arlene. "Style Wars and the New Lesbianism." In *Gay, Lesbian, and Queer*

Essays on Popular Culture, ed. Corey K. Creekmur and Alexander Doty. Durham: Duke University Press, 1995, 476–83.

Stein, Judi. "lesbian rap." Letter. *off our backs*, April 1974, 17.

Stevens, Wendy. Rev. of *The Women's Room* by Marilyn French. *off our backs*, February 1978, 18–19.

Stimpson, Catherine. "The Case of Miss Joan Didion." *Ms.*, January 1973, 36–41.

St. Louis Women's Collective. "Birth Control and Abortion, Some Things to Worry About." *off our backs*, 26 February 1971, 8–9.

Stokes, Terry. Rev. of *Fear of Flying* by Erica Jong. *New York Times Book Review*, 11 November 1973, 40–41.

Sylvander, Carolyn W., "Ralph Ellison's *Invisible Man* and Female Stereotypes." *Negro American Literature Forum* 9, 3 (Fall 1975): 77–79.

Tannenhaus, Beverly. Rev. of *Burning Questions* by Alix Kates Shulman. *Chrysalis* 7 (1979): 104–109.

Taylor, Verta, and Leila J. Rupp. "Women's Culture and Lesbian Feminist Activism: A Reconsideration of Cultural Feminism." *Signs* 19, 1 (Autumn 1993): 32–61.

Tax, Meredith. "Woman and Her Mind." In Koedt, Levine, and Rapone, 23–35.

Tennenbaum, Silvia. *Rachel, the Rabbi's Wife.* New York: Morrow, 1978.

Thom, Mary, ed. *Letters to Ms.* 1972–1987. New York: Holt, 1987.

Tiptree, Jr., James. [Alice Sheldon]. "The Women Men Don't See." In *The New Women of Wonder*, ed. Pamela Sargent. New York: Vintage, 1978, 176–217.

Tompkins, Jane. *Sensational Designs: The Cultural Work of American Fiction 1790–1860.* New York: Oxford University Press, 1985.

Trumbo, Sherry Sonnett. "A Woman's Place Is in the Oven." In Koedt, Levine, and Rapone, 419–24.

Tucker, Lindsey. "Alice Walker's *The Color Purple*: Emergent Woman, Emergent Text." *Black American Literature Forum* 22, 1 (Spring 1988): 81–95.

Turner, Alice K. "What Your Favorite Authors Are Working On." *Ms.*, December 1977, 58–59, 108.

The Turning Point. Dir. Herbert Ross. 1977.

Tyler, Anne. "Starting Out Submissive." Rev. of *The Women's Room* by Marilyn French. *New York Times Book Review*, 16 October 1977, 7, 38.

An Unmarried Woman. Dir. Paul Mazursky. 1978.

Updike, John. "Jong Love." Rev. of *Fear of Flying* by Erica Jong. *New Yorker*, 17 December 1973, 149–51.

Van Gelder, Lindsy. "A Year Later: The Lure of 'The Women's Room.'" *Ms.*, April 1979, 38+.

Wainwright, Hilary. "Introduction." *Beyond the Fragments: Feminism and the Making of Socialism*, ed. Sheila Rowbotham, Lynne Segal, and Hilary Wainwright. 1979; rpt. Boston: Alysoun, 1981, 1–20.

"The Waiting Game." Rev. of *Down Among the Women* by Fay Weldon. *Times Literary Supplement*, 10 September 1971, 1075.

Walker, Alice. *The Color Purple.* New York: Washington Square, 1982.

———. "Finding Celie's Voice." *Ms.*, December 1985, 71–72, 96.

———. "*One* Child of One's Own: A Meaningful Digression within the Work(s)." 1979. Rpt. *In Search of Our Mothers' Gardens: Womanist Prose.* New York: Harcourt, 1983, 361–83.

———."In Search of Our Mothers' Gardens." 1974. Rpt. *In Search of Our Mothers' Gardens: Womanist Prose.* New York: Harcourt, 1983, 231–43.

———. "In the Closet of the Soul: A Letter to an African-American Friend." *Ms.*, November 1986, 32–35.

Walker, Lisa M. "How to Recognize a Lesbian: The Cultural Politics of Looking Like What You Are." *Signs* 18, 4 (1993): 866–90.

Walker, Rebecca. "Becoming the Third Wave." *Ms.*, January/February 1992, 39–41.

———. *To Be Real: Telling the Truth and Changing the Face of Feminism.* New York: Anchor, 1995.

Wandersee, Winifred D. *On the Move: American Women in the 1970s.* Boston: Twayne, 1988.

Weisstein, Naomi. " 'Kinde, Kuche, Kirche' as Scientific Law: Psychology Constructs the Female." 1969. Rpt. in R. Morgan, 228–45.

Weldon, Fay. *Down Among the Women.* 1971. Rpt. New York: Penguin, 1973.

———. *Praxis.* 1978. Rpt. London: Coronet, 1980.

Wesley, Richard " 'The Color Purple' Debate: Reading Between the Lines." *Ms.*, September 1986, 62, 90–92.

Whittier, Nancy. *Feminist Generations: The Persistence of the Radical Women's Movement.* Philadelphia: Temple University Press, 1995.

Wiley, Jennifer. "Crossing the Bridge: A Historical Perspective of Feminist Generation Gaps." Paper given at "Feminist Generations, Bowling Green State University, February 1996.

[Williams], Brooke. "feminist conference: porn again." *off our backs*, November 1979, 24–27.

———. Rev. of *Woman's Fate: Raps from a Feminist Consciousness-Raising Group* by Claudia Dreifus. *off our backs*, January 1975, 18.

Williams, Brooke and Hannah Darby. "business vs. revolution." *off our backs*, March 1976, 28.

Williams, Sherley Anne. *Dessa Rose.* 1986. Rpt. New York: Berkley, 1987.

Willis, Ellen. "Comment" [Response to Catherine A. MacKinnon, "Desire and Power: A Feminist Perspective"]. In *Marxism and the Interpretation of Culture*, eds. Cary Nelson and Lawrence Grossberg. Urbana: University of Illinois Press, 1988, 117–21.

———. "The Conservatism of *Ms.*" In *Feminist Revolution*, 2nd ed., ed. Redstockings. New York: Random House, 1978, 170–71.

———. "Feminism without Freedom." In *No More Nice Girls: Countercultural Essays.* Hanover, N.H.: University Press of New England, 1992, 151–58.

———. "Radical Feminism and Feminist Radicalism." In *The 60s Without Apology*, eds. Sohnya Sayres, Anders Stephanson, Stanley Aronowitz, and Frederic Jameson. Minneapolis: University of Minnesota Press, 1984, 91–118.

Willis, Sharon. "Hardware and Hardbodies, What Do Women Want?: A Reading of *Thelma and Louise.*" In *Film Theory Goes to the Movies*, ed. Jim Collins, Hilary Radner, and Ava Preacher Collins. New York: Routledge, 1993, 120–28.

Wolf, Christa. "Selbstversuch: Traktatt zu einam Protokoll." 1972. Rpt. *Frauen in der DDR: Zwanzig Ehrzalungen*, ed. Lutz-W. Wolff. Munchen: Deutscher Taschenbuch, 1976, 224–47.

Wolf, Naomi. "Our Bodies, Our Souls." *New Republic*, 16 October 1995, 26–35.

The Women's Room. Dir. Glenn Jordan. 1980.

Woolf, Virginia. *A Room of One's Own.* 1929. Rpt. New York: Harcourt, n.d.

———. *Three Guineas.* 1938. Rpt. New York: Harcourt, n.d.

Yamada, Mitsuye. "Invisibility Is an Unnatural Disaster: Reflections of an Asian American Woman." In Moraga and Anzaldúa, 35–40.

Zia, Helen. "How Now?" *Ms.*, July/August 1996, 49–57.

Zimmerman, Bonnie. "Feminist Fiction and the Postmodern Challenge." In *Postmodern Fiction: A Bio-Bibliographic Guide*, ed. Larry McCaffery. New York: Greenwood Press, 1986, 175–88.

———. *The Safe Sea of Women: Lesbian Fiction, 1969–1989*. Boston: Beacon, 1990.

Index

Acknowledgments

When you work on a book for nine years, your list of institutional and individual debts gets very long. This book developed in part from my dissertation; I want to thank my committee, Diane Middlebrook, David Halliburton, Sandra Drake, and especially Estelle Freedman, who suggested some of the strategies I pursued in reconceptualizing the project. The Department of English at the University of Cincinnati granted release time from teaching and supported me for tenure even before the book was completed; the Taft Memorial Fund gave me a Summer Research Grant. The Center for Women's Studies provided a steady stream of able research assistants, and I am especially grateful to Dawn Dreisbach and Pilae Kim; to Quote Check Grrl, Norah Salmon; and to the Queens of Microform, Susan Freeman and Jennifer Ridenour.

Portions of this book first appeared in *American Literary History* (part of Chapter Four), *Journal of the History of Sexuality* (Chapter Three), and *Women's History Review* (Chapter Six); I am enormously indebted to those journals' editors and reviewers for their high standards and tough-mindedness.

Lots of smart people have read portions of this book, and lots more have argued about it with me at various stages of my thinking; my thanks to my tenure reviewers, Mary DeShazer, Barbara Gelpi, Tania Modleski, Peter Rabinowitz, and Bonnie Zimmerman; to students, colleagues, and friends, Beth Ash, Shay Brawn, Leslie Brody, Elaine Chang, Gary Dyer, Amy Elder, Marcy Knopf, Mike Mitchell, Robin Sheets, and Marty Wechselblatt; and to my editor at Pennsylvania, Patricia Smith. I am grateful as well to my students, especially my graduate students in Feminist Theory, for studying the seventies with me and for their speculations about alternative arenas for consciousness raising. My particular thanks to the Friday "bar night" crowd for providing another space for thinking and arguing.

No one has had as great an impact on this book as my former colleague and dear friend Bonnie Dow, who lent me books, sent me articles, fought out the fine points, and read the entire manuscript with her vicious red pen in hand. Bonnie and her husband, John Murphy, also took excellent care of me and of this book through difficult times. Every idea in this book is better for the days spent on their screen porch in North Dakota. Still, what's stupid, sloppy, or just plain wrong here is all my own.

A specific form of material support came from my beloved canine companion, Felix, who took me for walks to clear my head when sentences would not cooperate. My family's love and support has been generous, immediate, and profound. My sister, Chris, has taught me more about sisterhood in all of its forms than anyone else. To my grandmother, to my father and Caroline, to Rick, Robin, Megen, and Emily, and to Chris and Anne, I owe more than I can say. Finally, this book is dedicated to my mother. I miss her.

The author gratefully acknowledges permission to reprint material from *The Female Man* by Joanna Russ, © 1975 by Joanna Russ, reprinted by permission of Beacon Press, Boston; from *Fear of Flying* by Erica Jong, © 1973 by Erica Jong, reprinted by permission of Henry Holt, Inc.; from *Ella Price's Journal* by Dorothy Bryant, © 1972 by Dorothy Bryant, reprinted by permission of The Feminist Press.